International Intervention and Local Politics

International peace- and state-building interventions have become ubiquitous in international politics since the 1990s, aiming to tackle the security problems stemming from the instability afflicting many developing states. Their frequent failures have prompted a shift towards analysing how the interaction between interveners and recipients shapes outcomes. This book critically assesses the rapidly growing literature in International Relations and Development Studies on international intervention and local politics. It advances an innovative approach, placing the politics of scale at the core of the conflicts and compromises shaping the outcomes of international intervention. Different scales – local, national, international – privilege different interests, unevenly allocating power, resources and political opportunity structures. Interveners and recipients thus pursue scalar strategies and socio-political alliances that reinforce their power and marginalise rivals. This approach is harnessed towards examining three prominent case studies of international intervention – Aceh, Cambodia and Solomon Islands – with a focus on public administration reform.

SHAHAR HAMEIRI is Associate Professor of International Politics and Associate Director of the Graduate Centre in Governance and International Affairs, School of Political Science and International Studies, University of Queensland. He is co-author of *Governing Borderless Threats* (Cambridge University Press, 2015) and author of *Regulating Statehood* (Palgrave Macmillan, 2010), and has published in leading journals. He tweets @ShaharHameiri.

CAROLINE HUGHES is Head of the Department of Peace Studies and International Development at the University of Bradford, UK. She is the author of *Dependent Communities: Aid and Politics in Cambodia and East Timor* (Cornell SEAP, 2009) and *The Political Economy of Cambodia's*

Transition, 1991–2001 (RoutledgeCurzon, 2003) and co-author of *The Politics of Accountability in Southeast Asia* (Oxford University Press, 2014).

FABIO SCARPELLO is a scholar and consultant focusing on issues relating to the security development nexus. He is an Associate Fellow of the Asia Research Centre, Murdoch University, Australia, and an associate consultant at VJW International, Strategika Asia Pacific, Conow and the London Centre of International Law Practice. His academic work has been published in journals such as *International Studies Review, Contemporary Politics* and the *Journal of Contemporary Asia*.

International Intervention and Local Politics

SHAHAR HAMEIRI
University of Queensland

CAROLINE HUGHES
University of Bradford

FABIO SCARPELLO
Murdoch University

CAMBRIDGE
UNIVERSITY PRESS

CAMBRIDGE
UNIVERSITY PRESS

University Printing House, Cambridge CB2 8BS, United Kingdom

One Liberty Plaza, 20th Floor, New York, NY 10006, USA

477 Williamstown Road, Port Melbourne, VIC 3207, Australia

4843/24, 2nd Floor, Ansari Road, Daryaganj, Delhi – 110002, India

79 Anson Road, #06–04/06, Singapore 079906

Cambridge University Press is part of the University of Cambridge.

It furthers the University's mission by disseminating knowledge in the pursuit of education, learning, and research at the highest international levels of excellence.

www.cambridge.org
Information on this title: www.cambridge.org/9781108416894

DOI: 10.1017/9781108416894

First published 2017

Printed in XXXXXXXXXXXXXXXXXXXX

A catalogue record for this publication is available from the British Library.

Library of Congress Cataloging-in-Publication Data

ISBN 978-1-108-41689-4 Hardback
ISBN 978-1-108-40341-2 Paperback

Shahar Hameiri:

To Lee Jones, between the pessimism of the intellect and the optimism of the will.

Caroline Hughes:

To public servants everywhere.

Fabio Scarpello:

To Inga and Malena.

Contents

Acknowledgements

This book greatly benefited from the generous support of institutions and our colleagues, friends and families.

We are grateful, first and foremost, for the financial support we received from the Australian Research Council through Discovery Project grant DP130102273, 'The Politics of Public Administration Reform: Capacity Development and Ideological Contestation in International State-Building'. This book could not have been written without it. We are also thankful for the financial assistance we received from Murdoch University's Strategic Research Fund.

The writing of the book benefitted from the help of numerous colleagues. In particular, we are grateful to Dr Lee Jones, whose razor-sharp insights have been instrumental in the development of this book. We are forever indebted to his intellectual generosity. Colleagues at the Asia Research Centre, Murdoch University, where Caroline is a former Director, Fabio was a postdoctoral fellow and Shahar was located until moving to the University of Queensland in 2016, have been a constant source of support and inspiration. We would especially like to mention Professor Garry Rodan, Dr Jacqui Baker, Professor Vedi Hadiz, Professor Kevin Hewison, Dr Jane Hutchison, Professor Kanishka Jayasuriya, Emeritus Professor Richard Robison, Dr Ian Wilson and Dr Jeffrey Wilson. We are also grateful to the two anonymous reviewers who closely read our manuscript and provided many useful comments that helped improve the final product. The book benefited greatly from interaction with many academic colleagues around the world. We would especially like to thank Nicolas Lemay-Hébert, Joanne Wallis, Oliver Richmond, Volker Boege, Anne Brown, Matthew Allen, Miranda Forsyth, Sinclair Dinnen, Srinjoy Bose and Charlie Hunt. We also thank the many other colleagues who engaged with our ideas in conferences, seminars and workshops, and regret our inability to name them all here.

Cambridge University Press' commissioning editor John Haslam provided us with constant support and professional guidance throughout the process, as has the Press' excellent production team. The final version of the book benefited greatly from the attentive editing of Dave Prout, while Christopher Leite prepared the index. Sia Kozlowski guided us through the administrative labyrinths of Murdoch University, providing much appreciated administrative support.

Our research assistants made our tasks markedly easier and our fieldwork trips more productive. We are grateful to Anna Chapman and Melissa Johnston at the Asia Research Centre; Aidan Moniopolo in Solomon Islands; Eng Netra in Cambodia; and Ririn Sefsani and Fahmi Yunus in Jakarta and Aceh, respectively. We also express our appreciation to the dozens of sources who talked to us in Solomon Islands, Cambodia, Jakarta and Aceh, both on and off the record. It is through these conversations that we sharpened our observations and developed our analysis.

Our most heartfelt thank-you goes, however, to our families. They are the ones that often need to keep the boat steady as we excuse ourselves for lengthy fieldtrips. Shahar is particularly grateful to his wife, Meggan, for her love and encouragement, and to his children, Josh, Theo and Nina, for their peculiar brand of chaotic fun. Caroline acknowledges the important support of her husband, Richard, and her daughters Alice, Hephzibah and Beth. Fabio is grateful to his wife, Ingebjørg, and his daughter, Malena, for their support and patience.

Abbreviations

ACDF	Aceh District Response Facility
ADB	Asian Development Bank
AGSI	Aceh Governance Stabilisation Initiative
AGTP	Aceh Government Transformation Programme
ALGAP	Aceh Local Governance Programme
AMM	Aceh Monitoring Mission
AusAID	Australian Agency for International Development
BKPP	Provincial Personnel, Training and Education Agency (Indonesia)
BRR	*Badan Rehabilitasi dan Rekonstruksi NAD-Nias*, or Agency for the Rehabilitation and Reconstruction of Aceh and Nias
BSIP	British Solomon Islands Protectorate
CALGAP	Canada/Aceh Local Government Assistance Programme
CBSI	Central Bank of Solomon Islands
CDFs	Constituency Development Funds (Solomon Islands)
CED	Customs and Excise Division (Solomon Islands)
CEWG	Core Economic Working Group (Solomon Islands)
COMFREL	Committee for Free and Fair Elections in Cambodia
CPP	Cambodian People's Party
CSOs	Civil Society Organisations
DAU	*Dana–Alokasi–Umum*, or central–provincial–local transfers
DFID	Department For International Development (UK)
DFW	Department of Forestry and Wildlife (Cambodia)
EFRP	Economic and Financial Reform Programme (Solomon Islands)
FAO	Food and Agriculture Organization

FKKA	*Forum Komunikasi Pemerintahan Kabupaten dan Kota se Aceh*, or Communication Forum of Local Governments and Legislatures
FUNCINPEC	*Front Uni National pour un Cambodge Indépendant, Neutre, Pacifique et Coopératif*
GAM	*Gerakan Aceh Merdeka*, or Free Aceh Movement
GNI	Gross National Income
ICG	International Crisis Group (European Union)
IFIs	International Financial Institutions
IMF	International Monetary Fund
IPE	International Political Economy
IRD	Internal Revenue Division (Solomon Islands)
KDP	*Kecamatan* Development Programme (Aceh)
KPA	*Komite Peralihan Aceh*, or Aceh Transition Committee
LGSP	Local Governance Support Programme (Aceh)
LoGA	Law on Governing Aceh
LOGICA	Local Governance and Infrastructure for Communities in Aceh
MBPI	Merit-Based Pay Initiative (Cambodia)
MDF	Multi-Donor Trust Fund for Aceh and Nias
MDGs	Millennium Development Goals (UN)
MEF	Ministry of Economy and Finance (Cambodia)
MIGAS	*Minyak dan Gas Bumi*, or oil and gas revenue (Indonesia)
MOFOR	Ministry of Forestry (Solomon Islands)
MoFT	Ministry of Finance and Treasury (Solomon Islands)
MoHA	Ministry of Home Affairs (Indonesia)
MoU	Memorandum of Understanding
MP	Member of Parliament
NGOs	Non-Government Organisations
NZIRD	New Zealand Inland Revenue Division
OAG	Office of the Auditor-General (Solomon Islands)
ODA	Official Development Assistance
OECD	Organisation for Economic Co-operation and Development
OIE	World Organisation for Animal Health (originally, *Office International des Epizooties*)

OTSUS	*Dana Otonomi Khusus*, or Special Autonomy Fund (Indonesia)
PA	Partai Aceh
PAC	Public Accounts Committee (Solomon Islands)
PAR	Public Administration Reform
PFM	Public Financial Management
PIF	Pacific Islands Forum
PKI	*Partai Komunis Indonesia*, or Communist Party of Indonesia
PPP	*Partai Persatuan Pembangunan*, or United Development Party (Indonesia)
PRK	People's Republic of Kampuchea
PRSPs	Poverty Reduction Strategy Papers
PSBIs	Peace- and State-Building Interventions
PWC	Post-Washington Consensus
R2P	Responsibility to Protect (UN)
RAMSI	Regional Assistance Mission to Solomon Islands
RSIPF	Royal Solomon Islands Police Force
SAPs	Structural Adjustment Programmes
SDGs	Sustainable Development Goals (UN)
SIG	Solomon Islands Government
SIGOV	Solomon Islands Economic and Public Sector Governance
SSCs	School Support Committees (Cambodia)
TCU	Timber Control Unit (Solomon Islands)
TNI	*Tentara Nasional Indonesia* (Indonesian military)
UNDP	United Nations Development Programme
UNSC	United Nations Security Council
USAID	United States Agency for International Development
WHO	World Health Organization
ZILS	*Zona Industri Lhokseumawe*, or Lhokseumawe Industrial Zone (Indonesia)

Introduction

Since the early 1990s, international peace-promotion efforts have increasingly involved intrastate intervention.[1] Dubbed 'peace-building', these interventions have encompassed diverse activities, including military intervention, transitional justice and public administration and economic reform. In the 1990s, Western governments and international organisations operated largely on a naïve interpretation of the 'liberal peace thesis', assuming that stabilising 'fragile' and post-conflict states required rapid democratisation and marketisation.[2] However, from the 2000s, as failures of outcome and implementation abounded, peace-building has increasingly been delivered through 'state-building', which denotes a 'broad range of programs and projects designed to build or strengthen the capacity of institutions, organisations and agencies – not all of which are necessarily part of the state apparatus – to effectively perform the functions associated with modern statehood'.[3] Peace-building is thus frequently combined with state-building in a common effort to reshape target societies, polities and economies towards more peaceful outcomes.

Notwithstanding initial optimism, however, by the middle of the new millennium's first decade, the inability of these Peace- and State-building Interventions (PSBIs) to attain many of their objectives, despite the mobilisation of often significant resources, became widely recognised by practitioners, leading to considerable soul-searching. Publications as diverse as the United States Army's counterinsurgency manual[4] and the World Bank's *World Development Report 2011*[5] have questioned the hitherto widely accepted view that the key to alleviating conflict in fragile and post-conflict states and societies in the long term is the promotion of liberal, 'good governance' and/or democratic institutions. Instead, these publications and others have

[1] Bellamy et al. 2004. [2] Paris 2004. [3] Hameiri 2010: 2.
[4] Department of Army 2006. [5] World Bank 2011a.

argued that interveners must learn in some cases to accommodate customary institutions, leaders and values as the price of stabilisation and development. Likewise, in the field of international development assistance, which closely intersects with the practice of PSBIs,[6] established aid modalities, also premised on the promotion of (neo-)liberal economic policies and institutions, have been challenged by persistent failures of implementation and outcome.[7] These failures have led to calls to jettison the conceit of aid's technocratic neutrality and take the politics of recipient societies more seriously when designing and implementing aid programmes.[8]

Amid this apparent crisis of confidence for international interventionism and development aid orthodoxy, many peace-building and development scholars have begun to look more closely at the way international interventions and donors interface with target states and their populations and how this interaction shapes intervention outcomes. Undoubtedly, PSBI outcomes range widely across countries, as well as within countries across different areas of policy and governance. In Solomon Islands, for example, some apparent successes in improving state revenue are matched by notable failures in reining in public expenditure.[9] In other cases, such as Iraq and Afghanistan, despite considerable efforts and substantial funding, interveners have not even been able to prevent widespread violence and to promote the rule of law. This unevenness demanded explanation, and scholars have become increasingly convinced that it could in part be understood by looking at the precise interaction between interveners and the intervened. This was a welcome and much-needed shift from the earlier preoccupation by both policy-oriented and critical scholarship with refining or critiquing the ideas and modalities of interveners.

Reflecting the diverse fields examining various aspects of PSBIs, a variety of approaches to studying the interaction of international intervention and local politics have emerged, divided primarily between literatures on peace-building and the politics of development. Despite their similar subject-matter and broad objectives, these literatures have largely developed separately, with limited interaction. Peace-building scholars, who are largely based in the field of International

[6] Duffield 2001. [7] OECD 2010.
[8] Carothers and De Gramont 2013; Hutchison et al. 2014.
[9] Fraenkel et al. 2014.

Relations, have primarily advanced the concepts of hybridity and friction, viewing the outcomes of intervention as stemming from conflict and accommodation between the agendas, institutions and values of liberal internationals and non-liberal locals.[10] Meanwhile, scholars of the politics of development have focused on the effects of international aid programmes on domestic politics and economies, e.g. elite political settlements.[11]

This emerging research agenda improves on earlier conceptions and critiques of PSBIs in that it takes seriously recipient states and societies when examining interventions and their outcomes. It seems odd that the agency of those targeted by intervention had previously been relatively neglected. However, although each approach has distinct strengths, collectively they fall short, in different ways, of adequately conceptualising and theorising the outcomes of international interventions. Their core weakness is that they neglect to understand the manner in which these interventions affect not only the nature and outcome of social and political conflict in recipient states and societies, but the very terrain upon which it takes place. The main objective of this book is therefore to engage with this latest wave of scholarship on international intervention and advance an alternative framework better able to theorise and conceptualise the important relationship between international interventions and local politics, and hence to explain diverse intervention outcomes in given contexts. As we elaborate, the way in which PSBIs operate means that the *politics of scale* invariably becomes a crucial dimension of the socio-political struggles shaping political and governance outcomes.

Public Administration Reform and the Politics of Scale

We have elected in this book to focus on a particular subset of PSBI and aid programming – public administration reform (PAR). This is, in part, for practical reasons, to make comparisons across case studies more meaningful by honing in on similar programmes. It is also because PAR is an especially prominent aspect of aid programming, where considerable funds and efforts are funnelled. Assessing total annual aid spending on PAR is difficult, as it is an 'ad hoc

10 Belloni 2012; Mac Ginty 2011; Richmond and Mitchell 2012.

11 Hutchison et al. 2014; Khan 2010; Parks and Cole 2010; Unsworth 2009.

categorisation of various reforms' that cut across the OECD's Development Assistance Committee's aid-by-sector statistics.[12] Nonetheless, the available evidence suggests it is substantial. According to one assessment contained in a report by the World Bank's Independent Evaluation Group,[13] one-sixth of the World Bank Group's lending and other support between 1999 and 2006 was directed at PAR. Indeed, PAR programming reflects, for interveners, the very essence of what the state is supposed to be and how state functions should be performed. As such, it is an important lens on key intellectual and programmatic developments in both the peacebuilding and development agendas in recent years. PAR was also selected, however, because it is a counterintuitive test case for our framework. PAR is often officially aimed at strengthening national capacity and legitimacy. As we will show, however, in the context of PSBIs, these programmes actually seek to fragment the national scale, leading to new struggles over the scale and mechanisms through which important public policy issues are governed.

Sometimes called 'public management reform' or 'public sector reform', PAR has been broadly defined as: 'Deliberate changes to the structures and processes of public sector organizations with the objective of getting them (in some sense) to run better'.[14] It has been a core pillar of many international donors' aid programmes in recipient countries for over two decades, as part of the broader shift towards supporting 'good governance' as a precondition for development.[15] Aid agencies have funded and encouraged PAR as a means of creating conditions seen as supportive of economic growth, development and subsequently security and political stability. It incorporates a wide range of programmes, including: changes to the organisational structure of state agencies; devolution of budgets and responsibilities to subnational authorities; creation of merit-based public service appointment, promotion and dismissal processes; and introduction of mechanisms for holding officeholders to account by citizens or other government agencies.[16]

Though donors and other international agencies have promoted PAR in many recipient countries, it has been a particularly prominent

[12] Scott 2011: i. [13] World Bank 2008: xiii.

[14] Pollitt and Bouckaert 2011: 2.

[15] Grindle and Hilderbrand 1995; Scott 2011.

[16] Heredia and Schneider 2003: 3; Pollitt and Bouckaert 2011.

aspect of the PSBI agenda in so-called fragile states, where the urgency of getting public administrations to function 'better' appears to be acute for humanitarian, developmental and security reasons.[17] Especially after the September 11 terrorist attacks, development agencies have developed a keen interest in working in fragile states.[18] In 2011 alone, US$53 billion, or 38 per cent of total official development assistance (ODA), is estimated to have been delivered in fragile states.[19] In the context of PBSIs, public administrations working better usually means improving the delivery and quality of public services in key areas, such as policing, health, education and basic infrastructure.[20] The typical official rationale for making PAR central within PSBIs, grounded in a liberal-pluralist conception of statehood, is that a state capable of fairly and efficiently delivering basic services to the population it governs will win over people's allegiance from more particularistic sources of authority, such as kin groups or anti-government rebels, thus becoming legitimate. This is seen as crucial since, as an Asian Development Bank (ADB) report on state performance in the Pacific argues, although the 'state is not an answer to everything ... [it is] best placed to resolve important collective action problems' essential to development.[21]

However, as with many other forms of international intervention, available evidence suggests that PAR programmes rarely achieve the intended outcomes.[22] Donor explanations for failure often emphasise technical matters, such as capacity, resourcing and sequencing.[23] Critics, including within major aid organisations, have instead begun to stress the folly of treating PAR, and development aid in general, as a technical issue, emphasising its inherently political nature. This reflects the broader 'political economy turn' in development aid, which, although highly visible in the literature, is yet to have substantial impact on actual aid programming.[24] Hillman, for example, argues that, particularly in post-conflict situations, 'even apparently straightforward reforms to personnel management are inherently political and

17 Brinkerhoff and Brinkerhoff 2002.
18 Marquette and Beswick 2011.
19 Gisselquist 2015: 1269.
20 Brinkerhoff 2005; Fukuyama 2004; Ghani and Lockhart 2008; Hillman 2013; World Bank 2011a.
21 Laking 2010: 8.
22 Gisselquist and Resnick 2014; Hillman 2013.
23 E.g. World Bank 2008.
24 For an overview, see Carothers and De Gramont 2013; Hutchison et al. 2014.

prone to controversy'. [25] Relatedly, scholars and practitioners have also increasingly questioned the assumption of a linear relationship between state capacity, legitimacy and the efficient delivery of public goods and services. They have emphasised that state legitimacy, while essential for long-term stabilisation, often has other, more deeply ingrained, sources.[26] The hybridity literature in peace-building has also questioned the liberal conception of state legitimacy. For these authors, legitimacy results from greater accommodation of truly local or everyday institutions and values in governance, not necessarily from the construction of liberal polities.[27]

We accept that PAR programmes are indeed inherently political and contested, because they necessarily involve attempts to reallocate power and resources.[28] However, we argue that a core dimension of the social and political struggles shaping how power and resources are allocated following international intervention is over the territorial scale at which particular issues are to be governed. This is implicitly recognised by the hybridity scholarship, with its focus on local–international interactions. But hybridity scholars wrongly treat local, national and international as pre-given categories of actors, institutions and/or values, rather than as contested, and hence changeable, scales of governance that actors produce. Consequently, many hybridity scholars misunderstand the role the politics of scale plays in shaping the outcomes of PSBIs.

In political geography, scale refers to vertically differentiated, hierarchised social, political and economic spaces, each denoting 'the arena and moment, both discursively and materially, where socio-spatial power relations are contested and compromises are negotiated and regulated'.[29] Scales may reflect existing political tiers within a state, such as a village or the nation, or cut across them, e.g. bio-regions, transgovernmental networks or 'the global'. In all cases, however, they are not natural, but produced through strategic political action and socio-political contestation.[30] Whether local, subnational, or indeed

[25] Hillman 2013: 2.
[26] E.g. Batley et al. 2012; Brinkerhoff et al. 2012; Fukuyama 2013; Hillman 2013; Krasner and Risse 2014; McLoughlin 2015; OECD 2010; vom Hau 2012.
[27] Belloni 2012; Boege et al. 2009; Johnson and Hutchison 2012; Lemay-Hébert 2009; Mac Ginty 2011; Richmond and Mitchell 2012.
[28] Heredia and Schneider 2003; Hillman 2013.
[29] Swyngedouw 1997: 140.
[30] Brenner 2001: 592; Smith 2010.

national and global scales are part of a single social whole, they 'do not exist in mutual isolation but are always interconnected in a broader, often-changing inter-scalar ensemble'.[31] In turn, the 'politics of scale' – a concept first coined by Neil Smith[32] – denotes contestation over the construction of scales, as well as over differentiation and ordering among various scales.[33]

The scalar arrangement of political life is always contested because different scales afford different configurations of actors, power, resources and political opportunity structures.[34] Shifting scales – *rescaling* – can change these configurations, potentially changing political outcomes.[35] For example, Gibson[36] shows how authoritarian subnational elites strive to keep issues 'local', since at this scale their interests prevail. Conversely, their opponents often try to transform issues into 'national' matters, since they can find more allies and resources at this scale to tilt the balance against local strongmen. Similarly, 'scale jumping'[37] to a regional or global scale is a strategy often used by weaker socio-political groups to advance political objectives undermined by powerful interests dominating another scale.

The politics of scale is a crucial focus of socio-political conflict relating to PSBIs and PAR programmes, because these interventions essentially operate through *state transformation*.[38] Donors are not simply trying to build national capacity and legitimacy, leaving the form and function of the state otherwise unchanged, but rather to internationalise or transnationalise strategic parts of the apparatuses of target states. Their aim is to rescale parts of the ostensibly domestic administrations of recipient states so that these become not so much responsive to local demands, which are often viewed as pernicious or dysfunctional, but to international governance agendas, geared towards meeting international targets and aspirations.[39] Donors often attempt, for example, to intervene in parts of the bureaucracy responsible for designing budgets and disbursing funds, to limit the control of local elites, seen as corrupt and self-serving, over the public purse and redirect funds to objectives that they deem more appropriate, such as primary education or paying off interest on public debt. In Solomon Islands, as we show in Chapter 3, a Core Economic

[31] Brenner et al. 2003: 16. [32] Neil Smith 2010.
[33] Brenner 2001: 599–600. [34] Hameiri and Jones 2015. [35] Gough 2004.
[36] Gibson 2013. [37] See Smith 1992. [38] Hameiri 2010.
[39] Hameiri 2010; Harrison 2004.

Working Group (CEWG) was established at the demands of donors and the International Monetary Fund as a forum for the government to discuss its economic policy with the main donors, as well as for monitoring the implementation of agreed reforms. However, the Solomon Islands Ministry of Finance and Treasury, which represents Solomon Islands on the CEWG has itself been heavily rescaled through the secondment of donor and Overseas Development Institute personnel.

These efforts, which are perhaps ironically justified as supporting state capacity and enabling self-governance, reflect a broader trend in international politics away from conceiving of national sovereignty as autonomy from external interference, towards its reinterpretation as responsibility vis-à-vis the international community.[40] They also reflect a concurrent shift from intervention to governance in international development aid delivery, whereby donor programming is not imposed from the outside and temporary, but becomes deeply embedded within the ostensibly domestic apparatuses of recipient states, whose formal sovereignty remains intact but where substantive authority is shifted to the transnationally networked technocrats and regulators.[41] Similarly, interveners have more recently attempted to rescale subnational – even village or community – governance in response to the apparent failure of efforts to produce desired outcomes through the central state's bureaucracy. Most notably in Iraq, following the evident failure of centralised state-building efforts,[42] the US military sought to alleviate the deadly sectarian civil war of 2005–6 by supporting sheikhs and other local strongmen through transfers of weapons and funds, to establish order in their localities and excise al-Qaeda.[43] This was combined with efforts to link these groups with the Baghdad government to ultimately bring them under centralised authority.[44] Thus, although PSBIs work through states, not by undermining or supplanting them, they tend to produce fragmented forms of multi-scalar statehood.

However, because rescaling is so pivotal to PSBIs in general and PAR specifically, scalar strategies have become also integral to the way that domestic actors respond to these programmes, as they struggle to

40 Bickerton et al. 2007; Chayes and Chayes 1995.
41 Hameiri 2010; Williams 2013. 42 Dodge 2005. 43 Kilcullen 2009.
44 Biddle 2008.

promote governance outcomes favourable to themselves. These groups often seek to promote or constrain the rescaling of governance, as well as shape the actual functioning of rescaled apparatuses, in ways that best serve their interests and normative agendas. As such, powerful actors and groups will typically attempt to resist rescaling or modify the operation of rescaled institutions when rescaling is seen to undermine the basis of their power, by threatening its material underpinnings and/or the ideology rationalising it. They will support rescaling when it is seen to reinforce their interests and normative agendas and undermine their opponents.[45] Therefore, as we elaborate in Chapter 2, analysing the outcomes of PSBIs requires attending to the intra- and inter-scalar contestation – material and ideological – that results through, and in response to, these programmes, and specifically to the relative power of the coalitions mobilising to promote, resist or modify rescaling in particular contexts. As we shall see, even when the material preponderance of interveners appears overwhelming vis-à-vis domestic social forces, their capacity to attain desired policy and governance objectives is powerfully mediated by the scalar strategies of recipients, especially of recipient governments. In other words, how public administrations function and the capacities of their different agencies to pursue particular policy agendas in the context of PSBIs are invariably established through struggles between coalitions of socio-political forces, in which the politics of scale is a key aspect.

Domestic groups' scalar strategies in response to donor PAR programmes can take one of three forms. The first and second strategies relate to the agency of recipient governments. Because PSBIs maintain the formal sovereignty of target states, the implementation of PAR programmes necessitates at least the tacit consent of recipient governments. Governments thus retain a key role as 'scale managers',[46] able to harness national sovereignty claims to affect what interventions are allowed in, and in what ways. One possible response by recipient governments is to completely reject PAR programmes, thus preventing the rescaling of apparatuses altogether. Outright rejection of all foreign assistance is quite rare because the resources offered by interveners are typically attractive to embattled governments in poor countries. A second, and particularly significant, response is selective adoption. This entails the use of the state's scale management function, not to

[45] See Hameiri and Jones 2015: 51–74. [46] Peck 2002: 340.

reject intervention wholesale, but to selectively admit or constrain PAR programmes and rescale in ways that bolster the authority and control over resources of existing elites who dominate the national scale. This may also involve efforts to affect the ways that apparently rescaled institutions function, as well as to shift resources from rescaled to non-rescaled parts of the bureaucracy. But this selectivity is not simply a matter of choice; it reflects the broader political economic context, shaping socio-political power relations more generally, and the role of political and bureaucratic elites within this. The elites dominating the national scale will thus adopt or resist rescaling efforts not just to advance narrow, pecuniary interests, but often out of ideological conviction, to protect important allies or to undermine ideological or political rivals.

A third response, which often occurs alongside the second, is localisation. Usually, localisation is attempted by relatively weak groups, seeking to contest the power of elites dominating the national scale, by attempting to harness PSBIs' fragmenting of the national scale and the attendant blow to the authority of national elites to shift governance downwards, thereby bolstering their power and control over resources. Localisation is not only a weapon of the weak, however; it could also be attempted by powerful elites when rescaling to a subnational level is seen as potentially reinforcing their power against donors and domestic contenders. These efforts often involve ideological appeals to the legitimacy of modes of governance based in socio-culturally organic subnational communities, versus that of apparently 'transplanted' postcolonial institutions like the state. Related is the call that local groups and governance structures should enjoy greater autonomy and improved resource-allocation. Localisation efforts are sometimes reinforced by the donors' ubiquitous government decentralisation agenda.[47] They are sometimes also supported by what scholars of peace-building have identified as the 'local turn' – interveners' promotion of apparently customary institutions and forms of authority to stabilise recipient societies.[48]

An important part of this localisation agenda, typically missed by those endorsing it from outside, is that defining the local and its scope of governance and authority is inherently contested. While those supporting localisation seek to bolster their power, this is likely to be

[47] See Hadiz 2010. [48] Mac Ginty and Richmond 2013.

vigorously challenged by groups standing to lose out, including by challenging their claim to customary authenticity. Much like the upwards rescaling associated with donor PAR programmes, these localisation strategies involve an active effort to 'unravel' the state,[49] but within a broader context shaped by international intervention and uneven development. Struggles that may superficially appear to be about the relative merits of traditional and modern governance are fundamentally concerned with the scalar distribution of power and authority.

To explain the precise and typically uneven outcomes of PSBIs, we combine the politics of scale with insights from Gramscian state theory. This approach rejects the dichotomisation of state and civil society, viewing both as related arenas in which unequal power relations are embedded and contested. From this vantage point, state formation and transformation are understood as the contingent outcomes of unceasing social and political struggles over power and resources, which span state and civil society. State institutions' form and operation reflect conflicts and compromises among historically specific socio-political coalitions rooted primarily in the political economy – classes, class fractions, distributional coalitions and other social groups, such as ethnicity- or religion-based organisations.[50] These coalitions, often straddling the state–society divide, struggle to make and remake key political, economic and social institutions, especially of the state, to entrench their own power and wealth and marginalise their opponents.

In this view, the state can never be seen as neutral, not even in theoretical abstraction. Rather, states, as well as institutions generally, exhibit a 'strategic selectivity': they are structured to be systematically more open to some social forces pursuing certain social and political agendas, through certain strategies, while marginalising others.[51] Careful historical-sociological analysis is required to uncover the strategic selectivity of different parts of the state, and how this affects the response of key groups to particular donor programmes or projects. This in turn allows for identifying the coalitions agitating for or against particular scales and attendant modes of governance, and their relative capacities to attain their objectives, including by harnessing the scalar strategies discussed above.

[49] Hooghe and Marks 2003. [50] Hewison et al. 1993: 4–5.
[51] Jessop 2008.

Using this approach, we do not find that village-based actors will necessarily favour customary modes of governance or that local resistance to international agendas is the main dynamic shaping PSBI outcomes, as the hybridity scholarship would have it. Nor do we necessarily see domestic political economy relations as determining intervention outcomes, since one of the potential consequences of the politics of scale accompanying PSBIs is the transformation of what domestic, local, national and so on actually mean in concrete terms. Instead, we recognise that actors notionally located at various territorial scales often act and form alliances across these scales to advance their interests or defeat their rivals, and therefore place these alliances at the centre of our account.

Structure of the Book

The following chapter provides a brief account of the changes in the theory and practice of PSBIs since the end of the Cold War, placing particular emphasis on the relatively recent emergence of various approaches seeking to deal with the apparent failings of these interventions. We will then critically evaluate the key approaches that have emerged to examine how international interventions interact with local politics and societies. The discussion will be divided into approaches in development studies and peace-building. In particular, we will emphasise how these approaches' neglect of the politics of scale weakens their capacity to adequately conceptualise and theorise the politics of international intervention and hence explain the uneven outcomes of PSBIs within and between states.

The second chapter will outline our alternative approach. We begin by discussing the relevant insights of Gramscian state theory and the political geography literature on the politics of scale. We then proceed to discuss the four key elements of our method for studying the interaction of international interventions and their recipients: first, focus on a particular project or programme and identify the politics of scale involved; second, identify the precise forces and coalitions contesting the outcomes of this particular project and establish their relative power relations by reference to the broader political economy structures in which they are embedded; third, identify the strategies, especially scalar strategies, they pursue to attain their objectives; fourth and final, trace how struggles over the extent of governance rescaling constrain the extent and efficacy of governance changes.

This method will then be used for three detailed case study chapters. Solomon Islands, Cambodia, and Aceh (Indonesia) were selected for two main reasons. First, each is an emblematic case of international intervention, seen as a relative success story. Focusing on supposed successful cases allows us to fully capitalise on an approach that explains unevenness within different aspects of the intervention. The Australian-led intervention in Solomon Islands was held up as a case of best practice for international state-building,[52] though more recent assessments have been less glowing.[53] Indeed, Solomon Islands has not descended back into violent conflict and has achieved relatively consistent economic growth in the period since the intervention commenced in 2003. Cambodia's terrible modern history is well known, though since the arrival of peacekeepers in the early 1990s it has avoided wide-scale violent conflict, and following two decades of rapid economic growth, the once desperately impoverished country is approaching middle income status. The 2004 tsunami that devastated large swathes of the Indonesian province of Aceh was the catalyst for the 2005 peace agreement signed between the secessionist Free Aceh Movement (GAM, or *Gerakan Aceh Merdeka*) and the Indonesian government, ending a 30-year-long war. The province has remained largely peaceful since. Second, these cases reflect differing levels of international assistance relative to the resources available to the government and the size of the economy as a whole. Solomon Islands was the focus of an extensive Australian-led state-building intervention, for a decade from 2003 and continues to receive high volumes of international aid. From 2009 to 2011 it was considered the world's second most aid-dependent country, as measured by aid to gross national income (GNI).[54] Cambodia also receives very high levels of international assistance, though it is not ranked among the world's top twenty most aid-dependent countries. Nonetheless, from 2002 to 2010, almost 95 per cent of total spending on public services was donor-funded, though about half of this was spent on technical assistance.[55] The recurrent parts of the budget are funded through domestic sources, however, and by most accounts the Cambodian People's Party (CPP) regime is supported by resources obtained and distributed outside the

[52] OECD 2006. [53] Fraenkel et al. 2014. [54] Pryke 2013.
[55] Ear 2013; Sokunpanha You 2013.

official government system.[56] In Indonesia, foreign aid disbursements are miniscule in aid-to-GNI and per capita terms, although Aceh has received over US$5 billion in international aid following the 2004 tsunami.[57] We find, however, that contrary to expectations, higher levels of aid-dependence do not linearly correlate with donors more easily attaining their preferred objectives. In other words, material inequality between donors and recipients, our case studies show, does not explain the outcomes of intervention. Rather, we must pay attention to the precise coalitions assembling to support or resist particular programmes or projects and to their scalar strategies.

In Chapter 3, we examine Solomon Islands – an excellent case study for our argument because it clearly highlights the importance of scalar strategies of existing nationally dominant elites' for determining the outcome of PSBIs (even where donors are incredibly materially preponderant relative to all other groups). PAR and state capacity building were at the very core of the Regional Assistance Mission to Solomon Islands (RAMSI) and remain central to subsequent aid programming following its partial withdrawal in 2013, mainly through the multi-donor, Australia-dominated Solomon Islands Economic and Public Sector Governance (SIGOV) programme. Despite these extensive and relatively well-funded efforts, it has recently been recognised that many of the donors' governance objectives have not been met in Solomon Islands.[58] But rather than a blanket failure, RAMSI and subsequent programming's efforts to rescale state apparatuses and insulate them from 'undesirable' political and societal pressures have achieved profoundly variable results, shaped by a politics of scale related to decades of highly uneven capitalist development.

In Solomon Islands, the dominance of the national scale has historically required centralising rents within the capital Honiara from economic activities, mainly resource-extraction, occurring in provincial parts of the archipelago. National political leaders then redistribute some of these resources back to remote areas, in a discretionary manner, to secure essential electoral support-bases. This structure has meant that although the national scale has been overwhelmingly dominant, inter-scalar conflict has been rife in Solomon Islands, as marginalised groups have demanded a greater share of the benefits or even

[56] Ear 2013. [57] BRR 2009.
[58] Fraenkel et al. 2014; Hayward-Jones 2014.

autonomy, often asserting the legitimacy of local identities and customs over the supposedly foreign nation-state.

Donor attempts to rescale core state functions beyond domestic political control and societal influence have thus carried uneven implications for Honiara-based political elites. They have responded by harnessing the state's scale management capacity to adopt or resist international programmes and by shifting resources to non-rescaled parts of the state that they control. Donor PAR programmes aimed at improving revenue-collection have been successful since they increase the resources at the disposal of national elites. However, as controls over discretionary spending are deeply threatening, not only to the political survival of individual members of parliament (MPs) but to the very primacy of the national scale, donor attempts to dominate spending ministries, many of which are responsible for core services, and procurement processes have largely failed.[59]

Crucially, the achievements of revenue collection have been harnessed by national elites, through the massive expansion of Constituency Development Funds (CDFs) – discretionary funds available to MPs to spend in their constituencies – to overwhelm persistent demands from below to rescale governance downwards and reallocate resources to the local level. This exemplifies the use of selective adoption – the second strategy discussed above – to attain governance outcomes advantageous to national elites, which preserve the dominance of the national scale as the main locus of power and wealth.

In Chapter 4, we examine Cambodia. Successive crises of state institutions over the past 50 years have caused Cambodia to be the target of a series of internationally assisted state-building initiatives, culminating since the 1990s in a Western donor-assisted liberal peacebuilding programme, incorporating 'good governance' as a key theme. The present Cambodian elite in the ruling CPP emerged from the ruins of the Khmer Rouge revolution in the early 1980s and has worked consistently under the cover of both Vietnamese and international intervention to promote its own class interests through selective adoption of internationally directed state-building initiatives. However, as these interests have changed, and as Cambodia's economy has transformed, this has entailed quite radical shifts in the way that space, territory and power have been conceived.

[59] Fraenkel et al. 2014: 64.

Since the 1980s, the cultivation of networks of loyal village and commune chiefs has been central to the CPP's strategy of, first, maintaining centralised control over the national territory, and following the UN intervention, ensuring electoral success in the context of UN-sponsored multi-party competition. Simultaneously, the CPP elite has centralised control over the issuing of licences for the exploitation of the country's natural resources, as a way of buying the loyalty of tycoons and the military, and as a means of accumulating resources to distribute down to local officials as a form of patronage. The civil service meanwhile was also co-opted through the enabling of opportunities to benefit from bribes and economic opportunities available through public servants' formal roles. These imperatives have shaped the CPP's engagement with donor initiatives for much of the post-conflict period. For example, the introduction of commune elections in 2002, lauded by donors as the first step towards meaningful decentralisation of government, in reality reflected a localisation strategy by the leadership to shift political competition to a scale it was able to effectively control via its network of loyal local officials, to counter the growing power of opposition parties in the cities.

However, changes in Cambodia's political economy over recent decades have had a significant impact on the characteristics of the local scale and its relationship with the centre in Phnom Penh. The rise of an increasingly landless young population, working in factories in the cities or abroad, along with big improvements in communication technologies and transportation, have weakened the capacity of local chiefs to ensure the loyalty of rural voters to the CPP. Meanwhile, the primitive accumulation development strategies that have facilitated much of Cambodia's economic development have begun to encroach increasingly on more densely populated regions, thus undermining the CPP's popularity even further. Increasingly better educated and mobile voters are also voicing their growing displeasure with the corruption and inefficiency characterising Cambodia's public administration.

When the CPP suffered a significant decline in the 2013 national election, the concerned leadership has responded by implementing many PAR programmes long advocated by donors, such as improving public servants' pay and setting up user groups to promote better accountability for service delivery. Yet, deep tensions endure between the objective of improving service delivery and government efficiency, on the one hand, and maintaining the multi-scalar relationships that have kept the CPP in power for decades, on the other. It seems the CPP's long-standing scalar strategies are losing their efficacy.

In Chapter 5 we look at the Indonesian province of Aceh and specifically at the Aceh Government Transformation Programme (AGTP), a project funded by the World Bank-managed Multi-Donor Trust Fund for Aceh and Nias (MDF). The MDF was established in April 2005, following a devastating earthquake-tsunami on 26 December 2004. The tsunami also paved the way for the end of a 30-year civil war, formalised in the signing of the Helsinki Agreement in 2005 between the GAM rebels and the national government in Jakarta.

AGTP was aimed at addressing perceived capacity gaps in the provincial government's ability to assume the tasks and responsibilities from the Agency for the Rehabilitation and Reconstruction of Aceh and Nias (BRR, or *Badan Rehabilitasi dan Rekonstruksi NAD-Nias*). The BRR was the ad hoc government agency tasked with the coordination of the overall reconstruction effort and the implementation of most Indonesian government-funded projects. It closed in 2009, though the transition of responsibilities to the provincial government started much earlier.

The AGTP became particularly contentious as some of its components included important rescaling attempts by donors that got entangled in power struggles between various political factions in Aceh, and between the United Nations Development Programme (UNDP) – the partner implementing agency – and the European Commission (EC) and the World Bank, the key members of the MDF. The contentious nature of the project emerged from its outset.

Intra-donor conflict led to the UNDP establishing a transversal, tactical alliance with former-rebel-*cum*-newly-elected-governor Irwandi Yusuf, which de facto rescaled decisions on the project components and administrative arrangements to Aceh and away from the MDF office where the EC and the World Bank would have held more sway. One of the controversial results of the Irwandi-UNDP alliance was the establishment of the *Tim Asistensi* – 60 advisors handpicked by the governor to, essentially, bypass the local bureaucracy that Irwandi distrusted. In the chapter, we explore the significance of *Tim Asistensi* within the political economy dynamics that emerged post-conflict.

The scalar strategies of Acehnese leaders have been powerfully shaped by the province's political economy and inter-scalar tensions with the government in Jakarta and with district-based elites, and are crucial for explaining the successes and failures of the AGTP. In particular, we focus on donors' attempts to: internationalise the recruitment and training of civil servants, and rationalise and discipline access to, and the spending of, budget resource streams. We show that donors' efforts to reform the bureaucracy were resisted because they clashed with the rules of the game of how provincial elites contest for power. Conversely, donors were able to exploit Acehnese elite fragmentation to introduce limited, yet important, reforms that rescaled some state functions related to the access, outlay and monitoring of budget resources beyond the local, corrupt-ridden context.

Finally, in our concluding chapter, we identify and discuss cross-cutting themes emerging from our case studies. We also draw out some policymaking implications of this research for practitioners of international development. While our approach has clear implications for policy design and implementation, it is only when we can fully explain the outcomes of intervention, and therefore whose interests they serve or marginalise, that we can meaningfully assess their normative implications. Our study reveals that the actions of the elites dominating the national scale are especially important shapers of the outcomes of PSBIs, because their scale management capacity provides them with considerable power to affect what areas of governance are rescaled or not, and how. Thus, where the nationally dominant elite group is highly cohesive, even exceptionally well-resourced international interventions will likely end up reinforcing the power of those elites and the national scale's dominance over other scales, as the example of Solomon Islands clearly shows. However, where elites dominating the national, or another dominant, scale are more fractured, there are often opportunities for donors and other actors to form alliances in support of both upwards and downwards rescaling, by aligning tactically and/ or strategically with factions of nationally dominant elites that have access to state power. The example of Aceh is instructive here. In Aceh, Governor Irwandi was able to capitalise on divisions among national government agencies and among the donors to advance his own interests and capture considerable power and control over resources. This finding shares some resemblance with the literature on 'political settlements' and 'elite pacts', which also sees the cohesion or fragmentation of state elites as a key factor shaping policy directions, democratisation and reform.[60] However, by anchoring our analysis in Gramscian state theory and the politics of scale, we are better able to explain the cohesion or fragmentation of nationally dominant elites as the historically specific product of socio-political struggles with an inherent scalar dimension. We can also systematically analyse the scope and dimensions of contested and shifting scalar constructs, such as 'national' or 'local'. These take on different meanings and political significance not only between countries but also in different historical moments and between different areas of governance and issues. This fine-grained framework allows us to explain clearly why these structures survive or fall apart in particular historical moments.

[60] Parks and Cole 2010; Slater 2010.

1 *Existing Approaches to International Intervention and Local Politics*

In this chapter we critically evaluate the various approaches that examine the interrelations between international interventions and local politics. These approaches, although studying similar phenomena, have emerged in different subfields, especially in peace-building studies and the development assistance literature, with partial overlap. Our argument is that by neglecting the politics of scale, it is not possible to adequately conceptualise and theorise the manner in which interventions affect, and are affected by, local politics in recipient states and societies. Nor is it possible to approach and systematically account for interventions' highly uneven outcomes within and between states. This is because Peace- and State-building Interventions (PSBIs) not only affect relations between different groups contesting power and resources within a given territorial terrain, or across pre-defined and fixed territorial spaces; rather, the production and manipulation of space, especially territorial space, are core dimensions of the ways in which different groups, including the interveners, attempt to attain preferred political and governance outcomes. Consequently, contestations over scale – whether an issue should be governed at e.g. the local or national level, what the scope of these scales is, through what instruments it should be governed, and by which actors – tend to intensify, becoming a key dimension shaping the outcomes of international interventions.

In the area of international development assistance, building 'effective' states has been a core concern since the shift from structural adjustment to 'good governance' and the so-called post-Washington consensus (PWC) in the 1990s.[1] Although typically construed by practitioners as a technical exercise of designing optimal governance systems, failures of implementation and outcome have led to growing realisation in both academia and the donor community that these

[1] Goldfinch et al. 2013: 51.

interventions are inherently political endeavours and that therefore, to be successful, interveners must also 'engage politically'.[2] Nonetheless, considerable disagreement remains over what the relevant political or political economy context is and what engaging politically entails in practice. While an improvement on earlier work, these approaches remain scale-blind because they operate from a point of methodological nationalism that treats the societies within a state's borders as natural units of inquiry.[3] Therefore, their chief emphasis has been on how domestic social and political relations shape the outcomes of public administration reform (PAR) programmes. International interventions' effects on these domestic conflicts are seen to be limited to their capacity to provide resources and material support to some groups at the expense of others. However, donor interventions do not occur in an otherwise undifferentiated national territorial space, but involve attempts to transform the scope and significance of existing scales and/or produce new governance scales, to which local groups respond in ways that alter the spatial terrain of socio-political conflict and often the nature of the conflict itself, thus potentially altering governance outcomes too. For instance, decentralisation programmes or efforts at strengthening national institutions (i.e. effectively insulating them from undesirable societal or political pressures) are significant interventions in the spatial organisation, and hence in the distribution, of power in society. Reinforcing or marginalising particular scales of governance can have significant effects on the capacity of particular groups to promote their interests and preferred normative agendas.

In the peace-building literature, scholars have become interested in understanding processes of state formation, which are seen to be slow, non-linear and messy, as opposed to internationally driven, top-down state-building, which assumes linear progress.[4] Some scholars have been particularly interested in understanding the interrelations between intervention and recipients. Especially popular here has been an emphasis on the hybrid forms of peace and governance produced through the interaction between top-down state-building and bottom-up state formation. A related scholarship has studied the 'friction' produced through this international–local interaction.[5] Scale is an implicit concern for some scholars in this burgeoning literature,

[2] Carothers and De Gramont 2013. [3] Wimmer and Glick Schiller 2002.
[4] Bliesemann de Guevara 2010; Egnell and Haldén 2013. [5] Hughes 2013.

because of its interest in 'local agency' and the 'everyday'.[6] It remains limited, however, by the binaries its core concept imposes on the analysis. Although significant efforts have been made in recent years to avoid reinscribing binaries, such as between traditional/illiberal local and modern/liberal international actors and institutions, hybridity scholars ultimately perpetuate them. This framing then leads to analyses that seek to pinpoint the extent to which particular forms of peace or modes of governance reflect local or international agendas. This tends to ignore the fact that the interests of particular groups (whether ostensibly local or international), the scalar modes of governance they pursue and the alliances they form, cannot be captured within the local/international dichotomy internalised by hybridity and friction approaches. By developing a conception of the politics of scale, premised on work in the political economy school of political geography and grounded in Gramscian state theory,[7] we are able to overcome these problems. For us, 'local', or 'national' and 'international', are not predominantly actor categories, but mutually constitutive, dynamic and flexible arenas of politics, power and contestation. We develop this approach in Chapter 2.

In the present chapter, we begin with a brief overview of the changes in peace-building and aid orthodoxy since the end of the Cold War, leading to the current debates over the relationship between international intervention and local politics. We will then describe the principal characteristics and assumptions of the dominant state-building modality, of which more recent approaches are critical. We will especially focus on the important role PAR plays within this. Then, in turn, we will examine the critiques of this state-building paradigm emerging in peace-building and development scholarships, which emphasise the significance of local politics, identifying their contributions and their limitations.

International Intervention: From Triumphalism to Despair?

In this section, we trace the broad contours of the historical transformations in both international peace-building practices and the realm of international development assistance since the end of the Cold War. Our aim is not to explain why particular shifts have

[6] Mac Ginty and Richmond 2013. [7] Jessop 2008; Smith 2010.

occurred, as this would be a very large undertaking beyond the scope of this book,[8] but rather to identify the key changes in this period as necessary background for our subsequent discussion. Development assistance and peace-building came to be increasingly entangled in theory and practice in the post-Cold War era, especially during the 2000s through the human security agenda and state-building interventionism.[9] Despite their increasing assimilation, however, the fields remain somewhat separate as domains of practice, professionalisation and scholarly inquiry. In both areas, considerable optimism in the early 1990s had turned to scepticism and even despair during the first decade of the new millennium, in light of persistent and evident failures of implementation and outcome. These failures have led to the development of new foci for research and practice, and new approaches and ideas, critically discussed in subsequent sections, focusing on local societies and politics.

The end of the Cold War was declared 'the end of history' by Francis Fukuyama,[10] because of the widely held view that it heralded the triumph of liberal democracy and free market capitalism over other forms of social, political and economic organisation. Announcing the rise of a 'new world order', then-US President George H. W. Bush (1991) argued that the prevailing paralysis of the UN Security Council (UNSC), related to superpower rivalry, was over and that it could finally become the effective tool for collective international security it was intended to be.[11] This change was reflected in the UNSC-mandated war against Saddam Hussein's Iraq, which invaded Kuwait in 1990. In 1992, then-UN Secretary-General Boutros Boutros-Ghali released an influential report, entitled *An Agenda for Peace.*[12] The report was novel in discussing a range of interventions *within* countries to both ameliorate existing conflicts and reduce the likelihood of future conflict. The concept of 'peace-building' was mentioned by Boutros-Ghali in the report for the first time, referring to 'rebuilding the institutions and infrastructures of nations torn by civil war and strife'. The report also identified as necessary for stabilisation addressing the deeper causes of conflict – 'economic despair, social injustice and political oppression'.[13] Dealing with these issues reinforced the view in the UN and key capitals that intervention was required within

[8] See Carroll 2010; Hameiri 2010. [9] Duffield 2001. [10] Fukuyama 1992.
[11] Barnett 1997. [12] Boutros-Ghali 1992. [13] Boutros-Ghali 1992: 2.

target states and their societies. *An Agenda for Peace* was not mere talk. It was published at a time in which the UN found itself at the centre of several such large-scale peace-building missions in the former Yugoslavia, Cambodia and Somalia.[14] These interventions reflected, some claimed, an epochal shift from 'Westphalian' to 'post-Westphalian' peacekeeping, or from an underlying assumption that war was between states to one which saw state weakness as the key source of conflict and human insecurity.[15] They also indicated, it was argued, an increasing willingness to intervene within states by a new generation of liberal leaders committed to 'ethical foreign policy', as opposed to Cold War *realpolitik*.[16]

Meantime, in the realm of international development, the end of the Cold War meant sharply declining budgets, as aid was traditionally used as a Cold War tool to cement support in the Third World.[17] Intellectually, however, mainstream development orthodoxy was also in a triumphant mood, confident in the veracity of the neo-liberal paradigm. To many it appeared that the problem of how to promote development in poor countries was resolved and all that was required was full implementation of structural adjustment.[18] The World Bank and International Monetary Fund (IMF) had already in the 1980s promoted structural adjustment programmes (SAPs), entailing massive privatisation of publicly owned companies and assets, trade and financial liberalisation and deregulation of economic activities across large parts of the developing world.[19] With many developing countries, especially in Africa and Latin America in urgent need of financial assistance following the debt crisis of the early 1980s, the international financial institutions (IFIs) used aid 'conditionalities' to coerce recipient governments into accepting SAPs in return for the release of much-needed funds.[20] In the course of the 1980s, and especially at the end of the Cold War, the international development agencies of industrialised states also adopted the structural adjustment mantra.[21]

The worlds of peace-building and development assistance began to partly merge in the leading peace-building modality of the 1990s, which Paris described as combining quick democratisation, economic liberalisation and the departure of international forces.[22] This approach was

[14] Mayall 1996. [15] Bellamy et al. 2004. [16] Stedman 1992/1993.
[17] Lancaster 2007. [18] Craig and Porter 2006; Toye 1987.
[19] SAPRIN 2004. [20] Pender 2001. [21] E.g. Essex 2013; Rosser 2008.
[22] Paris 2004.

based on the assumptions of the liberal peace thesis and democratic peace theory that democracy and liberal market economics were the best guarantee against internal and international conflict.[23] Crucially, in this view, the particular social, economic, political or cultural characteristics of recipient societies and states were of little consequence to the objectives and design of intervention. The recipe for interveners was clear and constant across all cases. Joseph Stiglitz notes, for example, how World Bank and IMF prescriptions were literally copied and pasted from one country to the next. This was revealed when in one case a particular country's name was carried over into a document relating to another country.[24]

However, in the course of the 1990s and early 2000s, the implementation and outcome failures of both peace-building and development assistance had become too numerous to ignore.[25] In peace-building, already by 1993 the US-led mission to Somalia had run into serious difficulties, symbolised by the widely televised images of the bodies of American soldiers being dragged through the streets of Mogadishu by an angry mob. Subsequently, the US government became reluctant to commit troops to UN missions, including Rwanda in 1994, where a terrible genocide took place. And even though international interventions in war-torn countries did not stop completely, confidence in the rapid 'democratise–privatise–leave' approach was shaken. In the domain of foreign aid, SAPs had been so unpopular with recipients, and so unsuccessful in promoting development, that the World Bank's legitimacy as the world's premier development organisation was at risk of being significantly compromised.[26] A series of economic crises in the 1990s – Mexico, Russia, East Asia – also posed a challenge to the so-called Washington consensus on structural adjustment. This was not least because Mexico and post-Soviet Russia were considered faithful neo-liberal disciples.[27]

Subsequently, in both peace-building and development aid, the state became the core focus of attention, leading to even closer convergence between the fields of peace-building and development assistance. But rather than change the overarching aims of intervention, practitioners and scholars have endeavoured to develop new modalities and techniques around the concept of state-building that implement essentially

[23] See Doyle 1986; Richmond 2005. [24] Stiglitz 2002.
[25] Carroll 2010; Paris 2004. [26] See SAPRIN 2004. [27] Stiglitz 1998.

the same programmes. In the aid domain, state-building interventionism was already evident in the 1990s with the appointments of James Wolfensohn as president of the World Bank and Joseph Stiglitz as its chief economist. Backed up by widely cited studies linking the effectiveness of aid in promoting economic growth to the quality of governance in recipient countries,[28] the Bank's new leadership sought to promote a 'new development paradigm'.[29] This was to be implemented especially through Poverty Reduction Strategy Papers (PRSPs), which recipient governments were meant to develop in consultation with donors and civil society.[30] Known colloquially as the post-Washington consensus (PWC), this development agenda did not abandon the earlier preference for deep economic liberalisation, or any of the Washington consensus' substantive objectives. Rather, it sought to specify and promote the political, economic and social institutions required for liberal market-led development to succeed. In other words, the focus in development policy has shifted from destroying the state, under the assumption that markets would then flourish, to building the state up in market-supporting ways – in other words, to state transformation.[31] As we elaborate below, it is under this transition in development orthodoxy that PAR programmes became an especially important component of donor interventions,[32] alongside the broader focus on promoting good governance.

The apparent failure of external 'conditionalities' to force recipient governments to adopt donor-preferred economic policies and promote meaningful change led to a shift towards embedding liberal market-supporting governance within the state. Donors aimed to use aid to establish and/or empower key units within the administration of recipient states, staffed by donor representatives and/or like-minded technocrats. They then attempted to isolate these technocrats from undesirable political and societal pressures, which were seen to undermine efforts to institutionalise 'good governance', a term that essentially refers to liberal market-supportive institutions, such as property rights, the rule of law, transparency and accountability.[33] This internalisation of donor programming within the recipient state

[28] Burnside and Dollar 1997. [29] Stiglitz 1998. [30] Craig and Porter 2006.
[31] See Carroll 2010; Craig and Porter 2006. [32] Grindle and Hilderbrand 1995.
[33] Hout and Robison 2008.

has been described as a move from temporary *intervention* to ongoing *governance*.[34]

In the peace-building field, too, state-building became a more explicit object of international intervention, especially following the September 11 attacks in the US. This agenda cannot merely be seen as a direct descendent and natural evolution of earlier peacekeeping and peace-building modalities, since it emerged out of a concern, not with supporting peace as such, but with managing the security risk that poor governance and lack of control in so-called fragile states appeared to pose to developed states and their populations.[35] The 2002 US National Security Strategy paper clearly identified failing states as a major source of international insecurity, in that they were seen to permit the spread of trans-border security problems like al-Qaeda–style terrorism.[36] Similar assessments were made in the same period by the European Union[37] and the UN.[38] Indeed, international state-building interventionism extends well beyond war-torn and post-conflict countries, to be seen as applicable to developing countries more broadly.[39] Nonetheless, state-building became the dominant delivery device for liberal peace-building in the late 1990s and 2000s, and as a result the two became almost synonymous in the 2000s.[40] The UN's Responsibility to Protect (R2P) norm, which aims to prevent genocide and mass atrocities, has also adopted state-building as a core implementation mechanism. This is especially evident in R2P's Pillar II, which focuses on 'capacity building', as a means of preventing the development of domestic environments conducive to mass atrocities.[41]

As with the state-building turn in international development aid, the state-building agenda in peace-building did not indicate a serious reconsideration of the objectives of the earlier intervention projects, only of the means to achieve them. The new agenda was aptly characterised by Roland Paris as one of 'institutionalisation before liberalisation'.[42] Rather than rush to liberalise the economy of target countries and democratise their political systems, it was argued that interveners should focus on developing the institutional capacity of the intervened states seen as prerequisites for successful democratisation and liberalisation – a change in sequencing, not goals. The result has

34 Harrison 2004; Pender 2001; Williams 2013. 35 Hameiri 2014a.
36 White House 2002. 37 EU 2003. 38 United Nations 2004.
39 Bickerton 2007. 40 See Paris and Sisk 2009; Paris 2010.
41 E.g. United Nations 2013b. 42 Paris 2004.

been an even closer melding of the international aid and peace-building agendas. With the theory and practice of state-building already well developed in the field of development aid, more security-focused interventions have latched on to these templates for establishing 'effective' states.[43] In one prominent example, the 'light footprint' neo-conservative ideology underpinning Iraq's initial occupation by the US and allied forces gave way within one month to a neo-liberal state-building approach, which provided far clearer guidelines on how to restructure the Iraqi state and economy.[44] Ironically, the good governance agenda in aid and development was initially used to reduce aid delivery to 'poorly performing' states.[45] However, once policymakers determined that leaving failing or fragile states alone was too risky, aid agencies began to use similar interventions to those deployed elsewhere since the late 1990s.[46]

State-Building Interventions and Public Administration Reform

In this section, we introduce readers to the core ideas underpinning contemporary state-building and associated PAR programmes and to these interventions' key elements, as background for its critique and attempted revision by development and peace-building scholars. As we shall see, the mainstream state-building approaches do not generally tailor intervention objectives to the particular social, economic, political or cultural characteristics of target states and their societies. Rather, the focus is on specifying the kinds of generic institutions *and* capacities required for functioning, 'effective' statehood. Attaining positive outcomes is seen largely as a question of technocratic capacity. Politics, if it is considered, is accorded a limited role to provide support for predetermined governance programmes and marginalise resistance to these.

International state-building interventions are invariably premised on some notion of what a functioning state looks like, although this is rarely made explicit. These notions of ideal-typical statehood can be grouped into two main camps, based on either neo-liberal or neo-Weberian variants of new institutionalism, with the former finding greater expression in the work of development organisations.

[43] Duffield 2007. [44] Dodge 2009. [45] Hout 2004.
[46] E.g. DFID 2005; USAID 2005.

Despite their differences, both perspectives essentially concur that state fragility or failure is a problem of state capacity and political will, with the latter viewed as a secondary problem to that of capacity.[47]

State capacity began as a neo-Weberian concept, in the 'bringing the state back in' literature of the 1980s and 1990s.[48] For neo-Weberian scholars, state capacity has horizontal and vertical dimensions. Horizontally, it reflects the capacity of the agencies and organisations of the state apparatus to penetrate and mould society towards the attainment of shared goals – akin to Mann's notion of 'infrastructural power'.[49] This necessarily entails the capacity to overpower recalcitrant elements challenging state authority, if required. Vertically, a state's capacity is assessed in terms of its organisational coherence, relative to an ideal-typical, rational Weberian state, and consequently its ability to turn policy goals into reality.[50] Neo-liberal institutionalists, who are dominant within mainstream development organisations, have basically adopted the horizontal notion of state capacity from the neo-Weberian scholarship, but have a narrower conception of vertical capacity, focusing on whether a state provides 'good governance' for liberal market-led development.[51]

Crucially for our purposes, both notions of capacity as applied in PSBIs to-date maintain a broadly liberal, social contract understanding of state-society relations.[52] Citizens, it is assumed, will give their allegiance to the state, rather than other centres of authority, such as clans, tribes or warlords, if the state upholds its side of the social contract. Legitimate state authority, as opposed to brutal coercion (assumed to be less sustainable), is seen to require the delivery of 'political goods' to citizens. This is the distinction Zartman draws between 'strong' and 'hard' states,[53] or that Mann draws between 'infrastructural' and 'despotic' power.[54] It reflects a long-standing preoccupation dating back to Weber himself with the sources of legitimate authority.[55] In conventional forms of international state-building, state capacity and legitimacy are thus seen as inherently linked, with the former seen as a precondition for the latter.[56] In practice, this led to an emphasis by practitioners, alongside the broader good governance agenda, on supporting the capacity of target states to provide basic

[47] Hameiri 2010. [48] Evans et al. 1985; Weiss 1999. [49] Mann 1993.
[50] Fukuyama 2013; Krasner and Risse 2014. [51] See Hameiri 2009.
[52] Von Einsiedel 2005. [53] Zartman 1995. [54] Mann 1993.
[55] Seabrooke 2002. [56] Batley et al. 2012: 137; OECD 2010.

public services, like policing, health, education, infrastructure and even jobs.[57] State-builders have also focused on improving target states' capacity to generate domestic tax revenue, as an effective tax system is also seen to reinforce the social contract between state and society by making states more responsive to taxpayer demands.[58] Since state-building has been typically understood through the lens of a liberal social contract, PAR has become a key plank of this agenda.[59] The emphasis on PAR has been reinforced by the UN's Millennium Development Goals (MDGs), which also identified effective public administrations as crucial for service-delivery towards meeting the MDGs.[60] This remains a core feature of the Sustainable Development Goals (SDGs), which started to replace the MDGs in 2015.

Public Administration Reform and Service Delivery

The rationale for focusing on PAR is clearly expressed by Fukuyama: 'Governance [viz. a government's ability to make and enforce rules and to deliver services] is about execution or what has traditionally fallen within the domain of public administration, as opposed to politics or public policy'.[61] The key to the quality of government, Fukuyama adds, 'is the result of an interaction between capacity and autonomy. That is, more or less autonomy can be a good or bad thing depending on how much underlying capacity a bureaucracy has'.[62] In other words, capable public administrations require, in Fukuyama's view, greater autonomy from societal and political pressures, while ineffective ones need to be pressured from the outside, with donor support, to improve. State legitimacy is seen from this vantage, perhaps ironically, to be premised on the bureaucracy's *lack* of responsiveness to society, at least where societal demands are unrelated to more efficient service-delivery or liberal governance. Reform failure, in turn, is explained not in terms of PAR programmes' unsuitability to target societies, but as emanating from illegitimate resistance by 'vested interests', poorly designed institutions or from poor implementation by donors.[63]

[57] OECD 2010; Vaux and Visman 2005.
[58] Bräutigam et al. 2008; Everest-Phillips 2010; Moore 2004.
[59] Brinkerhoff et al. 2012: 274; Goldfinch et al. 2013: 97.
[60] Batley et al. 2012: 133. [61] Fukuyama 2013: 351.
[62] Fukuyama 2013: 360. [63] Bergling et al. 2010; Cornell 2014: 193.

Indeed, the conventional literature on PAR has long been dominated by public choice theory,[64] and by theories of institutional design.[65] Public choice theory promotes a view of the state as an ahistorical entity, engaged in a process of 'getting to Denmark' – i.e. efficient functioning that promotes stability and economic growth and, therefore, peace and human development. This is hampered by the self-interested actions of vested interests and rent-seekers – politicians, public servants and distributional coalitions – who seek to advance their own power through blocking flows of information and services, rather than facilitating these. Such an approach is exemplified in a United Nations Development Programme (UNDP) review which reported: 'Civil servants are in general understandably mistrustful of reforms that threaten their jobs and the benefits and perks that may have been a deciding factor in remaining in poorly paid employment. Politically influential public sector unions might fear losing their power through loss of membership, and oppose changes to pay structures that they have negotiated'.[66] This resistance has to be overcome, it is argued, for better governance outcomes to be attained. The public choice approach to reform focuses in particular on using various incentives to resolve these kinds of problems,[67] including positive incentives, such as performance bonuses, or negative incentives, such as censure by independent accountability and anti-corruption agencies. The reforms to public administrations inspired by public choice theory reflect, for some, the internationalisation of the so-called New Public Management model, which emerged in some developed countries in the 1980s and 1990s.[68] This approach promotes international intervention into target states' public administrations, because foreign and internationally trained technocrats are seen to be above the local fray and therefore as less likely to advance their own narrow interests ahead of 'good' public policy.[69]

The institutional design approach regards ineffective governance as the result of a historical accretion of bad decisions and failures to change with the times. These affect the structure of institutions, which in turn determines how public servants react. The 'new institutionalism' assumes that the behaviour of public servants, politicians

[64] Batley 2004; Brinkerhoff 2008; Gelb et al. 1991; Pritchett and Woolcock 2004.
[65] Levy 2004; Reilly 2006; Rodrik et al. 2002. [66] UNDP 2004: 20.
[67] Fukuyama 2013: 349. [68] Minogue 2001.
[69] Hutchison et al. 2014: 17–18.

and citizens is formed in large part by the political, economic and social institutions prevailing in particular societies, and therefore prospects for change are limited unless external intervention can impose new rules of the game to which players become habituated over time.[70] As with public choice theory, an important aspect of new institutionalism is the identification of informal institutions or networks operating within the state to promote particular sectional interests, which undermine formal processes of accountability and representation. These approaches have promoted a Weberian portrayal of PAR as the rationalisation of institutions bloated and hampered by cultures of patrimonialism.[71] Despite many similarities, institutionalist approaches are often more pessimistic than their public choice counterparts about the likelihood of change. Mary Shirley says 'new institutional economics is not good news for foreign aid . . . And most of what we know about aid confirms this pessimistic view. History suggests that institutions change slowly, and mostly endogenously'.[72]

In practice, therefore, both approaches have converged in PAR programmes that seek to make public administrations responsive not to domestic political leaders and citizens, who are assessed as either opposed to reform or unable to bring it about, but rather to predetermined international agendas and objectives. These programmes seek to circumscribe the range of political choices available to the leaders and populations of target societies by empowering technocrats within public administrations over other potential sources of authority.[73] Insulating public administrations from contending political and ideological agendas, in the interests of promoting good governance reforms and service-delivery, is precisely what the oft-used term 'capacity building' means in the context of PSBIs.[74] As we shall later see, this effort to 'rescale' strategic parts of public administrations – to insulate them from their domestic context and link them to international agencies empowering them to discipline other parts of their states and societies – tends to fragment the state, producing new forms of scalar politics that often lead to outcomes radically different to those desired by interveners.

[70] Carothers 1998: 96; Kaufman 2003: 36; Levy 2004; Stedman 1997.
[71] Carothers 1998. [72] Quoted in Booth 2011: S11; see also Ottaway 2003.
[73] Hameiri 2010. [74] Hameiri 2009.

However, even proponents of this form of state-building and associated PAR programmes have had to recognise in recent years that they are often unsuccessful. Already in 2004, a UNDP review concluded that PAR 'is as infrequently entirely successful as it is vitally important'.[75] Likewise, Fritz and Menocal, citing a wide range of World Bank, Asian Development Bank (ADB) and European Commission reports, claim:

> [S]ubstantial resources have also been devoted to the reform of core functions of the state – the civil service, public financial management and wider public administration. More than $4 billion of aid was spent on 'improving government administration' in 2005, according to the OECD's aid database. However, a general perception is that such 'public-sector reforms', as well as capacity-building efforts more generally, have fallen short of expectations.[76]

Goldfinch et al. add: 'Although considerable resources and attention have been allocated to recent "good governance" public management reform in low income and fragile states, there is little evidence as to what degree this agenda has been implemented nor as to whether it has led to improved services and outcomes for populations ... We report that there is little, if any, empirical evidence that reform enhances service delivery'.[77] Large cross-country studies now even challenge the assumed correlation between good governance and poverty reduction, underpinning the World Bank's PRSPs.[78] Similarly, the number of publications proclaiming a crisis of liberal peace-building has spiked from the late 2000s.[79] Especially significant was the abject failure of the American-led efforts to establish liberal democracies – or even stable states – in Iraq and Afghanistan.[80] Subsequent efforts to pacify these countries were premised on support for local strongmen under the guise of working with customary forms of rule, quite a distance from the original aims of these operations.[81]

Despite these problems, state-building interventionism remains a core tenet of the international development and peace-building agendas. In 2013, the United Nations' High-Level Panel on the Post-2015 Development Agenda maintained that 'good governance

[75] UNDP 2004: 18. [76] Fritz and Menocal 2007: 544.
[77] Goldfinch et al. 2013: 49. [78] Kwon and Kim 2014.
[79] Cooper 2007; Paris 2010; Richmond 2009b; Zaum 2012.
[80] Dodge 2007; Suhrke 2007. [81] Kilcullen 2009.

and effective institutions' should remain a central component of thinking about development interventions.[82] Indeed, the Sustainable Development Goals (SDGs) developed to replace the Millennium Development Goals (MDGs) from 2015 maintain a clear emphasis on good governance and capacity-building.[83] Meanwhile, Carothers and De Gramont[84] detect little change in the way donors plan and implement their programmes despite the apparent flurry of critical reflection and emphasis on engaging politically.[85] Yet, state-building's evident failures of implementation and outcome have spawned a new round of criticisms and recommendations, which we will examine in the next section.

Interventions' Interaction with Recipients: Existing Approaches

The apparent failings of more conventional state-building approaches have led practitioners and scholars alike to look beyond technocratic explanations, as well as beyond bland invocations of deficient political will. Increasingly, they began to more closely examine the ways in which the social, political, economic and cultural structures of target states and societies interact with, and shape the outcomes of, PSBIs. The discussion below is divided into subsections on the development and peace-building literatures respectively, though overlaps exist. The separate discussions are merited since, although state-building interventionism has partly merged the fields of peace-building and development, they remain often distinct in practice, owing to their different historical, institutional and intellectual origins. This is evident in the fact that the critiques of conventional state-building in the two fields discussed below have largely emerged in mutual isolation and limited interaction. As we shall see, despite providing considerable improvement on the conventional institutionalist approaches to state-building described above, none adequately theorises international intervention and local politics, since they neglect the spatial dimensions of struggles over the political outcomes of intervention.

82 United Nations 2013a. 83 Weber 2014.
84 Carothers and De Gramont 2013. 85 See also Chhotray and Hulme 2009.

Peace-Building, State Formation and Hybridity

In the study of peace-building, recurring failures of outcome and implementation have over the past decade encouraged the growth of new scholarships dedicated to studying the interaction of international interventions with target states and societies. We have seen a renewed interest in understanding state 'formation', which focuses on bottom-up, non-linear processes of state-making in areas where interventions occur. The growth of scholarship on state formation has largely combined with a burgeoning and increasingly popular literature on hybrid peace governance, international/local friction and the local turn.[86]

The state formation literature seeks to go beyond the narrow, fixed conceptions of Weberian statehood common in the scholarship on international intervention. Instead it seeks to draw on the insights of sociological and anthropological approaches to state formation 'offering contextual bottom up, post-colonial and subaltern insights relating to questions of inequality and justice as well as agency'.[87] The main argument of this literature is that long-term, bottom-up processes of state formation limit the possibilities for short-term projects of top-down, externally driven state-building.[88] This is because the systems, institutions and values of interveners reflect developments and the state-formation experience in Europe and industrialised countries,[89] which, some argue, are different from the experience of developing societies. There, divergent ideas of peace, governance and statehood are deeply embedded and enjoy greater legitimacy. By insisting on promoting alien forms of statehood in the non-Western world, state-building interventions are rendered 'failed by design'.[90] The best that these interventions could hope to achieve is a negative form of peace where the state acts as a container on social pressures from below.[91] This literature has also argued for some time that examining local agency is crucial, since target populations will tend to resist external impositions, either directly or more passively by erecting parallel informal systems. Indeed, rather than passively accept intervention programmes, recipients actively attempt to promote their own preferred form of statehood or governance.[92]

86 E.g. Richmond 2014. 87 Richmond 2014: 59.
88 Bliesemann de Guevara 2012; Egnell and Haldén 2013; Jung 2008.
89 Jung 2008. 90 Richmond 2014. 91 Mac Ginty 2006; Richmond 2014.
92 Bliesemann de Guevara 2010; Heathershaw 2008.

The emphasis on recipients' agency has led some scholars to attempt to develop ways of describing and analysing the outcomes of the interaction between exogenous state-building and endogenous state formation or peace processes. Especially popular in this literature have been the notions of hybridity and friction.[93] Whereas the development studies literature (examined below) is almost entirely scale-blind, this growing literature on hybrid peace governance and the local turn implicitly recognises the politics of scale; it appears to be more attuned to how local institutions and customs, not just at the national level, affect the outcomes of intervention. Yet, its problematic tendency to assume outcomes are produced along the lines separating local from international, and its incapacity to specify the local, are major limitations. Furthermore, the tendency to dichotomise international and local leads to problematic and narrow explanations of intervention outcomes that focus especially on where particular cases are placed on a continuum between ideal-typical modern/international and traditional/local alternatives. Merely locating PSBI outcomes on this spectrum does not explain why particular modes of governance emerge or whose specific interests they serve, which is the explicit aim of our approach.

The hybridity and local turn scholarship has emerged out of the earlier 'critique of the liberal peace' literature, which became ubiquitous in the 2000s.[94] These scholars drew largely on earlier post-structuralist and post-colonial studies, such as Michel Foucault's work on the local operation of power, especially his concept of governmentality,[95] Escobar's work on post-development and Homi Bhabha's writings on hybridity[96] to criticise the assumptions of the liberal peace thesis, expressly the view that the top-down promotion of liberal governance in non-liberal societies was conducive to peaceful outcomes. Richmond,[97] for example, argued that the evident failures of PSBIs reflected the fundamental incompatibility between the liberal institutions interveners promoted and the target societies' culture,

[93] Not all scholars of state formation have adopted hybridity and friction as core organising concepts. Some simply continue to emphasise the durability of the power relations shaping the historical state formation process, in a way that approximates the approaches we discuss in development studies.

[94] Campbell et al. 2011; Newman 2009; Pugh 2005; Richmond 2005; Tadjbakhsh 2011.

[95] See Li 2007. [96] See Richmond 2014. [97] Richmond 2005.

norms and institutions, which resisted changes to local customs and authority. More recently, this critique has morphed into attempts to analyse how international interventions interact with their local recipients and develop alternative prescriptions for policymakers. Policymakers, in turn, have developed considerable interest in the local turn and its applicability.[98]

As mentioned, the core concept harnessed by this literature is hybridity, which in the context of peace-building denotes:

> the way that local actors attempt to respond to, resist and ultimately reshape peace initiatives through interactions with international actors and institutions ... Unique, hybrid forms of peace arise when the strategies, institutions and norms of international, largely liberal-democratic peacebuilding interventions collide with the everyday practices and agencies of local actors affected by conflict.[99]

These everyday qualities are assumed to be non-liberal. Hybridity is thus 'a state of affairs in which liberal and illiberal norms, institutions, and actors coexist'.[100] It emerges because of a 'gap',[101] or 'agonism' between the agendas of liberal international interveners and those of non-liberal target societies.[102] Some have similarly used the concept of friction to describe 'the unpredictable and unexpected nature of this interaction'.[103]

This literature often slips between description and prescription, with hybridity used to describe intervention outcomes and to prescribe the incorporation of local priorities into PSBIs to achieve success.[104] Scholars suggest that hybrid outcomes, being more legitimate in the eyes of local people, are more effective in securing social order and peace,[105] or are even potentially 'emancipatory'.[106] Yet, many have recently become sceptical of interveners' capacity to purposely engineer legitimate forms of hybrid governance or peace.[107]

Before its adoption by peace-building scholars, the concept of hybridity was already widely used in other fields, especially cultural and postcolonial studies,[108] where extensive criticism of it had already

98 Hughes et al. 2015. 99 Richmond and Mitchell 2012: 8, 33.
100 Belloni 2012: 22. 101 Belloni 2012: 23.
102 Richmond and Mitchell 2012: 26. 103 Millar et al. 2013: 137.
104 Millar 2014: 501; Leonardsson and Rudd 2015.
105 Boege et al. 2009; Kumar and De la Haye 2012; Richmond 2014.
106 Mac Ginty 2010; Richmond 2011, 2014.
107 Mac Ginty and Richmond 2016; Millar 2014; Visoka 2012.
108 Peterson 2012; Richmond and Mitchell 2012.

generated an 'anti-hybridity backlash'.[109] Accordingly, peace-building scholars using hybridity attempted to avoid well-recognised pitfalls. In particular, they sought to counter accusations that hybridity is dependent upon, and thus reifies, pure social categories and identities, existing prior to intervention, much like colonial-era racial theory. This led scholars to deny that hybridity essentialises the international/local distinction, or essentialises, parochialises or romanticises local institutions and norms. However, in reality, since hybridity necessarily implies the existence of binaries, hybridity scholars actually continue to perpetuate the problems they claim to overcome.

In attempting to rebut criticism that hybridity reifies the 'local' and 'international', Mac Ginty argues that, rather than denoting the grafting together of two separate entities, hybridity is a *process*, resting on prior hybridity – 'a long history of interaction, fusion, competition, resistance and coalescence'. The liberal peace's policies, as well as their advocates, are themselves the product of prior hybridisation, and they are attempting to influence 'already hybridised environments that have experienced civil war or authoritarianism. Further hybridisation ensues as (the already hybrid) local and international interact, conflict and cooperate'.[110] For Boege et al., 'there are no clear-cut boundaries between the realm of the exogenous "modern" and the endogenous "customary"; instead processes of assimilation, articulation, transformation and/or adoption are at the interface of the global/exogenous and the local/indigenous'.[111] Hybridity scholars claim that hybridity actually disavows binaries like local/international, Western/non-Western, or modern/customary, emphasising their interaction instead.[112] Authors have similarly claimed that the local is 'neither monolithic nor necessarily incompatible with liberal norms'.[113] They are not romanticising the local as desirable, they add; only identifying its incorporation as essential for successful peace-building.[114]

Such caveats notwithstanding, hybridity scholars *do* in fact dichotomise and essentialise the local and the international, with the international typically reified as a realm of modern, liberal praxis and the local viewed as a domain of pre-modern tradition and customs.[115]

[109] Pieterse 2001. [110] Mac Ginty 2011: 8. [111] Boege et al. 2009: 15.
[112] Mac Ginty 2010: 397; Peterson 2012: 12.
[113] Belloni 2012: 23; Mac Ginty and Richmond 2013; Richmond and Mitchell 2012.
[114] Boege et al. 2009; Mac Ginty 2011. [115] Paffenholz 2015.

Thus, Boege et al.'s above-quoted rejection of binaries[116] is immediately undermined by the simultaneous presentation of another: the global/exogenous and the local/indigenous. Moreover, their caveat is followed by the statement, 'Nevertheless, the use of the terms "custom", "customary institutions" and so on is helpful because they expose specific local indigenous characteristics that distinguish them from introduced institutions that belong to the realm of the state and civil society'. Similarly, Mac Ginty states, 'Notions of hybridity move us away from the binary combinations ... [like] modern versus traditional, Western versus non-Western, legal-rational versus ritualistic-irrational',[117] yet immediately he reinstates the international/local binary:

> Hybrid peace [is] the result of the interplay of ... the compliance [and] incentivizing powers of liberal peace agents, networks and structures [and] the ability of local actors to resist, ignore or adapt liberal peace interventions ... [and to] present and maintain alternative forms of peacemaking.[118]

Essentialising binaries are particularly apparent when hybridity is used to explain particular cases. For example, in East Timor, a paradigmatic case for the hybridity scholarship, Hohe describes a 'clash of paradigms'[119] between the 'Western-style paradigm of statebuilding' and 'resilient traditional structures';[120] Wallis emphasises the merging of the liberal with the local;[121] Grenfell distinguishes between the donor-dominated 'state, as a modern institutional form of governance' and 'tribal-traditional' governance;[122] and Freire and Lopes dichotomise 'local dynamics' and 'external intervention'.[123]

Moreover, the definition of the 'local' in such accounts is slippery and lacking specificity.[124] Since hybridity proposes to understand PSBI outcomes as the interaction 'along the shared interface between the local and international',[125] this inability to clearly specify the local is a serious limitation. At times, it is implicitly everything that is not international, as in formulations focusing on the '"contact zone" ... between local and external'[126] or 'the melding of the "international"

116 Boege et al. 2009: 15. 117 Mac Ginty 2010: 397.
118 Mac Ginty 2010: 391. 119 Hohe 2002.
120 Chopra and Hohe 2004: 289. 121 Wallis 2012. 122 Grenfell 2008: 90.
123 Freire and Lopes 2013. 124 Hughes et al. 2015: 818.
125 Richmond and Mitchell 2012: 1. 126 Peterson 2012: 11.

with the "local"'.[127] Here, local seems to mean domestic or even national. Elsewhere, however, local seems to denote something more sub-national, as in dichotomous presentations of 'non-state indigenous societal structures and [externally] introduced state structures'.[128] Here, the local is understood as 'traditional, indigenous and customary',[129] denoting social relations 'at an individual or communal level rather than at the national level'.[130] However, interveners always engage *some* indigenous collaborators in constructing subnational and national institutions. Are these crucial actors not local? Is the national state built by state-builders not, in part at least, local? Hybridity scholars clearly struggle to engage these questions satisfactorily. Richmond[131] and Mac Ginty,[132] for instance, resort to especially awkward distinctions between 'international-locals' and 'local-locals'. Only the latter, in their view, are seen to be an authentic reflection of the kind of everyday beliefs, norms and institutions that PSBIs must find expression for if they are to avoid constructing top-down, failed-by-design states.[133] How these groups can be distinguished in practice is rarely made clear, and the distinction scholars necessarily make between genuine expressions of the everyday and other forms of agency in recipient societies are based on the same problematic top-down judgements they accuse more conventional peace-building approaches of deploying.[134]

The weakness of this dichotomising approach impedes hybridity scholars' capacity to accurately describe PSBI outcomes. Contrary to commonplace discussions of clashing local and international paradigms, our case study chapters show that local societies are not necessarily devoid of liberal or democratic practices or characterised by adherence to mystical beliefs and tribal authorities. They are highly variegated and conflict-ridden, with certain social groups supporting, and others opposing, the restoration of traditional values and structures, often for instrumental, but sometimes for ideological, reasons. Clearly, the dynamics shaping PSBIs' outcomes are too complex to be analysed in terms of local resistance to international projects; nor does labelling outcomes as multiple hybridisations bring us closer to an

[127] Millar 2014: 502. [128] Boege et al. 2009: 17. [129] Mac Ginty 2010: 391.
[130] Millar 2014: 502. [131] Richmond 2009a. [132] Mac Ginty 2011.
[133] Richmond 2014. [134] Randazzo 2016.

explanation. Instead, we see actors located at diverse territorial scales forging alliances to pursue their interests and normative agendas.

These problems of description stem from hybridity's intrinsically problematic nature. To identify a hybrid implies that two (or more) *distinct* entities have been combined. It is meaningless as a descriptive or explanatory device unless one can clearly specify the original entities, even if they are only heuristics, that combine to produce the outcome one seeks to explain. This is why scholars, despite repeatedly disclaiming the use of particular binaries, constantly substitute them with some other binary. The concept merely becomes a superficial label for extreme complexity – a 'whirr of hybridity' in Mac Ginty's words.[135]

Hybridity's tendency to reinstate binaries constrains what scholars can explain. Although scholars use diverse explanatory resources, drawn from a variety of disciplines, hybridity nonetheless structures their empirical analyses along dichotomising lines, presenting outcomes as an accommodation between the local and international. For example, in arguably the subfield's most sophisticated approach, Mac Ginty[136] focuses on liberal peace actors' compulsory and inducement powers as well as local actors' capacities to resist, subvert or substitute alternative projects. The balance between these defines the degree of hybridity observed between international/liberal and local/traditional ideal-types. Hybridity thus drives researchers to develop more sophisticated ways of *categorising* hybrid outcomes on this binary spectrum by developing more nuanced taxonomies[137] and/or identifying processes, types, 'levels' and 'degrees' of hybridisation.[138]

However, identifying where the outcome of a particular intervention sits on a spectrum between local/traditional and international/liberal not only rests on problematic dichotomies, it also tells us very little about the institutions established. Why did certain institutions emerge and not others? How do they actually function? And most importantly, whose interests and normative agendas do they advance? Merely categorising outcomes as melding the local and international does not answer these questions. As noted, not all locals feel well served by traditional practices; the incorporation of such practices into PSBIs

135 Mac Ginty 2010: 404. 136 Mac Ginty 2011.
137 Belloni 2012; Mac Ginty 2010, 2011; Richmond and Mitchell 2012.
138 Mac Ginty 2010; Millar 2014; Visoka 2012; Wallis 2012.

does not simply signify the local trumping the international, but rather a much more complex power struggle that hybridity lacks the theoretical apparatus to grapple with.

Development and Political Economy Analysis

Political and political economy analyses of aid programmes have become increasingly popular from the early 2000s among practitioners and scholars.[139] To be sure, critical International Political Economy (IPE) scholars have been studying international aid interventions for some time. Especially significant have been Marxist and neo-Gramscian approaches that see development assistance as part of either an attempt to complete the construction of the world market or alternatively to constitutionalise neo-liberal disciplines by limiting democratic controls within recipient countries in the interests of an emerging transnational capitalist class.[140] These earlier approaches identify important aspects of international development assistance, especially in its state-building phase. Yet, they pay relatively little attention to the precise nature of socio-political conflict shaping these interventions' outcomes in particular contexts, and in this sense, they are a mirror image of the dominant development paradigm discussed above.

Two particularly problematic assumptions are made by this literature – neither of which stands up to careful empirical scrutiny. First, these approaches presume that local societies and elites are often too weak to resist international forces, thereby becoming the servants of transnational interests. However, we find that although international interventions often lead to the establishment of modes of governance that superficially appear to approximate international agendas, how they actually function can deviate considerably, reflecting the enduring power of local interests. For instance, although the SAPs did lead to rapid and widespread privatisation in recipient countries, instead of developing neo-liberal markets, this process often led to the concentration of previously public resources in the hands of regime insiders.[141] Second, although critical IPE scholars often assume that conflict, when it emerges, takes the form of resistance to globalisation, far more common is for different factions within recipient societies to

[139] Carothers and De Gramont 2013. [140] E.g. Cammack 2004; Gill 1995.
[141] Hadiz and Robison 2005; Hibou 2004.

harness or resist aspects of the international intervention in selective ways that support their agendas or weaken their rivals. For example, in Indonesia the good governance agenda has been widely embraced by some sections of civil society seeking to limit the power of the country's powerful oligarchs, while other political leaders or aspirants have also claimed to support the concept while reinforcing predatory power.[142]

Our focus here, rather, is on those approaches that pay close attention to the recipients of intervention. This literature is broadly divided into two main camps – one, based on liberal-pluralist conceptions of state and society, sees development as a collective action problem, and therefore looks at international intervention as a means of overcoming some hurdles preventing the public good from being realised. Although somewhat distinct, we also include the growing political settlements literature in this camp. Another trend, broadly based on Gramscian state theory, views development as 'a historical process of contested structural change' within inherently unequal societies shaped by capitalist development.[143] It therefore emphasises the deeply ingrained nature of power relations and the very limited ways in which donors can promote change. As elaborated in Chapter 2, we find the latter approach more persuasive and build our own framework on a similar political theory. Both approaches, however, explain intervention outcomes as resulting from political economy contexts within given national territories to which interveners are essentially external. They are yet to consider systematically the manner in which international interventions alter not only power relations within fixed geographical terrains of struggles but also the terrains themselves, and hence the nature of social conflict. As this problem is common to both approaches, we will discuss its implications when examining Gramscian state theory.

Liberal-Pluralist Approaches

The recurring implementation and outcome failures of international development aid have led some within major development aid organisations and affiliated academic institutions – a group dubbed the 'political economy community'[144] – to place increasing emphasis on how the politics and political economy of recipient states and societies affect

[142] Airlangga 2016. [143] Hutchison et al. 2014: 78.
[144] Carothers and De Gramont 2013: 160.

the outcomes of aid programmes, and in turn, on how donors should interact with recipients to improve outcomes, especially in terms of service delivery and poverty reduction.

Despite their acknowledgement of the inherently political nature of aid, as well as of the existence of competing interests with unequal power within recipient countries, these approaches maintain a liberal understanding of development as a public good and a collective action problem, within a broadly liberal-pluralist conception of the state and of society. As a result, they continue to see the essence of engaging politically as finding ways to remove obstacles to collective action so that the whole of society is better off. Relatedly, they also view conflict over development programming and objectives as a sign of dysfunction – narrow interests prevailing over the public good – rather than an inherent aspect of the development process.[145] This perspective retains an emphasis on institutional, not structural, forms of power,[146] and continues to see institution-building to change elite incentives as remedy for development failure,[147] essentially tweaking the earlier institutionalist approach rather than substantially replacing it. This neglects the far deeper nature of socio-political and ideological conflicts relating to development in general and development assistance programmes in particular states and societies.[148]

As Carothers and De Gramont document,[149] the tacit acknowledgement of the role of politics in shaping development outcomes dates back at least to the emergence of the good governance agenda in the 1990s. This agenda saw marginalising political interference by rent-seekers and distributional coalitions as essential, and therefore focused on supporting the construction of governance institutions insulated from popular and political pressures deemed undesirable to market-led development. However, it soon became clear that this approach was no panacea.[150]

One response, associated with the 'aid effectiveness' agenda of the Organisation for Economic Co-operation and Development (OECD), has placed an emphasis on recipient country ownership of the development process, as well as on donor harmonisation, alignment and monitoring, but without significantly modifying the state-building

145 Hutchison et al. 2014: 57–58. 146 Hickey 2009: 146.
147 Batley et al. 2012. 148 Hickey 2012; Hutchison et al. 2014.
149 Carothers and De Gramont 2013. 150 Carroll 2010.

agenda of the PWC. This approach is the dominant one in practice. It has involved limited attempts to refine delivery modalities, including most recently the incorporation of some of the insights of behavioural economics, as evident, for example, in the 2015 *World Development Report: Mind, Society and Behavior*.[151] A second, less influential response has been to better understand the political economy of development.[152] This approach has emerged in direct opposition to the aid effectiveness agenda, which could not work, it was argued, because since

> local elites may be hesitant to engage in practices that could undermine the status quo or threaten established interests, many important governance reforms will essentially lack local ownership. In turn, without domestic political will, donor interventions are likely to be less effective than intended.[153]

As such, this group has questioned the assumption that recipient governments are necessarily developmentally inclined, as many are focused on political survival first and foremost, and that there is consensus over policy direction in recipient countries that could underpin effective action on development along the lines of the aid effectiveness agenda.[154]

This has led the political economy community to question the 'getting to Denmark' *problematique* of conventional state-building modalities and to increasingly focus on understanding the relevant domestic context shaping development outcomes.[155] Instead of 'getting to Denmark', Merilee Grindle argued for a refocus towards 'good enough governance', viz. 'the minimal conditions of governance to allow political and economic development to occur'.[156] For Fritz and Menocal,[157] good enough governance is less normative and more situational and pragmatic than the good governance agenda. Rather than setting general and often idealised governance benchmarks, it directs attention to the steps to be taken, 'given the state of affairs and the political opportunity structure in a country'. Similarly, Andrews questions the wisdom of donors' tendency to look for best practice solutions for problems of poor governance and administration

151 World Bank 2015a. 152 Dahl-Østergaard et al. 2005: 26.
153 Gisselquist and Resnick 2014: 144. 154 Faust 2010.
155 Gisselquist and Resnick 2014: 144–5. 156 Grindle 2004: 526.
157 Fritz and Menocal 2007: 538.

in recipient countries that are derived from developed countries with radically different contexts.[158] Thus, instead of assuming all fragile states are the same, Gisselquist recommends typologising fragile states, with a particular focus on whether fragility is temporary or longer-term.[159] Reviewing the institutionalist literature on development, Booth states:

> Indeed, prescribing for poor countries the institutions which now prevail in those countries, at the end of their process of development, is equivalent to 'kicking away the ladder' with which countries climbed up in the past ... As confirmed by recent developmental successes in East and South-East Asia, the institutions that are good for obtaining growth and reducing poverty in the poorest countries may be quite different from the 'best practice' arrangements that have proven their worth in moving forward from middle-income starting-points.[160]

A growing research agenda emanating from the above has focused on how donors could support 'developmental states', widely seen as responsible for East Asia's economic 'miracle' of the late twentieth century.[161] Reviewing the literature, Routley identifies four basic developmental state characteristics:[162] a capable, autonomous, but embedded bureaucracy; a political leadership oriented towards development; a close, often mutually beneficial symbiotic relationship between some state agencies (often discussed as pilot agencies) and key industrial capitalists; and successful policy interventions promoting growth. The crucial element is distilled by Leftwich, who argues that developmental states are not only those achieving high growth rates, 'but rather growth rates alongside with a perception of reasonably widespread *legitimacy*'[163] (emphasis added).

This has several implications. First, this literature questions the assumed relationship between Weberian-rational statehood and development success. Rather, in some cases neo-patrimonial structures may be conducive to development.[164] Just why such relationships are good for development in some contexts but not others remains a puzzle, however.[165] Second, the linear relationship between bureaucratic capacity, service delivery, and state legitimacy, has also been questioned by

158 Andrews 2012. 159 Gisselquist 2015. 160 Booth 2011: S7.
161 Leftwich 2000; Stubbs 2009. 162 Routley 2012: 8.
163 Leftwich 2000: 166–7. 164 Booth 2011; Hickey 2012.
165 Routley 2012: 22.

the political economy community. Derick Brinkerhoff and co-authors have argued that the availability of services is 'necessary but not sufficient to build legitimacy'.[166] McLoughlin further specifies: 'rather than there being a universal threshold of service access or coverage that can secure a state's legitimacy, it is the alignment between citizens' home-grown expectations of what the state should deliver and the state's capacity to meet these expectations that matters for legitimizing effects'.[167] In a similar vein, Krasner and Risse go as far as reversing the capacity–legitimacy relationship, arguing that legitimacy is in fact an important supporting condition for states to develop the capacity to deliver services.[168] This reflects, to use Lemay-Hébert's distinction, a shift from an understanding of legitimacy grounded in Weber, which emphasises organisational coherence and rationality, to one premised on Durkheim, which emphasises fit with societal values and institutions.[169]

Despite recognising the unevenness of power and opportunity in many societies and rejecting the idea of best practice development programming, the political economy community remains attached to liberal-pluralist conceptions of state and society. In this view society is 'a range of ad hoc and fairly fluid interest groups that contend on a reasonably level playing field to influence day-to-day policy decisions'.[170] Related is a tendency to view development as a common good and a collective action problem. The problem of attaining successful development is seen to be overcoming obstacles in the realisation of the common good, posed by self-serving elites and dysfunctional institutions. Achieving this requires institutionalisation, whereby 'those involved were able to devise, agree and enforce an institutional arrangement (a set of rules) that would require each of them to restrain in some degree their immediate and short-term pursuit of self-interest so that they would all be better off in the medium term'.[171] The benefits of institutionalisation are clear – providing 'predictability, justice, and opportunity for all'.[172]

In practice, the political economy community focuses on two intervention strategies. The first is one of supporting progressive, developmental leadership – mainly reform-oriented elites. This is the approach

166 Brinkerhoff et al. 2012: 277. 167 McLoughlin 2015: 344.
168 Krasner and Risse 2014. 169 Lemay-Hébert 2009.
170 Hutchison et al. 2014: 67. 171 Leftwich 2012: 7.
172 Hutchison et al. 2014: 67.

underlying, for example, the UK Department for International Development's 'drivers of change' approach[173] or the Developmental Leadership Programme.[174] This search for development champions goes beyond donors' earlier preference for supporting technocrats promoting neo-liberalism to look more broadly for actors with the will, legitimacy and capacity to act in the public good in specific contexts. The emphasis is not on individual reformers so much as those capable of mobilising coalitions. Alternatively, donors are directed to develop creative ways of incentivising otherwise predatory elites to act in the common good by seeking to capitalise on the fragmentation and financial bases of ruling coalitions. This is premised on the view that leaders want to stay in power and therefore will respond to incentives that support this aspiration or threaten to undermine their position.[175] The assumption herein, however, is that leaders are concerned with their own narrow personal or electoral gains, rather than driven by deeper ideological convictions and interests.[176]

Although clearly an advance on more technocratic approaches, there seems to be a fundamental contradiction in this approach: on the one hand, development is assumed to be in the interests of all. On the other, the political economy community recognises that development can be hampered by particular interests, which must be harnessed towards desired outcomes, or at the very least contained. It seems that like many liberal-pluralists the political economy community is caught in a bind between the recognition that powerful nefarious interests exist and the myth that interests potentially could (and should) be harmonious in the service of the greater good. Just why people and leaders consistently fail to make 'good' choices is never entirely clear, however.

And even if we ignore this contradiction, liberal-pluralist analysis is not particularly helpful in identifying who interveners should try and partner with and to what ends. Indeed, none other than Robert Dahl,[177] who pioneered pluralist state theory, ended up junking it later, conceding that inequalities in wealth and power actually dictate people's capacities to shape political outcomes. Without a structural view of power, how is it possible to identify 'champions' who can really deliver or 'bad guys' that must be bought off?

173 See Dahl-Østergaard et al. 2005. 174 Leftwich 2012.
175 Whitfield and Therkildsen 2011.
176 Hickey 2012; Hutchison et al. 2014: 72. 177 Dahl 1971.

In reality, there is no common good underlying development processes. Structural asymmetries of power and wealth are inherent to capitalist states and societies, as is spatially uneven development, an issue to which we will attend in Chapter 2.[178] This means that *fundamental and irreconcilable* differences of interest and ideology relating to development and its intended beneficiaries tend to exist that are not amenable to the kinds of interventions advocated by the political economy community.[179] Rather, development programmes are 'interventions into socio-economic realities and relations',[180] which will invariably be threatening to the interests of some groups, while advantageous to others.

A relatively recent addition to the political economy scholarship on development, emerging alongside the political economy community, is focused on elite political settlements.[181] This approach rejects the view of development as a public good. It adopts a historical institutionalist perspective that sees institutions as the product of power relations among elites, reflecting the nature of the broader political settlement in a country. Change in the outputs of institutions, from this view, happens only when there is change in the elite's 'common understanding of how power is organized and exercised'.[182] The question for donors, therefore, is how to help promote more inclusive, development-friendly, political settlements.

The political settlements literature's focus on the composition of elite groups and the struggles between them is a welcome departure from the liberal-pluralist assumptions of the political economy community. Indeed, we find in this book that the elites dominating the national scale play a crucial role in shaping intervention outcomes. When they are cohesive, it is practically impossible for interveners to change governance outputs in ways threatening to national elite interests. When they are fractured, however, many possibilities open up through tactical and strategic alliances with sections of the elite and other groups. Yet, this approach has limited capacity to explain why particular elites are powerful in given periods and how changes in elite composition and interests come about. It struggles to identify the conditions that make political settlements more or less durable.

178 Smith 2010. 179 Hutchison et al. 2014: 67.
180 Hutchison et al. 2014: 72. 181 Khan 2010; Parks and Cole 2010.
182 Parks and Cole 2010: 12.

This weakness relates to the absence of the necessary theoretical tools to explain broader socio-political change and the position of elites within this. Gramscian state theory's far broader social ontology overcomes this problem, as we elaborate.

Development as Contested Structural Change

An alternative to the liberal-pluralist approaches described above is the view of development as 'contested structural change'.[183] This view is broadly based on the insights of Gramsci's state theory,[184] as later developed by theorists such as Poulantzas[185] and Jessop.[186] It rejects the notion that society is basically an equal playing field, in which fluid groups and interests compete over policy choices within neutral, 'empty vessel' states and institutions. Rather, long-term historical processes of economic and social change, associated with capitalist development, produce structurally unequal societies, where power and wealth are unevenly allocated. In turn, different groups in society struggle to shape the state and its institutions in ways that privilege their own interests and marginalise their rivals, as well as promulgate ideologies justifying or denouncing these social and political orders. As such, states manifest 'strategic selectivity' – their institutions are structured to *systematically* promote the interests, ideologies and strategies of particular social forces over others.[187]

From this vantage point, development is not about economic growth, gross domestic product, or some other aggregate indicator of human welfare. At a far more fundamental level, it is seen to refer to unceasing struggles – over how resources are to be distributed, who is to benefit, and where power resides – between groups operating on unequal institutional terrains shaped by earlier similar struggles. In turn, the agency and strategies of groups contesting development outcomes, their relative power relations, as well as the changing nature of the economy, provide the structural context for future struggles.[188]

Crucially, in this view, aid programming 'is an intervention in this process [of development], but not a driver of it'.[189] Whereas conventional approaches to state-building tend, as we have seen, to largely

183 Hutchison et al. 2014: 78. 184 Gramsci 1971. 185 Poulantzas 1978.
186 Jessop 2008. 187 Jessop 2008. 188 Hay 2002.
189 Hutchison et al. 2014: 78.

neglect the particular characteristics of target states and societies, this approach provides the most powerful counterargument, foregrounding the way in which socio-political power relations in recipient states and societies definitively shape intervention outcomes. Since power relations in society are shaped by slow processes of social and economic change that donors have little capacity to transform significantly, donors are encouraged to set modest and achievable objectives that take into account the entrenched nature and resilience of the structures into which they seek to intervene.

By basing itself in a structural analysis of power, this approach provides a better guide for who interveners should partner with than its liberal-pluralist counterpart. In particular, this approach recommends that donors establish tactical alliances with powerful interests in target societies to advance particular and well-defined goals in areas where a convergence of interest is possible. Whereas, as mentioned earlier, donors tend to fixate on supporting ideologically compatible groups or leaders, it is argued that these are usually weak in the societies where interventions typically occur.[190] So, while strategic alliances with reformist groups are easier to form and more palatable, these alliances are unlikely to yield the results that donors desire. Alternatively, although some of the groups with which more limited and temporary tactical alliances could be formed are not ideologically compatible with the aid agenda, they may well have meaningful capacities to advance certain objectives, if they think that doing so is in their political or material interests.

In this book, we adopt this broad understanding of development and of intervention. As we elaborate in Chapter 2, our understanding of state transformation and of the politics of scale is premised on Gramscian state theory and on related approaches that view social and political conflict, and associated power relations rooted in the political economy, as underpinning how institutions are designed, formed and operate in practice. It is clear from all of our case studies that the societies and states in which international interventions are attempted are riven with deep structural cleavages and contested ideologies that are only explicable when viewed in broader historical-sociological perspective. As such, their

190 Hughes and Hutchinson 2012.

development trajectories do not reflect the dysfunctionality of local institutions in delivering the public good, but the historically specific outcomes of struggles over power and resources in those societies. These are shaped by the political economy context, including transnational processes, such as colonialism or capitalist relations of exchange, in which these societies have been embedded for generations, as well as the political strategies of dominant and dominated groups.

For example, as we shall see in Chapter 3, the efforts of Honiara-based elites in Solomon Islands to centralise resources in the capital and redistribute them to provincial supporters are a product of the particular pressures generated through the highly geographically uneven mode of development resulting from trade with Europeans in the pre-colonial era and the British Protectorate's own development strategies. With most Solomon Islander elites concentrated in the small national bureaucracy, which was dependent on income derived from economic activities in the provinces, the capture and redistribution of rents from resource exploitation became imperative to sustaining the country's administrative unity in the immediate post-independence period.[191] As a result, these political and bureaucratic elites have been deeply hostile to donor attempts to control public expenditure, developing creative ways to circumvent limitations imposed by the Regional Assistance Mission to Solomon Islands (RAMSI) and its successors.

Nonetheless, we also find that this approach to understanding the interrelations of international intervention and target states and societies is lacking in some important ways. Its main weakness, which is shared with the liberal-pluralist political economy community, is the presumption that the spatial terrain on which socio-political conflict occurs is fixed: the focus is on the national recipient state as a whole. Scholars thus implicitly operate from the assumption of methodological nationalism – the view that societies within states' territorial borders are natural objects of inquiry.[192] Although external processes, such as colonialism, the Cold War and capitalism, are seen as important, these are viewed as mediated by the power relations prevailing within a given, territorially bound society (Hameiri

[191] Allen 2013; Bennett 1987. [192] Wimmer and Glick Schiller 2002.

and Jones 2014). Territorial space – national, subnational or even municipal – is not theorised but implicitly understood as a single, unified site in which groups struggle for dominance and control over resources.[193] Therefore, international efforts to promote good governance here are essentially seen as the latest instance of external interference, whose outcomes are mediated by local power relations within a given national territory.[194]

This neglects the fact that these interventions seek to transform, not only the outcomes of socio-political conflict in target societies, but the very spatial and institutional terrain in which it occurs. Political geographers have long noted that the scale at which an issue is governed is not neutral, because different scales afford uneven resources, power and political opportunity structures for different groups in society. For instance, the palm oil producers benefiting from the large-scale use of fire to clear land for oil plantations in Indonesia have actively promoted, together with local political leaders, a subnational-district scale of governance for this issue to undermine efforts to impose greater controls on the use of fire by an international coalition seeking a regional governance scale.[195] Therefore, changing scales is also an attempt to shift the power balance on a given issue.[196] By attempting to transnationalise parts of ostensibly domestic state apparatuses and integrate these within regulatory networks at a regional or global scale, donors are essentially fragmenting these states, producing new dynamics of conflict taking the form of a politics of scale. As we see in the next chapter, groups in target societies respond to these attempts with other scalar strategies, also seeking to manipulate space to advance their own material and normative interests or marginalise their rivals. As the politics of scale is integral to the relationship between international intervention and local politics, ignoring it is detrimental to the capacity of this approach to account for the outcomes of international intervention.

[193] In the limited number of studies where territorial politics has been recognised, scholars have studied struggles between nationally and locally based elites in decentralised states, but without theorising the processes through which the scope of these scales as sites of governance and conflict is constituted; see Hadiz (2010).

[194] Carroll 2010; Hutchison et al. 2014; Rodan and Hughes 2012.

[195] Hameiri and Jones 2013. [196] Gough 2004.

Conclusion

In this chapter we have outlined the dominant state-building approach and its manifestation in PAR programmes. We have also critically examined the range of approaches that have emerged in recent years to analyse how these international interventions interact with the states and societies they target. As we have seen, existing approaches in development studies and peace-building provide an improvement upon earlier perspectives, which did not seriously examine the significance of the social, economic, political or cultural aspects of recipients for the political and governance outcomes of intervention. Nonetheless, these approaches also remain limited in their capacity to fully account for what they aim to investigate. The peace-building scholarship has shifted its focus on to state formation processes, with many scholars emphasising the emergence of hybrid forms of peace governance through the interaction between local and international actors. This literature gives implicit consideration to issues of scale, by looking at local agency and at conflicts between local and international actors. However, it maintains a problematic binary distinction between the supposedly modern/liberal internationals and the traditional/non-liberal locals, wrongly viewing the outcomes of intervention as the product of their interaction. Furthermore, the conception of the local is imprecise and slippery. The result is a tendency to focus on the degree to which particular modes of governance approximate either international-liberal or local-non-liberal heuristics, which provides limited insights into intervention outcomes. In development research, the political economy community has begun to consider ways to encourage reform, but remains limited by a liberal-pluralist conception of state and society and an erroneous view of development as a public good. These lead to neglect the deeper nature of the socio-political and ideological cleavages shaping development outcomes. The political settlements scholarship moves away from liberal-pluralism but also lacks a deeper social ontology, which would explain elite composition and relations. A critical political economy approach based on Gramsci's state theory provides a convincing view of development as a contested historical process of structured change. It is, however, limited by its implicit reification of the national territory, or at most subnational or urban administrative units, as the spatial arena in which struggle over development and its outcomes occur. This also leads this approach to view international interveners as essentially external to domestic power struggles.

Building on the political theory of the critical political economy approach and on insights from political geography, the next chapter outlines our framework for analysing the particular political and governance outcomes produced through the interaction between international interventions and target states and societies in given contexts.

2 International Intervention and the Politics of Scale

In this chapter we elaborate an approach that incorporates the politics of scale into an analytical framework, building on Gramscian state theory. This approach will then be deployed to examine three detailed case studies in subsequent chapters to demonstrate its utility in explaining the highly variegated outcomes of intervention.

We contend in this book that scale is a crucial aspect of the politics shaping the outcomes of Peace- and State-Building Interventions (PSBIs). Hybridity scholars implicitly acknowledge this, but their dichotomisation of local and international hinders their capacity to adequately analyse intervention outcomes. The scalar dimension is crucial because PSBIs seek to transform states by rescaling parts of their ostensibly domestic governance apparatuses, or other societal institutions, and to produce preferred governance outcomes. Interveners typically view political and bureaucratic elites in target states as rent-seeking and corrupt and the socio-political structures supporting these elites as pernicious, hindering development or peace. Yet, since they are unwilling, or sometimes unable, to introduce more direct forms of external rule, they seek to mediate their efforts through target states and societies. In the area of public administration reform (PAR) – a core aspect of most international interventions and the main empirical focus of this book – the aim is to produce transnationally networked and/or regulated departments or agencies within the national and/or subnational bureaucracies that are responsive to international agendas and targets (rather than domestic political and societal pressures) and that are capable of disciplining other parts of the state and society.[1] It is in this sense that public administrations are seen to be 'rescaled' through international intervention – removed from their hitherto strictly domestic context and inserted into networked modes of regulatory governance that extend beyond the borders of

[1] Hameiri 2010.

these states and the societies they supposedly govern.[2] The result is the emergence of fragmented, multilevel forms of statehood, in which some parts are rescaled while others are not.

This attempt to rescale target states' administrations, however, is typically met with domestic actors' scalar strategies that seek to promote their own interests and preferred normative agendas, or to marginalise their rivals, by supporting, rejecting or modifying interveners' rescaling efforts. Three responses are especially apparent. First, recipient governments can completely reject donor PAR programmes, thus preventing the rescaling of apparatuses altogether. Because PSBIs maintain the formal sovereignty of target states, the implementation of interveners' programmes requires the consent and cooperation of recipient governments. Governments thus retain a key role as 'scale managers',[3] able to invoke national sovereignty to prevent foreign aid from coming in, reinforcing the primacy of the national scale, which they and allied interests dominate. Outright rejection of all foreign assistance is, however, quite rare because the resources offered by interveners are typically attractive for embattled governments in poor countries. Indeed, as Reno argues in the African context,[4] sovereignty is often prized for helping those in government access many internationally derived resources less easily available to their rivals, such as foreign aid and armaments.

More common, however, are two kinds of responses that seek either to reinforce the national scale or shift governance downwards, producing inter-scalar conflict. A particularly significant response, evident in all of our case studies, occurs at the national scale. This entails the use of the state's scale management function, not to reject intervention wholesale but to selectively admit or constrain programmes in ways that bolster the authority and control over resources of the elites dominating the national scale. But this selectivity is not simply a matter of free choice; it reflects broader power relations in state and society and the position of political and bureaucratic elites within this. Another possibility, which often occurs simultaneously with the former, relates to efforts to construct a subnational or local scale. Typically, this 'localisation' involves weaker actors seeking to harness interventions' fragmenting of the national scale to shift governance downwards, where they hope to be able to bolster their own power.

[2] Hameiri and Jones 2015. [3] Peck 2002: 340. [4] Reno 1998.

These efforts often include ideological appeals to the legitimacy of modes of governance based in socio-culturally organic local communities, versus that of transplanted postcolonial institutions like the state. Related is the call that local groups and governance structures should enjoy greater autonomy and improved resource-allocation. This downward rescaling can be reinforced by the donors' ubiquitous decentralisation agenda,[5] as well as by the so-called local turn – support, including from donors, for apparently customary, bottom-up institutions and forms of authority.[6]

An important part of this localisation agenda, often missed or downplayed by those endorsing it from the outside, is that defining the local and its scope of governance and authority is inherently contested, as this always promotes or marginalises particular interests and normative agendas, including within apparently organic local communities. *Contra* the hybridity approach, it is not necessarily the case that local actors, such as traditional village elites, would prefer a customary mode of governance or that nationally based actors or international agencies would necessarily resist this. While those supporting localisation seek to bolster their power, this is likely to be vigorously contested by groups standing to lose out, whether based at the local or national scales, for example, by challenging their claim to customary authenticity. Struggles that may superficially appear to be about the relative merits of traditional and modern governance are fundamentally concerned with the distribution of power and wealth within and across scales. Therefore, the scope of the local scale and the range of issues governed through locally based governance mechanisms would tend to vary considerably and shift in relation to the dynamics of social and political conflict.

The kinds of interests and coalitions that mobilise in relation to rescaling would also vary depending on the particular programme or project attempted, as different interventions would have variable effects on the power of groups and interests in target societies. For instance, whereas a donor programme seeking to improve tax collection by the national government might be supported by national political leaders requiring resources to reinforce their position, it would likely be resisted by extractive industries seeking to minimise their tax liabilities. These industries could then form coalitions with

[5] See Hadiz 2010. [6] Mac Ginty and Richmond 2013.

communities in areas where they operate, supporting the demand that the central state keep its hands off 'their' resources so that rents can be localised. Further, the same industries could join forces with national politicians to prevent international regulation of environmental standards, for example, demanding a national scale there.

In contrast with the expectations of the hybridity scholarship, recipient groups seldom resist international intervention in its totality, but engage with different aspects of it in selective and often strategic ways to advance their own interests and agendas. In turn, the results of conflicts over implementation and the eventual outcomes of PAR interventions depend on the relative strength of coalitions to promote, resist or modify the functioning of rescaled institutions. This contestation is set against the backdrop of the broader structures of power shaped by historical patterns of development and state formation. These coalitions may, and often do, cut across the domestic/international divide and combine both strategic and tactical alliances.[7] As a result, international interventions attain highly uneven outcomes, not only across countries, but also particular programmes and projects. Our approach can accurately map and explain these results, as the case study chapters show.

In the first section below, we elaborate on the two key influences on our approach. The following section will then explain how these are combined and deployed to study the interaction between international intervention and local politics.

State Power and the Politics of Scale

Our approach combines two core theoretical elements – Gramscian state theory and the political geography scholarship on the politics of scale. The former enables an analysis of the nature of power and socio-political struggle in given states and societies, while the latter allows for clearly identifying the often contested and shifting terrain on which the outcomes of these conflicts take place. We discuss both below.

Gramscian State Theory

In his posthumously published *Prison Notebooks*,[8] Antonio Gramsci had the valuable insight that state and civil society are parts of a single

[7] See Hughes and Hutchinson 2012. [8] Gramsci 1971.

social whole. In liberal political theory (like de Tocqueville's), civil society constitutes a private realm of social and political organisation autonomous from, and providing a counterbalance to, state power. For Gramsci, however, the unequal power relations running through state institutions were also manifest in civil society.[9] The latter is seen as an important arena for the dissemination of ruling elites' ideologies and hence for embedding their power. It is also, however, an important site for ideological and political resistance by forces seeking to undermine the existing social and political order.

This fundamental insight was later developed by Nicos Poulantzas,[10] and especially Bob Jessop.[11] Both rejected the reification of the state as separate to society, instead arguing that the state and its institutions were expressions of social power. Against the then-fashionable neo-Weberian 'Bringing the State Back In' scholarship, Jessop stated:

> If one posits the need to choose between the state and society as the independent variable in social analysis, one implies that both exist as independent entities which are fully constituted, internally coherent and mutually exclusive and that one always unilaterally determines the other. This would reify and absolutize what is really an emergent, partial, unstable and variable social distinction.[12]

From this vantage point, state formation and transformation are understood as the contingent outcomes of never-ending social and political struggles over power and resources, which span state and society. State institutions' form and operation reflect conflicts and compromises among historically specific socio-political coalitions rooted primarily in the political economy – classes, class fractions (different sections of the same class), distributional coalitions and other social groups, such as ethnically or religion based organisations.[13] These coalitions, often straddling the state–society divide, struggle to make and remake key political, economic and social institutions in order to entrench their own power and wealth and marginalise their opponents.

In this view, again in contrast with liberal-pluralist approaches, the state can never be seen as neutral, not even in theoretical abstraction. Rather, states, and institutions more generally, exhibit a 'strategic selectivity' – they are structured to be systematically more open to some social forces pursuing certain social and political agendas,

[9] Ehrenberg 1999. [10] Poulantzas 1978. [11] Jessop 1990, 2002, 2008.
[12] Jessop 1990: 287. [13] Hewison et al. 1993: 4–5.

through certain strategies, while marginalising others.[14] For example, capitalist states systematically privilege capitalist interests and agendas over those of other groups. However, precisely what fractions of capital are ascendant within state institutions, what strategies are favoured, and indeed what strategies and tactics by weaker groups are likely to yield better results, can and often does vary. How the state and its institutions function, and in whose interests, is the outcome of dynamic social and political conflict between groups whose emergence and relative power is the product of earlier transformations in the political economy and associated struggles and compromises. The outcomes of these struggles are specific in both a spatial and temporal sense, and cannot be assumed a priori to be functional to capitalist development as a whole or even, in extreme cases, to the survival of the state as a single polity.[15] In short, the state's strategic selectivity, as well as the form and function of important institutions, is not static. It may, and often does, shift, in response to the changing political economy and the strategies of social forces both within and outside the state.

A significant example for the social roots of the state's strategic selectivity and how it can change is the slow, partial and uneven shift from the post-war welfare state in developed countries towards more regulatory forms of statehood today. The welfare state, based on Keynesian economics, was a manifestation of an institutionalised compromise between domestic capital and organised labour, following the upheavals of the Great Depression and Second World War, against the broader international backdrop of the Cold War, which Hobsbawm dubbed a 'global civil war'.[16] To prevent further worker radicalisation, core state institutions were restructured to help broker an accommodation between the main social classes of industrial society – capital and labour – with this cleavage also dominating electoral party politics. Although the post-war state in Europe, North America and Australasia retained a basic preference for the interests of capital, especially domestic industries, it afforded the interests of organised labour considerable expression, permitting a rising social wage and improved working and material conditions for most social strata, on a level unprecedented in human history. From the mid-1970s onwards, however, a stagflation crisis began afflicting developed economies, combining economic recession with rising inflation and unemployment. Wrought by productive

[14] Jessop 2008. [15] Hay 2006: 75–76. [16] Hobsbawm 1994.

over-capacity and falling business profitability in saturated domestic economies, this crisis began to eat away at the institutionalised class compact of the post-war era. Pathways out of the crisis involved a 'spatial fix' in the form of the globalisation of trade, production and investment, designed to find new markets and reduce production costs,[17] alongside increasing downward pressure on the gains made by workers, including in some cases through negotiated, corporatist compromises with trade unions.

As globalising sections of capital have strengthened relative to other sections of capital and organised labour, especially in the United States, the state's strategic selectivity has tended to shift too. This manifested in considerable institutional change within developed states. Corporatist institutions, such as collective bargaining or industrial relations courts, were either dismantled or weakened, while core areas of monetary and fiscal policymaking were in many countries relocated into quasi-autonomous agencies insulated from representative democratic institutions.[18] Rather than mitigating the negative aspects of capitalist development, social policy and welfare institutions have been reconfigured to promote national competitiveness in a globalising economy.[19] The subsequent emergence of 'competition states' or 'regulatory states' out of the ashes of post-war welfare states,[20] even if partial and contested, is a clear reflection of the ascendancy of globalising sections of capital and the defeat of other interests, particularly organised labour and other sections of capital.

In many developing countries too, shifts in the global political economy over recent decades have had profound effects on the location of state power and how it is exercised. Many of the countries that international peace-building and aid interventions target are former colonies of European powers. The period of decolonisation coincided with the Cold War and the dominance of Keynesian economics. The most powerful capitalist state in the post-war era, the United States, had, unlike Europe's empires, preferred a combination of 'open doors' – to US investment and trade – and 'closed frontiers' – independence for former colonies within internationally recognised and stable borders.[21] This policy of respecting national sovereignty of decolonised states

[17] Harvey 2001. [18] Gill 1995; Streeck 2014.
[19] Cerny 1997; Jayasuriya 2006. [20] Cerny 1997; Majone 1994.
[21] Colás 2008.

reflected the requirements of supporting the above-mentioned class compromise domestically. It was also in part a reaction to the Soviet Union's support for Third World independence movements.

The international architecture developed in that era – the Bretton Woods institutions and the United Nations – all reinforced a state-centred international order, in which governments retained considerable capacity to control their national territories – an order dubbed 'embedded liberalism'.[22] Indeed, both state-socialist and Keynesian prescriptions for capitalist development emphasised the key role of the central state and its bureaucracy in leading national development. Modernisation theory, then the dominant Western perspective on how development in poorer countries was to occur, also stressed the need for a strong and capable central state, which would be able to mobilise the resources necessary for achieving economic 'take-off', even against societal resistance to change.[23] This view, which implied that authoritarian governments were best able to not only keep the lid on communist agitators, but to support economic development for the greater benefit of society, was most clearly expressed in Samuel Huntington's influential *Political Order in Changing Societies*.[24]

Under these nurturing international conditions, and in the typical absence of strong home-grown bourgeoisies, bureaucratic and military elites in many postcolonial states became very powerful, relative to other social forces. Import-substitution industrialisation, which was strongly promoted by organisations like the World Bank as a component of national development,[25] provided state elites with considerable resources. National elites were thus able to relatively effectively mobilise the central state apparatus for a variety of nation-building projects to cultivate a national identity, as well as for personal enrichment in many cases. This domestic, centralised political order was reinforced by the Western-backed destruction of Leftist oppositions, which in many societies were the most significant non-ethnic secular organisations. This has left a legacy of fragmented civil societies in many developing countries, often disconnected from political power and party politics, paving the way to the subsequent rise of more particularistic political agendas around religious and ethnic identities.[26]

22 Ruggie 1982.
23 Berger and Weber 2014: 62; see Myrdal's ideas in Easterly 2013.
24 Huntington 1968. 25 Toye 1987. 26 Hadiz 2016; Rodan 1996.

The conditions for state-led national development began to worsen in the 1980s as a debt crisis struck many developing countries. The structural adjustment programmes of international financial institutions (IFIs), upon which essential aid disbursements were conditioned, as mentioned in Chapter 1, saw many national institutions, services and industries privatised and public servants laid off. However, this wave of privatisations did not lead to the emergence of efficient liberal market economies as expected. Instead, many state industries were privatised by rulers and given to cronies, cadres and relatives.[27] The result has not been the withering away of states as much as a reconfiguration of state power and state–society relations. Access to state power, often requiring personal connections with state elites, remains crucial for the attainment of wealth in many developing countries, and vice versa;[28] but the benefits tend to accrue largely in private hands, including transnational corporations.

Crucial services, such as policing, water and electricity, are now often privatised, but typically through modes of governance in which state sanction continues to be a crucial factor. For example, although it is often noted that private security companies, including subsidiaries of multinational corporations, are widely used to protect extractive activities in countries like Nigeria, this is rarely done without governmental consent.[29] The distribution of contracts, licences and resources has, therefore, become a key mechanism for securing support for rulers from elites and key groups in society, as well as for attaining external resources from donors and companies, and hence crucial for keeping state elites in power. Consequently, what some construe as state dysfunction in fact often reflects a purposeful political strategy and a mode of governance that is entirely rational within a given socio-political context.[30] It is also, clearly, the product of a broader transformation in the political economy, not simply a result of elites' poor choices.

Yet, the weakening of state-building and nation-building projects, which were dependent a few decades after independence on the concentration of resources within the central state and their wider redistribution in society, has not been without costs. Challenges to national state elites have tended to multiply and intensify, as shown in our case study chapters. And as states have disaggregated, struggles over the

[27] Hibou 2004. [28] Bratton and van de Walle 1994.
[29] Abrahamsen and Williams 2011. [30] Chabal and Daloz 1999.

spoils of state power have tended to fragment too. They are now often waged not over control of the state per se, as in classic cases of revolution, but over control of particular state agencies, areas of governance, and subnational regions. Especially contested are those areas seen as potentially lucrative, like forestry and fishing, or the geographic regions where resources are concentrated. However, in the absence of mass organisations in civil society, capable of mounting concerted opposition across a broad range of issues, these challenges are typically either from breakaway factions of state elites or, if from weaker groups, take the form of localised claims for autonomy based on cultural, ethnic or customary uniqueness. However, for the latter to have traction, some alignment or accommodation with at least some factions of the elite is usually required. Also common have been powerful, but usually disorganised, 'people power' movements, which for a time concentrate popular resentment of established elites into disruptive protests. Again, lack of organisation and cohesion among protesters usually means that as the initial energy of the protests dissipates, politics-as-usual tends to return.

In tandem with this, as discussed in Chapter 1, mainstream donors, especially from the 1990s on, have become increasingly concerned about the development failures of many recipient countries, which were increasingly attributed to structural adjustment and to the worsening quality of governance that rapid economic liberalisation inadvertently reinforced.[31] Especially following the September 11 attacks, the security implications of weakening centralised controls became significant.[32] As a result, donors have advanced significant programmes of state transformation, designed to promote the establishment of institutional environments conducive to market-led development,[33] or in other words to change the state's strategic selectivity in ways that privilege particular strategies of accumulation based on liberal markets. In particular, they have sought to insulate core parts of the bureaucracy from the apparently nefarious influence of corrupt elites and societal interests through a range of measures, including capacity-building, decentralisation and secondment of international staff to key administrative roles. Their aim has been to set up 'governance states' staffed by capable, unyielding and dedicated technocrats,

[31] Stiglitz 1998. [32] Hameiri 2010. [33] Carroll 2010.

approximating the regulatory states emerging in the West over the same period.[34]

The result has been considerable evident change to the governance architecture of many developing countries, as well as the deepening of the linkages between their administrations and those of other countries and major international organisations. Yet, in the typical absence of powerful socio-political interests in recipient countries supportive of these modes of governance working as intended by their architects,[35] implementation is uneven, reflecting the tentative outcomes of power struggles over particular programmes and projects. In many cases, established elites have learnt to sustain their dominance through reconfigured state institutions.[36] Therefore, as we can see, the institutions of developing states are also strategically selective, but in ways that reflect the prevailing political economy conditions and socio-political power relations in those societies.

In sum, Gramscian state theory, especially as developed by Poulantzas and Jessop, directs us to identify how historically specific struggles between coalitions shape the strategic selectivity of state or societal institutions, and in turn, how the design and functioning of these institutions continues to be reshaped by the changing political economy, the strategies of powerful and weaker interests and conflicts or alliances between them.

The Politics of Scale

As we have seen in Chapter 1, many analyses using Gramscian state theory in development studies neglect the politics of scale, assuming the national state is the natural framing for social and political conflict. This is not a unique tendency. According to Neil Smith, in 'traditional social theory, space usually intrudes as the self-evident: as the site, the ground, the stable foundation that lets history move. It defines a fixed set of coordinates that renders historical change coherent'.[37] In the study of politics and international relations, specifically, methodological nationalism is prevalent. This refers to the tendency to take 'national discourses, agendas, loyalties, and histories for granted without problematising them, or making them an object of analysis in its

[34] Harrison 2004. [35] Hutchison et al. 2014.
[36] E.g. Robison and Hadiz 2004. [37] Smith 2010: 224.

own right. Instead, nationally bounded societies are taken to be naturally given entities to study'.[38] Indeed, methodological nationalism is so ingrained in political analysis that the distinction between the core sub-disciplines of International Relations and Comparative Politics is premised upon a differentiation of the spaces inside and outside the national territories of states.[39] International Relations tends to naturalise its units of analysis – states – and see them largely unproblematically as 'power containers' and as single actors in international politics.[40] Comparative politics, meanwhile, focuses on studying and comparing the internal characteristics of states, thus also reifying the inside/outside separation.

Methodological nationalism and scale-blindness are not always detrimental to political analysis. Many important social and political processes, especially since decolonisation, can be quite accurately captured without problematising space and territory within given states. However, in the context of PSBIs, scale-blindness is highly problematic because these interventions almost invariably involve efforts to shift the scale and associated modes of governance through which power and resources are distributed. This in turn produces responses from affected interests in state and society that also encompass a crucial scalar dimension. The latter point will be elaborated in the following section. Here, we articulate what we mean by a politics of scale.

Political geographers have long argued that space and society are mutually constituted. Power relationships run through the construction of space and, in turn, the spatial organisation of political and economic governance helps (re)produce particular power relations in society.[41] David Harvey's work, for example, shows that geographically uneven development, transformations in the built environment, and 'spatial fixes' to capitalist crises of over-capacity, which move contradictions around rather than resolving them, are an integral aspect of capitalism's history and the development of capitalist societies. Similarly, territorial space has crucial political significance. At the most basic level, the extent of the territory over which a state exercises sovereignty has enormous repercussions for the number of people sharing particular identities, the type and amount of natural resources available, the size of internal markets, the number of political actors

[38] Wimmer and Glick Schiller 2002: 304. [39] Walker 1993.
[40] Giddens 1985. [41] Harvey 2006.

with citizenship rights and the extent of their networks, and so on. Consequently, 'the extensiveness of a territory can play a crucial role in determining the balance of power among competing territorial groups and institutions'.[42]

In his seminal book, *State, Power, Socialism*, Nicos Poulantzas proclaims: 'Frontiers and national territory do not exist prior to the unification of that which they structure: there is no original something-inside that has later to be unified'.[43] In other words, the emergence of the territory of the state as the dominant arena for political action and domination occurred simultaneously with the development of the social and political relations that this territorial organisation reinforces.

As such, territorial politics forms a crucial, but oft-neglected, aspect of social and political struggle. Societal and state actors seek to manipulate space and its political consequences by adopting 'territorial strategies ... mobilizing state institutions to shape and reshape inherited territorial structurations of political-economic life, including those of state institutions themselves'.[44] These strategies are constrained by existing institutional arrangements, including established international borders, national sovereignty, and international law, which in themselves are manifestations of earlier contested processes of territorialisation. For instance, as the Poulantzas quote above indicates, the stronger territorial demarcation of European nation-states through the 'long nineteenth century' went hand-in-hand with the development of capitalism within these states, related to both the dynamics of capitalism itself and the necessities of increasingly more expensive war-making.[45] Yet, to the extent that territorial strategies transform the spatial configuration of political and economic rule, they can have profound consequences. For example, the designation of particular parts of the national territory as 'offshore' industrial zones is a direct intervention in social struggle, in that it disadvantages organised labour groups, which are reliant on national legal protections and bargaining institutions, while advancing the interests of corporations seeking to reduce the cost of production.[46]

It is in this context that the production of scale, and struggles over scale, must be understood. 'Scale' in political geography refers to

[42] Miller 2009: 54. [43] Poulantzas 1978: 105.
[44] Brenner and Elden 2009: 368. [45] Teschke 2003; Tilly 1990.
[46] Lillie 2010.

hierarchised social, political and economic territorial spaces, each denoting 'the arena and moment, both discursively and materially, where socio-spatial power relations are contested and compromises are negotiated and regulated'.[47] It is, in other words, a territorial space, existing in a hierarchical relationship with other territorial spaces, in which social, political and economic relations are organised and contested. Scales can be existing administrative tiers within a state, but they can also cut across them, manifesting, for example, in scales such as 'the global', 'bio-regions', 'eco-systems', or 'local communities'.

Scales are ubiquitous. However, Smith points out that although 'the division of the world into some combination of urban, regional, national, and international scales' is often taken for granted, we 'rarely if ever explain how they came about'.[48] The crucial point is that, as with space and territory, scales are never natural. Rather, they are produced through strategic agency and social and political contestation.[49] Smith describes 'spatial scales of social organization' as 'islands of absolute space in a sea of relative space'. 'Relative space' refers to how an 'absolute space' – a house, a bridge, a factory, a city and so on – relates to, and is positioned within, broader processes of development, the circulation of capital and the socio-political relations bound up in them.[50] As such, to produce a scale is to produce an apparent fixity, usually temporary, of absolute space, demarcated from the spaces around it, but always within the relative space of interconnected flows and relations.

For Smith, for example, the urban scale is at once an absolute space – an actual place that one could visit, with its administrative municipal boundaries and associated regulations – and a location in relative space – the city's position within broader processes of accumulation in the national or global capitalist economies. It is its location within relative space that greatly shapes crucial aspects of the urban scale's development, such as the size of the labour market, the kinds of jobs available to residents, the transportation connections available, and so on. These are not natural attributes, but the product of human agency in the context of uneven social relations.

The same is true for the national scale, which is perhaps naturalised more than any other. Conditions in the early post-war era were broadly

[47] Swyngedouw 1997: 140. [48] Smith 2010: 181. [49] Smith 2003.
[50] Smith 2010: 113.

conducive to the concentration of power and authority in the national scale – supporting 'the primacy of national economies, national welfare states, and national societies managed by national states concerned to unify national territories'.[51] More recently, however, shifts in the global political economy have 'relativised' the national scale. It is no longer taken for granted as the best level at which political, economic, or security issues should be governed. Yet, no other scale – local, regional, or global – 'has acquired a similar dominance. Instead, different economic and political spaces and forces located at different scales are competing to become the primary or nodal point of accumulation and/or state power'.[52]

That scales are simultaneously absolute spaces and locations within relative space means that scales – notwithstanding shorthand labels like 'local', 'subnational', 'national', 'regional', 'transnational' or 'global' – are not levels of analysis that can be seen as truly distinct arenas for social and political inquiry.[53] Nor are they equivalent to hybridity's binaries. Rather, they are part of a single social whole, existing not 'in mutual isolation but are always interconnected in a broader, often-changing inter-scalar ensemble'.[54] As, such they must be understood in dynamic, relational terms.[55]

The attempt to fix scales as absolute, apparently natural and unproblematic spaces is not incidental. It is an expression of efforts to organise space in ways that reinforce or challenge a particular distribution of power and resources. Different scales privilege different interests, unevenly allocating power, resources and political opportunity structures. This makes the production of scale an inherently contested process.[56] Recognising this, Smith coined the term 'politics of scale' to refer to conflicts over the production of scales and their scope.[57] He argues that 'the true contest concerns the locus of the power to determine the scale of the struggle: who defines [the place where events occur] . . . and its boundaries'.[58] Shifting scales – rescaling – can change these configurations of power, resources and political opportunity structures, therefore, potentially changing political outcomes in struggles over given issues.[59] For this reason, 'scale jumping' strategies have been common, especially by weaker groups, like labour or indigenous

[51] Jessop 2009: 99. [52] Jessop 2009: 99. [53] Peck 2002: 340.
[54] Brenner et al. 2003: 16. [55] Peck 2002. [56] Hameiri and Jones 2013.
[57] Smith 2010. [58] Smith 2010: 232. [59] Gough 2004.

people, seeking to find sympathetic allies elsewhere to undermine more powerful interests dominating a given scale.[60]

The centrality of the politics of scale to social and political conflict is demonstrated by Hameiri and Jones' recent work on non-traditional security governance.[61] Governments, experts and activists, hoping to ameliorate so-called non-traditional security threats, such as climate change, infectious disease and organised crime, have typically emphasised these threats' transnational character and the associated inability of individual states to deal with them unilaterally. This has been accompanied by efforts to construct transnationally scaled modes of governance that are seen to better map on to the scope of the problems. In most cases, this has involved the rescaling of ostensibly domestic state apparatuses to integrate these into transnational multilevel governance structures and network them with peers across borders, so that they would enact regulatory disciplines on other parts of their states and societies. Although portrayed as a common-sense, technocratic intervention to manage dangerous threats, these efforts, if successful, invariably also reallocate power and resources and therefore are contested by those who are likely to lose out from rescaling.

For example, following widespread outbreaks of highly pathogenic avian influenza caused by the H5N1 virus in 2003 and 2004, international organisations – the World Health Organization (WHO) and the Food and Agriculture Organization (FAO) – and wealthy states, especially the United States, promoted the considerable transformation and rescaling of Indonesia's domestic animal and human health bureaucracies. Primarily in the area of animal health, large-scale surveillance and intervention apparatuses were developed at the district level, where previously none had often existed, to tackle outbreaks in poultry. These were linked with agencies established at the provincial and national levels and ultimately with the broader global governance effort. Their aim was to place veterinarians in charge of managing outbreaks to implement best-practice interventions, as recommended by the FAO and the World Organisation for Animal Health (OIE, from the French *Office International des Epizooties*). This attempt to rescale Indonesian health governance was contested vigorously by Indonesia's powerful poultry industry and its supporters in government, who attempted to maintain control at the district level and under the purview of local

[60] Smith 1992. [61] Hameiri and Jones 2015.

livestock production officials. This resistance meant that rescaled state apparatuses were primarily focused on poor households owning 'backyard' chickens that were in fact infected by commercial farms.[62]

How to Study the Interaction Between International Interventions and Local Politics

In this section, we outline the precise manner in which the insights of Gramscian state theory and the politics of scale apply to concrete analysis of the outcomes of PSBIs in particular states and societies. Our method involves four interrelated steps: (1) focus on a particular project or programme and identify the politics of scale involved; (2) identify the precise forces and coalitions contesting the outcomes of a particular project and establish their relative power relations against the broader political economy structures in which they are embedded; (3) identify the strategies, especially the scalar strategies, they pursue to attain their objectives; (4) trace how struggles over the extent of governance rescaling constrain the extent and efficacy of governance changes.

A Programme/Project Methodological Focus

A clear implication of Gramscian state theory is that how institutions are designed and function, and in whose interests, is the dynamic outcome of social and political conflict, between coalitions rooted mainly in the political economy. Since donor programmes essentially intervene into this environment, not all governance projects attempted as part of these programmes will have similar social and political effects upon recipients. Rather, we find that different coalitions will come together or disband in relation to different projects, depending on how given social forces and groups see the potential for particular donor activities to affect their interests and agendas. Furthermore, forces in struggle will pursue different strategies and tactics depending on the challenges particular projects/programmes pose to their interests and/or ideologies, and the emerging balance of power. For instance, a donor project promoting fiscal decentralisation will threaten some elites, especially those benefitting from domination over the national scale, while

[62] Hameiri and Jones 2015.

empowering others, but both groups could combine to resist a project to introduce stricter environmental regulations over extractive industries. Since the nature of socio-political conflict often varies in relation to particular projects, PSBI outcomes are typically uneven.

We therefore diverge from conventional approaches that study interventions at the national or sectoral levels, emphasising instead the significance of having a programme or project focus, albeit set against the broader structures of power in which particular struggles are embedded. Our case study chapters focus specifically on PAR, as this is typically a major pillar of PSBIs, but we disaggregate PAR programmes and explain their variable outcomes in each of the countries investigated to reveal the precise realignment of power following international interventions.

The Forces in Contention

Our second step, again based on the insights of Gramscian state theory, is to identify the precise forces and coalitions in contention over given governance projects, as well as establish their relative power by reference to the broader political economy and its legacy in the use of state power and state–society relations. Importantly, these coalitions involve both domestic and international actors and can only be adequately understood through historical–sociological analysis.

Closely examining the make-up of particular coalitions avoids both the methodological nationalism of some approaches and the presumption of local resistance to international impositions common in the hybridity and friction perspectives. For instance, in our case study of Aceh, an alliance between the United Nations Development Programme (UNDP) and the province's governor – a former rebel leader – permitted the informal roll-out of a PAR programme that sought to strengthen the governor's position vis-à-vis local challengers, as well as resistance from a coalition involving the World Bank and the European Commission.

It is essential at this stage of analysis to locate the power relations relevant to struggles over particular governance projects within the specific historical processes of state formation and transformation pertaining to the state and society we are investigating, and the role particular socio-political forces have played. This entails undertaking an analysis of the structures of power prevailing in given states and societies at specific historical moments, focusing on uncovering the main lines of socio-political conflict, the strategic selectivity of state institutions and various interests' access to state power. Following Gramscian state theory, this analysis places special attention on understanding how the formation of and relations between social forces, such as classes, class fractions, distributional coalitions and even ethnic or religious groups, shape the use of state power and relate to the changing political economy.

Furthermore, a detailed historical-sociological analysis is crucial for understanding the interests and outlooks of particular groups. It is impossible a priori and without analysing the concrete circumstances of particular societies to know how actors, especially recipient governments and administrations, will respond to international intervention. *Contra* the public choice and institutional design literatures discussed in Chapter 1, these responses do not always simply reflect basic greed and narrow self-interest, but instead the need to maintain support of important allies and societal interests, or to prevent rivals from capitalising on international intervention to change existing power hierarchies. They can also manifest strongly held ideological agendas.[63] We find that particular groups assemble or join coalitions to both advance strategic objectives and for tactical reasons. Where their reasons are merely tactical, their commitment to the stated objective of the coalition they have joined will tend to be much weaker.[64] A structural analysis of the kind discussed above will also be able to distinguish between strategic and tactical alliances in given contexts.

Strategy and the Politics of Scale

A key innovation of this study is to add scalar strategies and the politics of scale to Gramscian state theoretical analysis. The politics of scale is frequently crucial to the outcomes of PSBIs because these interventions typically do not entail attempts to directly rule target states and societies. Rather, interveners seek to attain desired governance outcomes by using the political, economic and social institutions of the intervened state as mediators, while maintaining the state's formal sovereignty.[65] Particular emphasis is placed upon the institutions and apparatuses

[63] Hickey 2012. [64] Hughes and Hutchinson 2012. [65] Hameiri 2010.

of target states, especially their public administrations, since they are seen as important policymaking loci. But a range of other international interventions have been attempted, including subnational or community governance and transitional justice measures. What many of these interventions have in common is that they seek to rescale key institutions – take them out of their hitherto more strictly domestic or local contexts – in order to attain different governance outcomes. Public administration reform (PAR) specifically aims to rescale parts of the ostensibly national and subnational administrations of recipient states so that they become less responsive to local demands, which are often viewed as pernicious or dysfunctional, and more responsive to international governance agendas, geared towards meeting international targets and aspirations. This is done either through the insertion of externally funded international experts and technocrats into key roles in the administration, or through the transnational or international regulation of particular agencies of target states, using, for example, peer-review mechanisms or other forms of benchmarking against international standards. The unevenness of these interventions across the public administration, with some departments heavily rescaled and others not, produces fragmented, multilevel forms of statehood, where a politics of scale is built into how the state is internally organised. But, as already indicated, rescaling is in effect an attempt to reallocate power and resources, from those benefitting from existing institutional arrangements. As such, it would in most cases attract responses from those affected, seeking either to support or resist rescaling or to modify the functioning of rescaled institutions in ways that support their interests and marginalise their rivals.

Because PSBIs operate through state transformation and rescaling, responses to them also typically involve scalar strategies. These scalar strategies, as we elaborate below, can have pivotal effects on the outcomes of socio-political conflict relating to the adoption and implementation of particular programmes or projects. Three kinds of responses are especially apparent: total rejection of international intervention, selective adoption at the national scale and localisation. The first and second strategies usually involve the elites dominating the national scale, who have a privileged position when dealing with PSBIs, because of the preservation of recipient states' formal sovereignty. The second and third strategies often coincide, producing sharper interscalar conflict.

Total Rejection of International Intervention

Because PSBIs in most cases do not suspend the formal sovereignty of target states, intervention programmes typically require at least the tacit consent of the governments of those countries.[66] This means that recipient governments retain a key role as scale managers[67] and perform 'boundary-work' – the demarcation of territorial areas and the groups included and excluded within them.[68] They can, if so desired, prevent most forms of international intervention from coming in, thus maintaining the dominance of the national scale that they and their allies dominate. For example, in the case of the Regional Assistance Mission to Solomon Islands (RAMSI), international intervention is legalised through an act of the Solomon Islands Parliament that must be re-ratified each year.[69] The act provides international staff with legal immunity from prosecution under domestic laws, an important precondition for the mission's deployment, especially its policing and military components. In 2007, the relationship between RAMSI and the Solomon Islands Prime Minister, Manasseh Sogavare, deteriorated. Sogavare complained publicly at the time that RAMSI's control over key offices in the bureaucracy prevented him from carrying out his preferred development policies, even though he was the democratically elected prime minister of a formally sovereign state. Sogavare threatened on a number of occasions to not ratify the RAMSI Act, thus making the intervention illegal and effectively forcing its withdrawal. Had Sogavare acted on his threat, RAMSI would have had no choice but to leave. Indeed, this is exactly what happened to the Australian Enhanced Cooperation Programme in Papua New Guinea only a few years earlier. So, in a bid to prevent this outcome, then-Australian Foreign Minister Alexander Downer took the extraordinary step in July 2007 of having an open letter to the Solomon Islands people published in the country's main daily newspaper, *The Solomon Star*, urging Solomon Islanders not to let their leaders destroy the mission and its achievements.[70]

Nonetheless, that Sogavare never actually carried out these threats is telling. It is rare to find recipient governments totally rejecting international intervention. While donor good governance and decentralisation programmes can provide some challenges to the elites dominating the

[66] Hameiri 2010. [67] Peck 2002: 340. [68] Kyed and Albrecht 2015.
[69] Fry and Kabutaulaka 2008. [70] Downer 2007.

national scale, the resources offered by interveners are typically attractive for embattled governments in poor countries. It is not a coincidence that the government led by Sir Allan Kemakeza, in power when RAMSI was first deployed, was the first in Solomon Islands' history to complete a full-term in office.

Selective Adoption at the National Scale

This is a particularly significant response to international intervention. It entails using the state's scale management capacity to selectively admit or constrain international programmes in ways that reinforce the power and authority of elites dominating the national scale. Another element of this approach involves efforts to shape the manner in which rescaled institutions actually function, shifting resources from more heavily rescaled parts of the bureaucracy to areas that have not been rescaled. Selective adoption is important because the elites dominating the national scale in many developing countries are far from unchallenged. The resources deployed by interveners can make the difference between losing and maintaining power, both within the national scale and among existing elites.

Selective adoption is very common in all of our case studies. In Solomon Islands, for example, the power of the elites dominating the national scale has hinged since independence on their ability to centralise in the capital Honiara rents from foreign aid, as well as from logging and extractive activities in provincial areas, and then redistribute these back to supporters outside of the national capital. Because they support this basic strategy of rule, international programmes designed to improve state revenue by, for example, rescaling the Inland Revenue Division, have been remarkably successful, with tax collection increasing fourfold in the five years to 2011. However, programmes to control public expenditure have on the whole failed to achieve their objectives, because national elites have jealously guarded their ability to control resource disbursements to their supporters. Accordingly, the increases in revenue have largely been channelled into Constituency Development Funds (CDFs) – discretionary funds available to Members of Parliament to spend on local development in their constituencies. These have been used to maintain the power of the elites dominating the national scale and the national scale's dominance over subnational scales.

Crucially, which interventions are blocked or promoted is not a simple matter of free choice by recipient governments. It reflects the broader political economy context, the unequal social and political relations associated with it, and the position of political and bureaucratic elites within it. Indeed, in our Solomon Islands example, the rapidly growing CDFs are not simply a reflection of politicians' venality. In a context of highly fragmented politics where ideology plays a very limited role in elections or the formation of political coalitions and where state resources are the main source of funds,[71] discretionary ability to spend public funds is essential for political survival.

Localisation

Localisation refers to attempts to construct a local scale of governance and shift important capacities and resources downwards. This strategy is often, but not exclusively, attempted by marginalised groups seeking to wrest power and resources away from existing elites dominating the national scale. A local scale, as any other, could take almost infinite forms. It could, for instance, be organised around a subnational administrative unit of a state, or instead refer to a particular ethnic community, village or a river system. What makes it local is the claim that organising political life, economic relations and/or governance at that scale is superior or preferable to their location at a higher scale, especially that of the nation-state.

Crucially, and in contrast with the assumptions of the hybridity scholarship, localisation is not necessarily always pursued by local actors. We should not assume that village elites, for example, would necessarily seek a village scale of governance for all issues, because this would not always best advance their interests or agendas. Rather, the attempted construction of local scales is a context-specific effort to intervene in a particular struggle over power and resources. Although attempts to scale down power and control over resources are nothing new, in the context of PSBIs these often assume novel forms, as various interests in recipient states and societies respond to these interventions' fragmenting effects on the national scale, and thus, potentially, on the power relations this scale embodies and reinforces.

A particularly obvious example of PSBIs' effects on localisation is the ubiquitous decentralisation agenda of organisations like the World Bank. Decentralisation is sometimes promoted because it is seen to advance democratic accountability.[72] For development agencies,

[71] Steeves 2011. [72] Diamond 1999.

however, its main appeal, rooted in neo-institutionalist notions of good governance, is that it supposedly brings decision-making closer to those affected by it, thereby promoting greater governmental accountability to citizens in service delivery. Relatedly, it is also seen as a way of getting around existing forms of patronage and inefficiency entrenched in central states' bureaucracies and political institutions.[73] But as is always the case with the politics of scale, the actual outcomes of decentralisation reflect dynamic socio-political conflicts and may deviate considerably from their architects' intentions.

In Indonesia, for example, the international financial institutions and some local technocrats promoted a comprehensive process of decentralisation following the end of Suharto's authoritarian rule in the late 1990s. This has entailed devolving to the district level of government control over a significant proportion of the budget, as well as the authority to regulate key industries. Although the reform did not bring about the improvements in governance and service-delivery anticipated, Indonesia's decentralisation has undoubtedly had a profound effect on the scalar distribution of power.[74] Suharto's relatively coherent New Order regime was premised on a Jakarta-centred system of patronage penetrating down to Indonesia's remotest corners. This was maintained through the awarding of government contracts and resource-extraction concessions to key interests in state and society, including the military.[75] Decentralisation has greatly fragmented this order, though it has not fundamentally transformed the predatory nature of political power. The greatest beneficiaries from this shift have been locally based political and business elites, formerly junior players within the New Order regime. They have increased their dominance by capturing rents derived from locally based economic activities, which in some cases are conducted by transnational corporations, and establishing smaller-scale patronage networks. Thus, decentralisation has mainly led to the fragmentation and localisation of an essentially similar social order to that prevailing during the days of the New Order, albeit in a context of electoral democracy.[76]

The draining of power from the national scale has not gone uncontested in Indonesia. Political, bureaucratic and business elites dominating the now much weaker national scale have sought to rescale power upwards in various ways. These have included latching on to

[73] Grindle 2009. [74] Hadiz 2010. [75] Robison 1986. [76] Hadiz 2010.

international interventions, like efforts to combat transnational security threats emanating from within Indonesia, such as avian influenza and environmental pollution. In these cases, central ministries and politicians have claimed that lower level governments' incompetence or corruption has prevented the effective management of the threat. They have also used international funding and pressure for action to construct modes of governance that grab power back from lower-level governments. Their success has been limited, largely because the relevant industries – in these cases, poultry and palm oil – have endeavoured to maintain a local governance scale to avoid international regulation, tilting the power balance in favour of localisation. In the case of avian influenza, for example, the full brunt of the international effort to combat the disease in poultry was directed only at poor villagers keeping chickens in their backyards, while commercial farms, the real source of the disease, were almost entirely exempt.[77] As this example shows, international interventions have transformed and intensified the politics of scale in Indonesia by both reinforcing the initial decentralisation agenda and recentralisation attempts later on.

Although the decentralisation agenda is primarily rationalised by its architects as a means of advancing good governance in the neo-institutionalist mould, localisation efforts may also be promoted ideologically by reference to the legitimacy of unique ethnic, religious and/or customary authority of local leaders and modes of governance. These are contrasted with supposedly foreign, imposed modes of governance, especially the central state, but also those promoted by international peace-builders and donors. In Indonesia, Hadiz points out that although many of those benefitting from decentralisation used to be New Order apparatchiks, they have often reinvented themselves as localist leaders with claims to some traditional or ethnically based legitimacy.[78] This tendency is even more apparent when the construction of a local scale happens at a lower government level than that of a district or province, or does not map onto an administrative unit within a given state at all.

These assertions of legitimacy, based on supposedly unique local characteristics, and associated claims for autonomy and a greater share of power and resources, are foregrounded in the local turn scholarship, especially that working with the concepts of hybridity

[77] Hameiri 2014b; Hameiri and Jones 2015. [78] Hadiz 2010.

and friction. Scholars like Richmond, though careful to deny that they romanticise local institutions and ideas, nonetheless view the neglect of everyday ideas, institutions and customs within peace governance as the source of its failings.[79] Richmond also sees them as a potential source of emancipation for those affected by conflict and international interventions. To be sure, the authoritarian, repressive nature of many local forms of rule, especially their marginalisation of women and youth, has been widely noted.[80] But approaching this issue from the perspective of the politics of scale goes further: it avoids reifying the local, especially as international intervention plays a key role in its construction as a governance scale, and provides analytical tools for explaining its scope in given contexts. For example, the US counterinsurgency strategy in Iraq in 2006–7 purportedly reinforced traditional authority as a means of preventing sectarian bloodshed and stopping al-Qaeda. In reality, however, exactly who or what comprised local, traditional authority was not readily apparent, but tended to be contested and shaped by a long legacy of engagement with the colonial and postcolonial state.[81] According to David Kilcullen, one of the chief architects of the US counterinsurgency shift in Iraq, in one case, 'more than 162 leaders [were] claiming sheikhly status in northern Babil Province alone'.[82] Ultimately, local authority and its scope were determined by the capacity of particular leaders to use violence to establish order within given territories. Kilcullen describes a method of trial and error, whereby coalition forces would approach various individuals, typically those with overlapping jurisdictions (tribal, religious, official), eventually supporting those who could mobilise wider networks against the al-Qaeda-affiliated insurgency. This capacity to establish order through violence was strongly enabled by money and weapons derived from the United States, reinforcing the point that the construction of a local scale here cannot be merely described as an assertion of authentic local identity. Localisation and its outcomes are thus only legible if placed against the broader context of socio-political conflict and power relations, whereby the construction of local scales of a given scope is an attempt to attain particular political outcomes.

[79] Richmond 2014. [80] E.g. Paffenholz 2015. [81] ICG 2008.
[82] Kilcullen 2009: 158.

Analysing Intervention Outcomes

The final analytic phase is to bring together the previous three steps into a coherent analysis of governance outcomes in given contexts. Our analysis focuses on struggles over whether rescaling of particular parts of the administration should occur at all and, if it does, to what extent and, finally, over how rescaled institutions actually function in practice. The focus in our inquiry is not on whether outputs reflect the expectations of the architects of international intervention (though we also address this), but on explaining concretely in whose interests actual modes of governance operate. We also examine whether power and resources are displaced to non-rescaled parts of the administration in relation to the same struggles.

The outcome will depend on the balance of contesting forces in a given context, with particular significance being attached to the responses and strategies of elites dominating the national scale before and during the implementation of international programmes/projects. Their scale management capacity means that more than any other group contesting the outcome of PSBIs, they can harness international interventions selectively to bolster their power. However, Gramscian state theory makes it clear that we should not presume that the elites dominating the national scale, or any other actors, including the interveners, are necessarily unified or know exactly how to promote their interests in every given situation. Rather, intervention outcomes are produced through dynamic social and political conflict, shaped but not determined by the structural factors discussed above.

Conclusion

In this chapter we have advanced an alternative framework for analysing the outcomes of the interaction between international interventions and local politics. It has two key elements: Gramscian state theory and the politics of scale. Gramscian state theory draws our attention to the nature of socio-political struggle, in particular to the strategic selectivity of states and institutions.[83] The design of institutions and how they actually function is contingent on the outcomes of struggles between socio-political coalitions, whose make-up and relative strength is

[83] See Jessop 2008.

shaped by historical processes of state formation and economic development. Institutions are never neutral, but systematically privilege particular interests, agendas and political strategies over others. These coalitions routinely cut across the state–society divide, and in the context of international intervention also traverse the divide between the interveners and intervened. The forces aligning to promote or resist particular political outcomes are not necessarily the same across all programmes or projects attempted by interveners. Rather, different coalitions come together depending on how particular interventions and governance programmes affect the interests and normative preferences of various groups.

This approach is then supplemented by the introduction of the politics of scale as a key dimension of conflict over intervention outcomes. The significance of scale is implicitly recognised by the hybridity scholarship's focus on the relations between local and international, although the tendency to reify a dichotomy between the two is, as argued in Chapter 1, problematic. Drawing on political geography, we define scales as vertically differentiated, hierarchised social, political and economic spaces, each denoting 'the arena and moment, both discursively and materially, where socio-spatial power relations are contested and compromises are negotiated and regulated'.[84] They manifest the contingent outcomes of contested attempts to fix space in ways that promotes particular interests and normative agendas. They are therefore not entirely separate from other scales, but are part of a broader set of power relations.[85]

The politics of scale is important in the case of international interventions, since PSBIs seek not to govern target states and societies directly, but typically to produce particular governance and political outcomes by using state and societal institutions of the intervened as mediators. In other words, as we have argued, they seek to rescale these institutions – take them out of their hitherto domestic or local context and make them responsive to international agendas and targets. In the case of PAR, this is potentially threatening to existing elites dominating the national scale, whose power often depends on their capacity to control these institutions and their outputs. In turn, as we discuss in the second part of this chapter, a range of scalar strategies emerge to respond to PSBIs' fragmenting of the national scale – total rejection of

84 Swyngedouw 1997: 140. 85 Brenner et al. 2003; Smith 2003.

international intervention, selective adoption at the national scale and localisation. The significance of these strategies, and their success, depend on their position within the kind of socio-political struggles Gramscian state theory emphasises.

The following chapters provide three in-depth case studies of Solomon Islands, Cambodia and Aceh (Indonesia). They demonstrate the significance of the politics of scale as a key dimension of conflict shaping the outcomes of international interventions. The cases also show that international interventions yield highly uneven outcomes across different programmes, depending on the strength of the coalitions assembling to support or resist particular elements of the intervention and their scalar strategies.

3 Public Administration Reform and the Politics of Scale in Solomon Islands

The archipelagic state of Solomon Islands, population 560,000, has received high levels of international development aid since the Australian-led Regional Assistance Mission to Solomon Islands (RAMSI) started in July 2003. By 2009 it was the world's second most aid-dependent country.[1] RAMSI arrived at the Solomon Islands government's request following a period of conflict since 1998 that devastated the formal economy and emptied the state's coffers.[2] Solomon Islands was framed in the Australian capital, Canberra, at the time as a 'failing state', at risk of collapse. Its troubles were thought to be the result of the failure of post-colonial state institutions to deliver on the promise of independence. Captured by venal interests, it was argued, the state had lost the allegiance of most Solomon Islanders, who continued to give their support to more particularistic identities, such as kin groups or islands.[3] The task of intervention was thus to give the central state a second chance, by initially restoring law and order and budgetary controls, and then by rebuilding its governance capacity. A central state capable of promoting economic development and delivering basic services, it was expected, would become more popularly legitimate, securing sustained peace and stability.[4] Public administration reform (PAR) programmes have been at the heart of this state-building agenda. The main objectives of all of RAMSI's three pillars – law and justice, economic governance and especially machinery of government – were primarily to be achieved through PAR, aimed at 'capacity building'.[5] After RAMSI's partial withdrawal in 2013, PAR remains at the core of ongoing aid programmes delivered by bilateral and multilateral donors, as well as in RAMSI's continuing 'police-building' mission, which is due to end in 2017.

[1] Hayward-Jones 2014: 6; Pryke 2013. [2] Fraenkel 2004; Moore 2004.
[3] Wainwright 2003. [4] See Batley 2005; Coppel 2012: 6. [5] Hameiri 2009.

Despite the vast resources, relative to the size of the economy and the government's budget, donors have funnelled into Solomon Islands, their ability to implement PAR programmes and achieve anticipated governance results has been limited.[6] Explanations vary, but two main types are apparent: The first, working from the assumption that individuals are utility-maximising (understood to mean seeking pecuniary gain), sees resistance to RAMSI as driven by vested interests – corrupt politicians, public servants and affiliated business people benefiting from the status quo. Furthermore, the material incentives facing individuals at the village level and upwards are also seen to militate against electing the kind of politicians that would transcend their own self-interest and those of their followers.[7] This approach leads to an emphasis on external intervention as necessary for change. Haque, for example, argues that only donors are interested in and capable of instigating change because they do not benefit from the existing arrangements.[8] This is to be achieved through institutional redesign to locate decision-making beyond the reach of vested interests and change incentive structures by strengthening accountability mechanisms and the judicial system. RAMSI's failures are thus explained as stemming from its not being intrusive enough, since as an intervention 'invited' by the Solomon Islands government (SIG), it has been unable to seriously challenge vested interests and change incentive structures.

A second perspective sees RAMSI's problems in meaningfully reforming governance as emanating from the incompatibility between the liberal Western values and objectives of donors and Solomon Islanders' non-liberal culture and society, especially *wantokism* (a pidgin term referring to favouritism towards one's kin). Two strands are apparent in the cultural argument. Some observers, echoing modernisation theory, see Solomon Islands' culture as a problem to overcome, because it undermines the delivery of the modern state's essential political and administrative functions.[9] This perspective converges with the economistic approach in essentially viewing intervention to limit Solomon Islander control over policy, resources and service-delivery as the only means of surmounting entrenched and undesirable influences. A second strand, which is derived from the

[6] Fraenkel et al. 2014; Haque 2013; Hayward-Jones 2014. [7] Haque 2012.
[8] Haque 2012: 8. [9] Fukuyama 2008; Wainwright 2003.

local-turn literature discussed in earlier chapters, concurs that Solomon Islanders' culture and society are incompatible with the 'modern' state institutions donors are attempting to construct, and instead views RAMSI's own objectives as the problem. RAMSI is seen to have failed by neglecting important institutions outside the state, such as local communities and churches, as well as customary forms of authority, which are considered very important for maintaining social cohesion.[10] This approach thus advocates hybridity – combining introduced state institutions with local traditions and social forms.[11]

However, any explanation based on broad generalisations, whether relating to culture or bad incentives, is problematic. If Solomon Islands' culture is incompatible with, and resistant to, external state-building, or if incentive structures militate against reform, we would have expected the results of intervention to be largely consistent as well: all PAR programmes should have failed. In reality, results are uneven. Programmes aiming to improve revenue collection, for example, have been apparently successful, with state revenue quadrupling between 2006 and 2011; however, donor attempts to impose greater controls on public spending have been unsuccessful, with aid continuing to fund public services despite growing revenue.[12]

Our approach, outlined in Chapter 2, is capable of fully accounting for this variability. The outcomes of specific programmes or projects are shaped by struggles between coalitions in state and society, in which international actors are deeply involved, over the extent to which particular parts of the bureaucracy are rescaled and how rescaled institutions operate. Especially pivotal to the outcomes of these struggles are the scalar strategies of dominant elites at the national level. In turn, how these elites exercise their scale management capacities is shaped by a long-term process, beginning in the pre-colonial era, through which the national scale and its relations with subnational scales have been constituted. The dominance of the national scale requires centralising within the capital Honiara rents from economic activities, mainly resource-extraction, occurring in provincial parts of the archipelago. National political leaders then redistribute some of these resources back to remote areas, in a discretionary manner, to secure electoral support-bases. This structure has meant that although the national

10 Allen and Dinnen 2010; Morgan and McLeod 2006.
11 See Boege et al. 2008; Brigg 2009; Dinnen and Allen 2013; Richmond 2011.
12 See Fraenkel et al. 2014.

scale has been dominant, inter-scalar conflict has been rife in Solomon Islands, as marginalised groups have demanded a greater share of the benefits or even autonomy, often asserting the legitimacy of local identities and customs over the supposedly 'foreign' nation-state.

Donor attempts to rescale core state functions beyond domestic political control and societal influence have thus carried uneven implications for Honiara-based political elites. They have responded by harnessing the state's scale management capacity to adopt or resist international programmes and by shifting resources to non-rescaled parts of the state that they control. Donor PAR programmes aimed at improving revenue-collection have been successful since they increase the resources at the disposal of national elites. However, as discretionary spending is essential, not only to the political survival of individual members of parliament (MPs) but to the very primacy of the national scale, donor efforts to dominate spending ministries and procurement processes have largely failed.[13]

Furthermore, the Solomon Islands government has pursued its own PAR agenda. Designed to reinforce the primacy of the national scale, especially against localisation challenges, the government's reforms have funnelled revenue growth into the massive expansion of Constituency Development Funds (CDFs) – discretionary funds available to MPs to spend locally – putting at an MP's disposal resources far superior to anything available to their rivals.

The following section demonstrates that donor PAR programmes essentially seek to rescale parts of the Solomon Islands state. We will then, as a precursor to explaining the outcomes of donor PAR programmes from RAMSI onwards, provide the relevant historical-sociological context, focusing on the power relations produced by uneven economic development, and their manifestation in the state's strategic selectivity, as well as Solomon Islands' politics of scale. The final section will then explain the uneven outcomes of PAR.

International Intervention and the Rescaling of the State Apparatus

The arrival of RAMSI in Honiara on 24 July 2003 initiated a period of enhanced international engagement in Solomon Islands, with foreign

[13] Fraenkel et al. 2014: 64.

aid increasing from 16 to 30 per cent of GDP between 2004 and 2011.[14] RAMSI was deployed at the request of the Solomon Islands government, following a period of civil conflict (1998–2000), especially on the main island of Guadalcanal, between militias claiming to represent the island identities of Guadalcanal and Malaita, followed by a period of instability in which ex-militants dominated the state (2000–2003). Largely Australian-funded and led, though officially under the auspices of the Pacific Islands Forum (PIF), RAMSI was one of the most comprehensive state-building operations ever attempted. It was also very expensive, relative to the size of Solomon Islands' population and economy.[15] In July 2013 RAMSI's scope was reduced to a police-building mission, which is to last until 2017. However, the governance agenda it set in Solomon Islands is ongoing through bilateral and multilateral aid programmes, especially Australia's, which provides about three-quarters of total aid to Solomon Islands.

From the outset, RAMSI's objectives were defined as supporting the state's capacity to more effectively provide basic services, such as policing, health and education, as well as conditions suitable for private sector-led economic development.[16] Improving state performance in these areas was justified as necessary for rebuilding the state's legitimacy in the eyes of Solomon Islanders, thus ensuring longer-term social and political stability. Nicholas Coppel, the last RAMSI Special Coordinator of a full-capacity mission, wrote: 'The efficient and effective delivery of services throughout the country is important for its own sake, and to alleviate feelings of social injustice and exclusion'.[17] More recently, the likelihood of private sector-led development ever becoming sufficient for attaining adequate service delivery and improvements in living standards has been questioned.[18] However, the link between service-delivery and state legitimacy remains established in the objectives of the multi-donor Solomon Islands Economic and Public Sector Governance Programme (SIGOV) that has replaced RAMSI's economic governance and machinery of government pillars.

RAMSI officials and their Solomon Islander counterparts have consistently understood RAMSI's role as providing external support to

[14] Haque 2013: 13. [15] Hayward-Jones 2014. [16] Warner 2003.
[17] Coppel 2012: 6. [18] E.g. Haque 2013; World Bank 2014.

the development of *national* state capacity and hence *national* state legitimacy. This, as we have seen in Chapter 1, is very common in the context of Peace- and State-Building Interventions (PSBIs). For example, former Special Coordinator, James Batley, argued, 'we see RAMSI's core state-building agenda as providing an essential foundation or underpinning in which discussion about these basic national issues can take place. Just as RAMSI's work provides a platform for national economic recovery, RAMSI has succeeded in creating an environment in which this national discussion can occur'.[19] In the 2009 partnership agreement signed between SIG and RAMSI, RAMSI's overarching goal was defined as a 'peaceful Solomon Islands where key national institutions and functions of law and justice, public administration and economic management are effective, affordable and have the capacity to be sustained without RAMSI's further assistance'.[20]

Notwithstanding this rhetoric, the key aim of donor programming in Solomon Islands since RAMSI has been to reshape the objectives and function of public governance in Solomon Islands to make it responsive not to the demands of Solomon Islanders, which are typically viewed as corrosive of 'good governance', but to international agendas and objectives. The rescaling and internationalisation of public governance in Solomon Islands is multilayered, beginning at the highest level in the way that strategic policy objectives are formed, and running through many central agencies and line ministries.

A key mechanism at the strategic level has been the Core Economic Working Group (CEWG), which was established in 2009 at a time when Solomon Islands' fiscal position was badly affected by the global financial crisis and its government requested urgent assistance from donors and the International Monetary Fund (IMF) to avoid defaulting on the state's foreign debt. CEWG was formed as a condition for granting donor assistance to the government.[21] It includes all the biggest donors to Solomon Islands, as well as representatives from the Solomon Islands Ministry of Finance and Treasury (MoFT), the Central Bank of Solomon Islands (CBSI), the Office of the Prime Minister, the Ministry of Planning and the Ministry of the Public Service.

[19] Batley 2005.
[20] Pacific Islands Forum Ministerial Standing Committee 2009: 6.
[21] Brown et al. 2012.

The CEWG's main task is to monitor the Solomon Islands government's implementation of the Economic and Financial Reform Programme (EFRP). The EFRP is a matrix of policy objectives and benchmarks relating to economic and financial policy, set by the IMF and officially adopted through the CEWG framework. The policy objectives are the IMF's typical economic liberalisation ensemble including: fiscal stability; strengthening the government's revenue base; improving the budget preparation process, budget transparency and control over government expenditure; and enhancing the management of state-owned enterprises. Progress on the EFRP benchmarks is reviewed annually by a CEWG Joint Review Mission.[22] The EFRP also includes 'incentive funds', which are released or withheld depending on the attainment of IMF benchmarks.[23] Thus, when a recent review found that about half the policy objectives were not met in 2013, about A$4 million of donor funding was withheld, according to one donor representative.[24]

Though the CEWG is presented as a negotiating forum between donors and SIG, this view is problematic. First, donors' superior resources give them considerable power vis-à-vis the heavily aid-dependent government. Equally important, however, is the fact that key agencies on the Solomon Islands side of the CEWG are heavily rescaled, especially the lead agency, MoFT. An Australian government review of CEWG effectiveness notes:

> [T]he secondment of RAMSI staff, Overseas Development Institute fellows, and other technical expertise to MoFT has helped to bolster the Ministry's technical capacity and to develop more robust financial management systems and procedures. This capacity has allowed SIG to engage more effectively at a technical level with bilateral and multilateral partners and has served to reassure donors about MoFT's systems and procedures. As a close observer of CEWG noted: 'without RAMSI staff, SIG and donors wouldn't be on even footing'.[25]

This supposedly even footing has clearly been provided through the significant internationalisation of MoFT, which naturally leads it to endorse donor agendas through CEWG.

22 E.g. The Solomon Islands Core Economic Working Group 2011.
23 Brown et al. 2012: 5–6.
24 Author's interview with donor representative to Solomon Islands (name withheld), Honiara, 22 July 2014.
25 Brown et al. 2012: 11.

This is part of a broader pattern. Because RAMSI and other donors have been reluctant to assume formal sovereign authority over Solomon Islands, the main mechanism for attaining donor goals has been PAR, which seeks to transform key government agencies from within and, in particular, to insulate them from apparently undesirable political and societal pressures. This involves rescaling the governance of core state functions beyond the scope of domestic political contestation and control. Empowering the public administration to withstand pressure from above and below has meant that RAMSI was not a case of rolling *back* the state, like the ADB-promoted structural adjustment programme enacted in the late 1990s,[26] but rather the rolling *out* of a governance architecture insulated from the society it is meant to run.[27] Indeed, RAMSI and other donors have funnelled considerable resources into the Solomon Islands public administration. From 2003 to 2013 the public sector doubled in size to approximately 16,000 employees and public spending shot up 180 per cent.[28] Government expenditure now accounts for 60 per cent of GDP, with the public service payroll taking up 40 per cent of the recurrent budget.[29]

Donor attention and resources have not been evenly distributed, however. Particular emphasis, as mentioned, has been placed upon MoFT, the key institution responsible for managing public revenue and expenditure. MoFT receives the bulk of SIGOV's annual funds of A$60 million, and is 'dominated by expatriates'.[30] Donors have targeted state agencies responsible for basic service delivery, mainly the Royal Solomon Islands Police Force (RSIPF) and the Ministries of Health and Education, as well as public accountability institutions, mainly the Office of the Auditor-General (OAG). Many other ministries, such as the Ministry of Forestry, have been largely neglected. The assumption is that rescaled institutions will act as bureaucratic good governance 'enclaves',[31] which would deliver core services more effectively, thus strengthening society's allegiance to the state, and discipline rent-seekers in state and society.

One prominent example for the rescaling of Solomon Islands' public administration is the Internal Revenue Division (IRD) – responsible for taxation administration and compliance – within MoFT. Supporting

[26] See Knapman and Saldanha 1999. [27] Peck and Tickell 2002.
[28] Fraenkel et al. 2014: 79; Haque 2013: 5. [29] World Bank 2014: 30.
[30] Barbara 2014: 11. [31] Williams 2003.

revenue-collection capacity was seen as important to 'increase the Solomon Islands' self-sufficiency and thus reduce reliance on [donor] budgetary support'.[32] It was also thought crucial for improving state legitimacy, since, as mentioned in Chapter 1, taxation is considered important for 'establishing a functioning relationship between governments and tax paying citizens'.[33] However, as with public finances more broadly, the IRD's revenue-collection capacity was seen to be hampered by a corrupt 'culture where granting of [tax] concessions became "endemic"',[34] because of political pressure and public servants' own greed. Therefore, donors' main thrust in the IRD has been to insulate it from pressures for tax exemption and increase regulation of the exemption-granting process.

This has involved the agency's considerable internationalisation, mainly through the establishing of a direct relationship with the New Zealand Inland Revenue Division (NZIRD). Since 2005, NZIRD has been sending advisors, providing training and funding information technology (IT) upgrades, and from 2008 seconding a commissioner to the IRD.[35] This reflects the widely held donor view in Solomon Islands that 'the best performing organisations are all run by expats'.[36] Indeed, after NZIRD became directly involved, revenue collection quadrupled from SI$365.5 million in 2005 to approximately SI$1.7 billion in 2012.[37] Furthermore, a new process for approving tax exemptions and concessions was developed, whose aim was to 'remove [decision-making over exemptions] from the political level and give it to bureaucrats',[38] and then insulate these bureaucrats from political pressure. New legislation, promoted by the rescaled MoFT, led to the setting up in 2008 of a joint committee for approving tax exemptions, led by the IRD, and including the Customs and Excise Division (CED), and the Ministries of Planning and Commerce.

The exemptions approvals committee's first task was to develop guidelines and standards for awarding tax concessions or exemptions, as previously there were none and decisions were entirely at the

32 Murray et al. 2014: 141. 33 Murray et al. 2014: ix.
34 Murray et al. 2014: 134. 35 Murray et al. 2014: 134.
36 Shahar Hameiri's interview with senior donor advisor (name withheld) in the Solomon Islands bureaucracy, Honiara, 17 July 2014.
37 Murray et al. 2014: 135.
38 Shahar Hameiri's interview with senior donor advisor (name withheld) in the Solomon Islands bureaucracy, Honiara, 17 July 2014.

discretion of the Finance Minister and tax officials. It meets monthly to assess requests and publicises its decisions. By including CED, this committee was also part of an effort to rescale the granting of excise and duty exemptions by customs officials. The CED is widely viewed by donors and IRD officials to be underperforming relative to the IRD, because of the pernicious influence of logging-related interests, and its Solomon Islander leadership initially resisted the joint committee idea.[39]

Another area where considerable rescaling has been attempted is in public expenditure for basic services. Donors typically view the quality of public spending as quite poor and rife with adverse political interference.[40] However, despite substantial revenue growth over recent years, donors continue to heavily fund education, health and policing services, through tied grant funding and direct budgetary support.[41] Taxes are seen to 'just fund the public service [wage bill]. Aid pays for all the essentials such as roads, hospitals and schools'.[42] In health, for example, donors provided 50 per cent of the total budget in 2006, while the SIG reduced its own share by 33 per cent.[43] Likewise, 'Government expenditure on education is high, but financed almost entirely by donors'.[44] In the area of law and justice, which accounted for 83 per cent of RAMSI's total spending between 2003 and 2013, in-kind support to the RSIPF from the Australian Federal Police amounted to SI$564 million (US$76 million) in 2014,[45] or about two-thirds of the total costs of policing in Solomon Islands.[46]

Frustrated with their inability to channel SIG expenditure into public services, donors have pursued two rescaling strategies. The first has been to harness MoFT to discipline public spending. Solomon Islands' new Public Financial Management Act, mandated as part of the CEWG process, tightens rules relating to the use of public monies and, perhaps more importantly, orders the establishment of a network of accountants and financial controllers with expanded auditing and oversight responsibilities within every government agency and state-owned enterprise (SOE), whose role is to evaluate spending decisions and report misuse to MoFT and the Office of the Auditor-General (OAG).

39 Ibid. Also, Shahar Hameiri's interview with Eric Salea, Compliance Team Leader, Solomon Islands Internal Revenue Department, Honiara, 18 July 2014.
40 E.g. World Bank 2011b. 41 Craig and Porter 2014.
42 Murray et al. 2014: 144. 43 Asante et al. 2012: 169–75.
44 Whalan 2011: 237. 45 SIG 2014: 15. 46 Dinnen and Allen 2013: 233.

The Under-Secretary for Economic Policy in MoFT, argued: 'MoF[T] is very keen to ensure good quality of spending ... We can put people in other ministries under pressure [by] holding the budget and screening for some poor items'.[47] A second approach has been to more narrowly 'ring-fence' donor funds to prevent these from being misused.[48] Donor funds are clearly demarcated through a separate line in the Solomon Islands budget, and as part of the SIGOV programme donor financial controllers have been placed within the Treasury Division of MoFT, as well as within the Ministries of Health, Education and Infrastructure. They are required to sign off on every expense related to the donor-funded part of the ministerial budgets. One financial controller interviewed estimated that approximately 25–30 per cent of government funds were lost on corruption, including overcharging, fake tendering, and inappropriate petty cash payments. The same person said: 'I saw bullying of [Treasury] staff to give cheques to ministers and suppliers ... external input is essential ... if I wasn't here, monitoring would stop'.[49]

Finally, considerable rescaling of accountability institutions has occurred as well, especially of OAG. Until RAMSI's arrival, the OAG was practically completely dysfunctional. Subsequently, substantial donor resources have poured in, including the secondment of many in-line auditors and advisors from Australia and the training of Solomon Islander staff.[50] Expatriates have also served as Auditor-General twice: Eric Muir from 2006–2009 and Robert Cohen from 2013–2015. As a result, since 2005 the OAG has produced many publicly available reports on the finances of government ministries, public agencies and SOEs. The reports are tabled at the Public Accounts Committee (PAC) of the Solomon Islands Parliament, which is meant to take action. However, PAC is widely viewed within the OAG and donor circles as incapable of, or disinterested in, following up on OAG recommendations.[51] A recent World Bank report, for example, stated: the 'Public Accounts Committee of Parliament has limited capacity and

[47] Shahar Hameiri's interview with McKinnie Dentana, Under-Secretary for Economic Policy, Solomon Islands Ministry of Finance and Treasury, Honiara, 21 July 2014.

[48] Fraenkel et al. 2014: 65.

[49] Shahar Hameiri's interview with financial controller (name withheld) from an international development agency, Honiara, 23 July 2014.

[50] Hameiri 2010: 166. [51] Clark and Levy 2012: 57; Hameiri 2010: 167.

doesn't go beyond [identifying] spotted [typographical] errors'.[52] Likewise, former Auditor-General Robert Cohen said he hoped 'international agencies will be a bit harder on SIG' to get them to implement OAG recommendations.[53]

As we see, the main thrust of donor efforts has been to rescale public governance to make it responsive to their preferred agendas and objectives, not to the demands of Solomon Islanders as expressed through their elected political representatives. PAR programmes initiated since RAMSI's arrival have often had the explicit aim of insulating policy-making in key public agencies from political and societal 'interference', which is viewed as pernicious and illegitimate, and empowering technocrats, who are either expatriates, closely monitored by international agencies, or transnationally networked with their overseas counterparts. The variable results of these attempts, however, have been shaped by power relations within Solomon Islands society formed over decades of uneven development and socio-political conflict manifesting as a politics of scale. It is to this context that we now turn, as a necessary background to the subsequent analysis of the outcomes of donor PAR programmes.

Uneven Development and the Politics of Scale Before RAMSI

From the nineteenth century onwards, contact with Europeans began to intensify, culminating in the British Empire's colonisation of the Solomon Islands in 1893. The effect of this period on social and political power relations in Solomon Islands today and, specifically, on the prevailing form of scalar politics is considerable. First, it set in motion a longer-term pattern of uneven development based upon the exploitation of natural resources that are unevenly spread throughout the archipelago and, following colonisation, the concentration of rents within a central administration subordinating subnational scales.[54] Secondly, the period was significant for the emergence of new identities – especially, but not exclusively, defined in ethnic terms – which came to play an important part in the subsequent conflict of the late 1990s that preceded RAMSI's intervention. These identities and their

[52] World Bank 2011b: 8.

[53] Shahar Hameiri's interview with Robert Cohen, Solomon Islands Auditor-General, Honiara, 24 July 2014.

[54] Bennett 1987.

political salience, reflected especially in claims for local autonomy and a greater share of resources, are in no small part related to the geographically uneven pattern of development introduced through European contact and colonial rule.[55]

Before the intensification of European contact in the nineteenth century, the islanders typically lived in small kin-based communities, and their identities were therefore highly localised. They were often not even aware of the existence of many of the communities later incorporated into the British Solomon Islands Protectorate (BSIP). Their livelihoods mainly depended upon subsistence agriculture or fishing, bolstered by exchange with whalers occasionally passing through. Rulers, as in most of Melanesia, were typically 'big men' – influential individuals, selected for their capacity to organise the community and redistribute wealth, but not on a hereditary basis. The arrival of missionaries and the subsequent Christianisation of almost all communities on the islands was an important first step in establishing new relationships across island communities.

Perhaps more important, though, were two developments in the mid-nineteenth century. First, from the 1860s, European traders settled more permanently on the islands, trading mostly with communities in regions in what are now the western Solomon Islands that were richer in valuable resources like bêche-de-mer, goldlip shell, pearlshell, ivory nuts, tortoiseshell and copra. In return, these communities were able to obtain European goods, such as steel tools, guns and tobacco.[56] This was the beginning of a long-term pattern of economic disparity and uneven development across different regions, shaped by the availability of tradable natural resources. For the resource-rich communities, trade with Europeans provided relative material wealth, especially for big men, allowing them to remain on their land. A second important development in the same period was the commencement of large-scale international labour migration, indentured and free, initially to work on plantations in Australia, mainly from the relatively resource-poor but populous island of Malaita. The absence of tradable resources led Malaitans to exchange 'years of their labor, the only commodity they had that the white man wanted'.[57]

European contact, and the spatial inequalities it wrought, also created new social hierarchies within communities, based on

[55] Allen 2013. [56] Allen 2013: 69. [57] Bennett 1987: 78.

individuals' relations to the emerging capitalist economy. In labour-exporting regions, returnees brought with them valuable European goods, thus creating inequality within their communities and increasing the pressure for labour migration.[58] In resource-rich communities, whereas before the arrival of Europeans, reef and land resources were available to all members, when these resources became commodities, conflicts began to arise over who had control of them.[59] As a result, those within the community capable of controlling resources and benefitting from trade with outsiders became even more powerful.

In 1893 the islands were colonised by Britain, largely at the request of the Australian colonies, creating the BSIP. Because the BSIP was meant to pay its own way, colonial rule led to the emergence of 'enclave' plantation development, which reinforced the pre-existing pattern of uneven development. The colonial administration expropriated large areas in the relatively few regions suitable for plantations, especially in the north and west of Guadalcanal, but also in the Western Province and Russell Islands.[60] The establishment of large-scale, expatriate-owned plantations in Solomon Islands coincided with the end of international labour migration in 1910. Labourers from Malaita and other resource-poor areas, such as Guadalcanal's Weather Coast and Makira, migrated instead to work on plantations in the BSIP, providing almost the entire workforce, with Malaitans accounting for 68 per cent of the total. By 1932, 22 per cent of all adult Malaitan men were involved in wage labour elsewhere, mainly in the plantations.[61] This development pattern, whereby those with tradable natural resources could sustain a relatively comfortable life on their land, while those from resource-poor regions migrated and sent remittances back to their communities, was sustained well beyond the colonial era, creating marked differences in income per capita. Large-scale surveys conducted in the 1960s show that average income in some parts of the Western Province and Guadalcanal's resource-rich regions was up to five times that in resource-poor regions, with the latter relying heavily on labour migrants' remittances.[62]

As Allen persuasively argues,[63] the uneven and differentiated integration of different regions of Solomon Islands into the global capitalist economy in the colonial period was also associated with the

[58] Allen 2013: 70. [59] Bennett 1987: xviii. [60] Allen 2013: 70.
[61] Allen 2013: 71. [62] Allen 2013: 87. [63] Allen 2013: 15.

production of scales, which have allocated power and resources unevenly across the islands. It disrupted and transformed pre-existing relationships between people, places and identities, while creating new power relations and social hierarchies, as well as novel forms of social conflict. It is in this context that local claims for autonomy and resources, which began to be made at the time, must be understood.

One key example for an early use of a scalar strategy of localisation is the emergence of the concept of *kastom*. Although often portrayed as a demand for recognition of customary, pre-colonial social and cultural practices in contemporary governance, *kastom* was principally an 'ideology of resistance to external forces',[64] arising explicitly out of the colonial experience and the development patterns it wrought. It constituted 'a challenge to both the legitimacy of the colonial law and the exploitation of resources, including land by Europeans'.[65] *Kastom* emerged initially in the Malaitan Maasina Rule movement of the early post-war period, which at its peak unified almost all Malaitans in resistance to the colonial administration. The movement's key goals were to reject the low status of Malaitans relative to Europeans and work for social change and development in line with 'Malaitan sensibilities'.[66] Maasina Rule demanded that the colonial government institute regional autonomous courts and a Malaita-wide council, codify *kastom* law and improve working conditions on plantations. It later forbade Malaitans from working on plantations in other islands, requiring them to work for Malaita's development, through the establishment of larger settlements and the cultivation of communal gardening and cash-cropping.[67] It is perhaps not surprising that this ideology initially emerged among Malaitans, with their experience of plantation wage labour. It created a sense of relative disadvantage based on material inequality, vis-à-vis both European plantation owners and managers, and the landowning communities encountered. It also helped create an island identity among members of hitherto disparate communities brought together by their labour. A similar process led to the emergence on the impoverished Guadalcanal Weather Coast of the Moro movement, which shared many of Maasina Rule's characteristics.[68] Though the colonial

[64] Allen 2013: 16; Akin 2013; Keesing 1989. [65] Allen 2013: 82.
[66] Akin 2013. [67] Allen 2013: 78. [68] Allen 2013: Ch 3.

government eventually repressed Maasina Rule in the early 1950s, *kastom* has remained a powerful ideology of resistance to external influence, including contemporarily to the post-colonial central state and donors. But in every period it has reflected specific struggles and political agendas, shaped by Solomon Islands' changing political economy.

The post-World War II era heralded another important development in Solomon Islands' politics of scale. Honiara, which after the war was made the colonial capital, and its environs became a centre for considerable economic activity and investment. The British authorities institutionalised enclave development by explicitly basing their economic strategy upon a small number of foreign-owned, large-scale, export-oriented agricultural development projects, mainly on the Guadalcanal plains.[69] The British also decided to strengthen the BSIP's administrative capacity to drive development – in line with the era's dominant Keynesian economics – by developing the capital's infrastructure and the government's expertise base. Thus, in the 1960s and 1970s half or more of all public expenditure on infrastructure was spent in Honiara, creating a boom in public and private sector employment.[70] This attracted thousands of migrant workers, of whom unsurprisingly the vast majority were Malaitans. Malaitans took up most of the jobs in the capital and in the major agricultural development projects on Guadalcanal, and also began to permanently settle in and around Honiara on customary and public land.[71]

The increasing concentration of wealth and investment in Honiara had two important effects that became even more significant after independence in 1978. First, village development in resource-poor regions came to be partly dependent upon the villagers' capacity to secure resources from the government, or from Honiara-based kin – a capacity that itself was uneven within and across communities.[72] This created new social hierarchies based on villagers' relations with urban elites capable of commanding and redistributing resources. Because large industries were foreign-owned, these urban elites were mainly concentrated in politics or the bureaucracy. With the introduction of elections in 1976, it also became an important driver of electoral contestation in rural communities, as personal connections to people

[69] Kabutaulaka 2001. [70] Allen 2013: 86.
[71] Allen 2013: 86–91; Bennett 2002. [72] Herlihy quoted in Allen 2013: 88.

of authority at the national scale became crucial to local power and material well-being.[73] Tellingly, 80 per cent of Solomon Islands MPs in 1980 came from a public service career.[74]

Also significant was the growing resentment towards the central state in resource-rich areas. Many worried about their wealth being usurped by a central administration seen as dominated by Europeans and, after independence, by Malaitans, and hence as a foreign power. Consequently, calls for federalism abounded in the years before and immediately after independence, especially from the areas now in the Western Province, which even threatened secession. On Guadalcanal, too, the Malaitans' large settlement on land around Honiara, purchased in the post-war era from some landowners, created strong resentment among some youths who felt their future had been sold. The rancour of marginalised groups in both resource-poor and resource-rich regions has never abated, playing an important part in the eruption of violent conflict in the late 1990s.[75]

The tensions produced by the colonial legacy of uneven development came to a head in the early post-colonial period, producing policy responses from the SIG to reinforce the national scale's primacy. Unable to contain secessionist pressures, mainly from the west, Solomon Islands' first government, led by Peter Kenilorea, a Malaitan, collapsed after 14 months.[76] Kenilorea's successor, the savvy Solomon Mamaloni, sought to manage this problem through two significant legislative changes, designed to tie fissiparous local big men into the central state. The first was the Provincial Government Act of 1981, which created seven (later increased to nine) provinces, based on colonial administrative units, as well as lower level Area Councils, based on the colonial Native Councils. Although the provinces' administrative and political structures were modelled on the central government, with their own assemblies, executives and bureaucracies, the Act entirely denied them fiscal decentralisation, and they were made dependent upon central government allocations. Their functions and relationship with the central government were also left vague by the legislation, again making them largely dependent on their relationship with the central government.[77]

[73] Corbett and Wood 2013: 330. [74] Corbett and Wood 2013: 327.
[75] Allen 2013; Kabutaulaka 2001. [76] Alasia 1997: 8.
[77] Cox and Morrison 2004.

Perhaps more importantly, Mamaloni also introduced legislation to allow logging on customary land. As approximately 87 per cent of all land was customarily owned, opening it up for development vastly expanded the opportunities for logging. By 1985, 95 per cent of logging was conducted on customary land, mostly by Southeast Asian companies and often through 'joint ventures' with Solomon Islanders.[78] Logging in fact has exceeded the estimated sustainable yield by as much as eightfold every year since 1981.[79] As a result, logging's share of exports has risen from about 25 per cent in 1977–78 to around 60 per cent by 2008, or 16 per cent of GDP.[80] The industry has thus become indispensable to the Solomon Islands economy, as export earnings are hugely important for bringing hard currency into a country heavily dependent upon imports.

But beyond these figures, the changing political economy associated with Mamaloni's logging reforms has had a tremendous effect on the constitution and interrelations of the national and local scales. Because timber resources are often the only means for many communities to earn significant cash incomes,[81] access to logging-related rents became crucial to attaining power locally and nationally. Although forests remain communally owned by law, the emergence of logging as the main economic activity in many rural communities has created local hierarchies and conflicts over their de facto control, typically privileging those with better education and access to Honiara, who are able to arrange permits and liaise with foreign companies.[82]

A 2006 survey conducted by the Australian aid-funded Community Support Programme shows the logging's uneven benefits within communities: Only 38 per cent of respondents reported some income from timber and logging royalties. The survey also found little evidence for the creation of employment opportunities or reinvestment in landowning communities, a further indication of the fact rents are held by and disbursed at the discretion of powerful individuals.[83] Nationally, governments have been formed and sustained since the 1980s mainly through the glue provided by logging rents, used by well-connected politicians to bribe others into joining them in coalition governments. But, as Mamaloni intended, the rents from logging also worked to

[78] Bennett 2000: 235; Frazer 1997. [79] Allen 2011.
[80] World Bank 2010: 49. [81] Kabutaulaka 2006. [82] Scales 2003.
[83] MDP 2007: 4.

undermine the secessionist impulse among elites, though not necessarily the wider public, especially in the Western Province where many have benefitted handsomely from large-scale logging and thereby accumulated political power nationally. Indeed, as logging on customary land became a crucial source of hard cash, and as Honiara-based services sectors grew as well, relations with the private sector became important for election to office. Accordingly, by 2001 the share of national politicians with a public service background fell to 45 per cent, while the share of MPs with a private sector background rose from 20 per cent in 1980 to 62 per cent in 2001.[84]

The underlying shift in Solomon Islands' political economy began to condition from the 1990s emerging struggles over PAR. Although initially conducive to stabilising national politics, logging generated new power bases, independent of the public service, which began to colonise and transform the public administration to suit their interests. For instance, the central administration's capacity to tax loggers was severely undermined by affiliated politicians. Increasingly concerned about rampant deforestation and rising corruption more generally, donors attempted to rescale state apparatuses but were met with countervailing scalar strategies from the government.

The example of the Timber Control Unit (TCU) is instructive. The TCU was established in 1993 under pressure from Australia and other donors and with substantial Australian aid funding. Its role was to identify and report irregularities in the logging industry, such as the underreporting of exports and illegal harvesting practices.[85] Then Solomon Islands Prime Minister Francis Billy Hilly, who was not affiliated with loggers, accepted its establishment partly because of Australian threats to withhold foreign aid, which for a non-logging-affiliated politician carried considerable weight. Indeed, Hilly, who was unusual among Solomon Islands' political elites in seriously attempting to tackle the power of loggers, sought to use the international rescaling of forestry governance to strengthen his hand against logger-backed politicians. But this rescaled pocket of the administration was overwhelmed by logger-backed national politicians, who were able to construct logging-friendly national coalitions and local support-bases, and thus keep the governance of the industry at the national scale.

[84] Corbett and Wood 2013: 327. [85] Bennett 2000.

Attacking the transnationalised TCU became part of the political manoeuvring that enabled Solomon Mamaloni, 'the darling of the loggers', to remove Hilly with a vote of no confidence.[86] Mamaloni, whose 1990–93 government had 11 of 15 ministers closely affiliated with the logging industry, claimed Hilly was an 'Australian puppet, usurping the rights of landholders'.[87] He also used financial inducements provided by loggers to coax members of Hilly's already tenuous coalition across the floor, thereby becoming prime minister again in late 1994. The Mamaloni government quickly began using its scale management capacity to undermine the TCU, bringing it into direct confrontation with a resistant, rescaled forestry administration, as well as with the donors themselves. In September 1995, the Finance Minister, Christopher Abe, cancelled an extensive Price Waterhouse study of forestry taxation and downstream processing in Solomon Islands, which revealed the extent of tax avoidance and evasion by logging companies. In the same month, Mamaloni threatened to abolish the TCU because of its supposed 'inaccurate and erroneous reports of the real state of the country's forests'.[88] Mamaloni supplemented this by attacking the Australian government, telling Australian Prime Minister Keating to 'shut up and stop interfering with the domestic affairs of Solomon Islands'.[89] In response, the Australian Minister for Pacific Islands Affairs, Gordon Bilney, threatened to withhold aid funds, saying that providing aid to corrupt Melanesian governments was to 'encourage and condone malfeasance'.[90]

After the TCU reported that Solomon Islands' tax administration lost SI$24 million in 1995 due to various exemptions and remissions, the Australian government felt compelled to act, effectively ending its efforts to rescale forestry governance in Solomon Islands. It cut SI$7 million of its forestry sector grant, reducing its overall aid contribution to Solomon Islands from US$10.19 million to US$7.97 million in 1995, maintaining funding approximately at this level until 2000 (OECD DAC n.d.). For Mamaloni this was a golden opportunity to undermine the TCU even more, and he abolished it in January 1996.[91] Although the TCU was reinstated in 1997, following Bartholomew Ulufa'alu's election as Prime Minister, it has remained

[86] Bennett 2000: 340–41. [87] Bennett 2000: 344. [88] Bennett 2000: 351.
[89] Bennett 2000: 344. [90] Bennett 2000: 352. [91] Schultz 2012: 131.

systematically underfunded and toothless ever since.[92] In fact, funds became so scarce that the TCU's sole officer in Isabel Province had no money for petrol or even a phone.[93]

The eruption of violent conflict in the late 1990s between militias claiming to represent Guadalcanalese and Malaitans was directly related to the development patterns described above, and their manifestation in state–society relations and increasingly fraught inter-scalar disputes. The militias – the Isatabu Freedom Movement (IFM) and the Malaita Eagle Force (MEF) – drew on long-standing discourses of marginalisation. As Allen argues,[94] it is not a coincidence that the main sources of recruitment for both rebel groups were the disaffected and disadvantaged Malaitans and Weather Coast Guale. The conflict, targeted at the central state, represented the culmination of decades of resentment building up among those not benefiting from development. Although tensions were simmering for some time, the trigger was the collapse in logging exports following the 1997–98 Asian economic crisis which undermined the national scale's dominance and which unsurprisingly soon became overwhelmed by localist demands for autonomy, initially from within Guadalcanal, spilling into violence.[95]

To be sure, claims that an illegitimate, transplanted central state is corrupting and exploiting pre-political, organic, local communities are rife in Solomon Islands. For example, Solomon Islander academic Gordon Nanau argues that *wantokism* has been corrupted when it was taken out of its original local context and incorporated into modern politics.[96] But, as we have seen, claims to some pure form of 'genuine' *wantokism* or *kastom* are ahistorical as there is hardly a community on the islands that has not been substantially transformed over centuries of uneven development, colonialism and Christianisation.[97]

Another common claim regarding the relationship between the central state and peripheral communities, is that the former is very remote from the daily lives of the rural majority, playing 'a negligible role in the governance of rural localities'.[98] While this may be true if we focus the delivery of services like education, health and policing, it is fundamentally mistaken if we look at more substantive issues of power, its distribution and reproduction. The multiple scales and associated

92 See Hughes et al. 2010. 93 Bennett 2000: 356. 94 Allen 2013.
95 Fraenkel 2004; Hameiri 2007. 96 Nanau 2011: 46. 97 Lawson 1996.
98 Dinnen and Allen 2013: 226.

hierarchies produced by Solomon Islands' pattern of uneven capitalist development run through the remotest community. Power, including within communities, almost invariably requires access to material resources centrally to redistribute locally.[99] For instance, Corbett and Wood show that election to parliament is impossible without local support-bases, but election does *not* usually depend on any traditional leadership status.[100] In some cases, elected politicians have never even lived in their supposed home village.

In this context, assertions of local authenticity are not really about culture, but manifest strategic mobilisations of localist ideologies in concrete struggles over power and resources; they are always attached to demands that governance and control over resources should be rescaled downwards from the national scale. These demands are essentially attempts by structurally weaker groups, not necessarily physically based in villages, to improve their political standing and material well-being – claims which are made also *against some in their own communities* who are better connected to structures of power. But because of these groups' structural weakness, they typically fail to attain desired change – resources continue to be centralised and redistributed at the discretion of national politicians with connections to private industry, especially logging. As we shall see in the following section, the overwhelming alignment of interests among the elites dominating the national scale means that internationally driven rescaling efforts have only served to reinforce their power.

Public Administration Reform and the Politics of Scale After 2003

Solomon Islands governments since 2003 have attempted to harness state-building programmes to reinforce the primacy of the national scale and the attendant socio-political interests benefitting from this arrangement. This has meant using the central state's scale management capacity to continue to concentrate rents, whether from extractive industries or foreign aid, within Honiara and making these available to political elites to spend at their discretion, to form coalitions and to maintain their deep-reaching networks in provincial areas. Therefore, PAR programmes to rescale revenue collection have been

[99] Devesi 2013; Steeves 2011. [100] Corbett and Wood 2013: 329.

relatively, though not uniformly, successful, whereas programmes to rescale spending have generally been highly unsuccessful. But this is not all. Donors' PAR programmes have helped national politicians and their allies to undermine the widely popular decentralisation agenda, which involves efforts to scale down governance via changes to the constitution to delegate more authority and resources to provinces. Decentralisation has partly been undermined by politicians' stalling tactics, but more substantially through the funnelling of massive resources, generated through the expansion of government revenue, towards CDFs, which far outweigh the resources available to provincial governments or other locally based groups not part of dominant networks.

Despite their considerable material preponderance vis-à-vis SIG, RAMSI and other donors have been unable to attain their preferred governance reform outcomes because of the government's scale management capacities but, perhaps more importantly, because political and business elites form a cohesive ruling class in that nearly all are beneficiaries of the arrangements described in the previous section. Donors therefore have found no powerful constituencies with which to align, even tactically, in order to push through reforms that meaningfully threaten the existing social and political order. The main source of opposition emanates, as mentioned, from various groups demanding localisation, but these are typically weak and the decentralisation agenda is unpopular among donors in Solomon Islands. We begin by examining PAR's uneven results and then proceed to discuss the rise of CDFs and the marginalisation of the decentralisation agenda.

The Uneven Results of Public Administration Reform in Solomon Islands

The PAR programmes implemented as part of RAMSI and the subsequent SIGOV have yielded highly uneven results. These outcomes can be explained if viewed against the backdrop of efforts to strengthen the national scale and reinforce the socio-political power relations supportive of it.

Perhaps the best illustration is the discrepancy between the performance of different parts of the revenue-collection administration itself. Although revenue growth within the central state is advantageous to powerful elites, their connections particularly with the logging industry are essential for their ascendancy. Reform outcomes in the tax system are moulded closely around these imperatives. Clearly, the most significant revenue growth has been achieved in areas that do not interfere with the logging industry. Revenue has grown primarily because of taxes collected from foreign companies providing services in Honiara and its environs, often in the delivery of donor projects. By the IRD's own estimate, only around 30 per cent of companies lodge their tax returns in most tax categories,[101] and some sectors are particularly non-compliant, most notably the logging industry, which is why it was specifically targeted in the IRD's 2013–15 Compliance Focus.[102]

This pattern is even more obvious if we look at the CED, which has a far closer engagement with the logging industry because it is tasked with collecting duties on log exports. As a recent report concluded, 'Revenue lost through the port remains a significant issue for Solomon Islands'.[103] To be sure, the CED's revenue has grown, though far less sharply than the IRD, from approximately SI$392 million in 2006 to SI$796 million in 2013. But growth has been primarily achieved in duties on imports and excises rather than on exports. In 2006, while a precise breakdown by sector is not available, receipts from export duties were estimated by RAMSI officials at SI$220 million, while import receipts were estimated at SI$172 million.[104] In 2013, total CED revenue from duties on log exports was just over SI$408 million, whereas revenue from duties on imports and excises was approximately SI$370 million.[105] Thus, even if all of the export duty receipts in 2006 were from log exports, which is doubtful, export duty revenue had grown by only 85 per cent by 2013, while revenue from import duties had risen nearly threefold. Meanwhile, estimated timber export volumes had doubled, from about 1.1 million cubic metres in 2006 to just over 2.2 million cubic metres in 2013.[106] This means that revenue growth has actually failed to keep up with export volume growth, despite the claim that 'some semblance of order and functionality was restored to the [Customs and Excise] Division' by 2008.[107] Indeed, CBSI's 2013 annual report claims that 'only 60% of

101 MoFT 2014: 55. 102 IRD 2013. 103 Murray et al. 2014: 138.
104 See Fraenkel et al. 2014: 66. 105 MoFT 2014: 26.
106 CBSI 2014: 18; URS Australia 2013: 6. 107 Fraenkel et al. 2014: 67.

total export [duty] proceeds for 2013 were reconciled and received while the remaining 40% are still outstanding'.[108]

Because of the establishment of the aforementioned IRD-led joint committee for tax exemptions, the formal granting of duty remissions by the CED has declined in recent years. Nonetheless, considerable anecdotal evidence exists of pressure from companies and politicians on customs officials to allow goods to clear the ports untaxed. One particularly egregious example, provided off the record to the authors, allegedly occurred on Christmas Eve 2013. The DFAT-funded, expatriate Deputy Comptroller, who was on leave for the holidays, reportedly came in to the office unexpectedly, only to find that a very large number of hitherto unseen export invoices were being processed quickly by local staff in his absence in order to get them through the port without paying the relevant duties. In another recent example, in September 2014, the *Solomon Star* reported that 60 containers of tubi logs were stopped in the port following a High Court injunction, since the logging company's licence to export was cancelled more than nine months previously. However, the same company had, since then, managed to export five shipments of at least 144 containers of tubi logs worth millions of dollars without being stopped by CED officials, until a concerned landowner approached the High Court to stop the trade.[109]

Let us now turn to the general failure of PAR projects related to government expenditure. It is perhaps immediately apparent, in light of the discussion in earlier sections, why politicians, who depend on access to and redistribution of resource rents to their supporters, are keen to allow rescaling that improves government revenue but constrain programmes aiming to limit their discretion over spending. Indeed, to limit donors' ability to interfere, budgetary allocations are appropriated through Parliament,[110] and reflect mainly negotiations in Cabinet, not requests from the ministries themselves.[111] But the role of public servants in preventing the rescaling of expenditure is also significant. The public service, as mentioned, has been deeply embedded in Solomon Islands' politics of scale for decades. Apart from some high-level, ideologically committed bureaucrats in key

[108] CBSI 2014: 19. [109] Namosuaia 2014. [110] Fraenkel 2011: 314.
[111] Coventry 2009.

ministries and agencies, donors have generally been unable to win the active support of most Solomon Islander public servants.

Employing 7 per cent of Solomon Islanders in 2009,[112] the public service continues to function as an important form of redistribution to bureaucrats' kin groups, through both official salaries and opportunistic sources, such as skimming off departmental budgets and petty cash or bribes. This is especially the case in ministries responsible for regulating lucrative activities, such as the Ministry of Forestry (MOFOR).[113] For example, MOFOR's Human Resources officer said that employees 'don't depend on their salary … They're drinking here every day – where are they getting their money from?'[114] A donor-funded auditor of government expenditure has likewise argued that many public servants are very active in procurement scams of various kinds. For example, the auditor was aware of around SI$80 million in petty cash payments taken by public servants without any record of how they were used. Also common, said the auditor, was the use of fake quotes as a means of avoiding tendering standards to award government contracts to companies either directly owned by public servants or their relatives.[115] Thus, most Solomon Islander public servants share political elites' resistance to imposing spending or procurement controls.

In sum, the uneven outcomes of donor PAR programmes in Solomon Islands make sense if viewed through the lens of long-term struggles to maintain the primacy of the national scale, in the context of decades of geographically uneven development. To reinforce this argument, we will now turn to look at how the outcomes of donor PAR have been further harnessed by national political elites to undermine the decentralisation agenda.

Constituency Development Funds and the Defeat of Decentralisation

In development jargon, the term 'reform' typically presupposes a shift towards liberal, international standards of good governance. But as

[112] Corbett and Wood 2013: 327. [113] Hughes et al. 2010: 23–24.

[114] Shahar Hameiri's interview with Salome Ramo, Human Resources Officer, Solomon Islands Ministry of Forestry, Honiara, 22 July 2014.

[115] Shahar Hameiri's interview with financial controller (name withheld) from an international development agency, Honiara, 23 July 2014.

shown by the rapid expansion of CDFs in the Solomon Islands, administrative reform can be harnessed to promote a very different governance agenda – one focused upon reinforcing the capacity of actors dominant at the national scale to continue to extract wealth and concentrate power in a highly fragmented society.

Development funds for MPs to spend in their constituencies were first introduced by Solomon Mamaloni before the 1993 elections. At the time, they were worth SI$100,000 per MP. His successor, Francis Billy Hilly, doubled the funds to SI$200,000 per MP. The supposedly reformist Prime Minister Bartholomew Ulufa'alu increased the funds to SI$300,000 in 1998 and to SI$370,000 in 2000, with much of the increase funded by Taiwanese aid.[116] The collapse in government accounts during 'the tensions' limited CDF allocations to very small amounts in 2001 and 2002. Following RAMSI's arrival, CDFs were re-established with Taiwanese money, reaching SI$600,000 in 2006. From 2007 onwards, the rapid increase in government revenue created exponential growth in the size of CDFs – tripling to SI$2 million in 2008 and tripling again to SI$6 million per MP after the passing of the 2013 Development Funds Bill by Parliament.[117] In terms of spending in rural constituencies, CDFs now dwarf allocations to provincial governments by about seven to one.[118]

Crucially, CDFs' rapid recent growth reflects the diversion of considerable portions of Solomon Islands' own development budget, not just Taiwanese aid, into discretionary MP funds. Taiwanese aid, which used to account for the entirety of the CDF allocation, has remained at approximately SI$1 million per MP since 2008, so the exponential growth in CDFs is funded through domestic sources which, ironically, are only available because of the rapid growth in government revenue generated by RAMSI programmes.[119] As such, CDFs now represent 40 per cent or more of the government's total development budget, and about half of all new spending announced in recent budgets.[120] Even

[116] Solomon Islands is one of a small number of countries worldwide that formally recognise the Republic of China (Taiwan) over the People's Republic of China. In return, Taiwan has been providing Solomon Islands with large sums of foreign aid.

[117] Fraenkel 2011: 312–15; Solomon Islands National Parliament 2013: 6.

[118] Craig and Porter 2014: 23. [119] SIG 2014: 11.

[120] Fraenkel 2011: 306; SIG 2014: 33.

when floods hit parts of Solomon Islands in April 2014 and Tropical Cyclone Raquel struck in July 2015, government relief funds were distributed mainly in the form of CDFs.[121]

Aside from Taiwan's contribution of SI$50 million for Solomon Islands' 50 constituencies, there are 16 SIG-funded projects under the CDF rubric, with a cumulative value of approximately SI$250 million per annum. These have managed to escape the scrutiny of the RAMSI-dominated MoFT, because MoFT is only responsible for the 'recurrent' line in the budget. The development budget is prepared by the Ministry of Development, Planning and Aid Coordination, 'with little RAMSI input', while development funds, including for CDFs, are appropriated by Parliament.[122] CDF projects are officially recorded in the budget as being under the responsibility of several ministries and agencies, including the Ministries of Rural Development; Forestry; Education and Human Resources Development; Culture and Tourism; Energy and Rural Electrification; Home Affairs; Women, Youths, Children and Family Affairs; Agriculture; and the National Parliament Office.[123] In reality, however, these administrations have little control over the funds, which are directly provided to MPs' Constituency Development Offices. For example, two new projects – a reforestation programme and downstream processing, both of which supposedly aim to develop economic opportunities to replace income from declining whole log exports – are managed through CDFs, with MOFOR officials completely marginalised.[124] Even the Ministry of Rural Development, which was set up in 2007 explicitly to regulate CDF spending, has had little influence in reality over how funds are spent, often struggling to obtain information from MPs.[125]

The spectacular growth of CDFs has been driven by both supply of funds for elite politicking and voter demand, broadly in line with the perspectives on Solomon Islands politics and society discussed in the introduction. On the demand side, scholars have argued that national politicians remain 'embedded in networks and relationships that link

[121] ABC 2014; Morton 2015. [122] Fraenkel 2011: 314.
[123] Data collected by Transparency Solomon Islands and provided directly to Shahar Hameiri by TSI officer, Louise Hiele, Honiara, 22 July 2014.
[124] Shahar Hameiri's interview with Felix Koraimae, Undersecretary for Administration, Solomon Islands Government, Ministry of Forestry, Honiara, 22 July 2014.
[125] Based on Shahar Hameiri's interviews with high-level bureaucrats in the Ministry for Rural Development, Honiara, December 2014.

them to the communities they represent, including through families and churches, but also largesse and other forms of money politics'.[126] This relationship of clientelism is seen to be either based on cultural expectations[127] or corruption and self-interest.[128] Either way, politicians are subject to constant demands for redistribution, and it is this pressure that pushes them to find new income streams.[129] Others see CDF growth as driven by the supply of money and politicians' own greed. Fraenkel has argued[130] that CDF increases are typically associated with attempts to hold together fragile political coalitions, not with demands from below, and that they are driven by 'windfall gains associated with external economic or political engagements'.[131] Likewise, Haque views CDFs' growth as the product of 'a resources boom', reinforcing the pernicious incentive structure that 'corrode[s] the influence and legitimacy of central government institutions and deepen[s] the dominance of patronage-driven politics'.[132]

Though both perspectives are partly correct, at a more fundamental level, CDFs can only be properly understood as an intervention in Solomon Islands' politics of scale, designed to reinforce the national scale in a context of persistent uneven development and, during 'the tensions', escalating violent resistance. They are a primary means through which national elites have undermined localisation alternatives in Solomon Islands, which remain broadly popular. CDFs are part of a wider and longer-term effort to make locally based actors entirely dependent upon resources distributed through nationally based politicians.[133] Indeed, McDougall claims, in line with the argument made in this chapter, that the defunding and dismantling of lower level governments has gone hand in hand with the expansion of logging on customary land and reflects a deliberate attempt to remove obstacles to the centralisation of rents.[134]

Political and fiscal decentralisation has been a popular agenda in Solomon Islands since before independence. This is perhaps not surprising in such a highly geographically and ethnically fragmented archipelago, where subsistence livelihoods remain the norm. But localisation has in most cases been attached to claims on resources. As mentioned, calls for secession, especially from the western parts of

126 Allen and Dinnen 2010; Corbett and Wood 2013: 332.
127 Corbett 2013; Fono 2007. 128 Craig and Porter 2014; Hughes 2013.
129 Corbett 2013: 14. 130 Fraenkel 2011: 319. 131 Fraenkel 2011: 306.
132 Haque 2013: 8. 133 McDougall 2014: 4. 134 McDougall 2014: 5.

the archipelago, played an important part in both the permission of logging on customary land and the establishment of provinces in the early 1980s. Increasingly, however, and especially after 'the tensions', many have been demanding a new federal constitution and more devolution of resources and authority to lower levels of government, especially to the provinces. Consultations and surveys conducted by UNDP (2003), MPs (2004) and the Constitutional Congress (2007–10) consistently reveal very high levels of support for 'state governments' among ordinary Solomon Islanders around the country.[135] Yet, despite some apparent gains, better-resourced interests, benefitting from the existing scalar hierarchy, have consistently stalled this popular agenda.

A major focus of the decentralisation and localisation agenda has been a demand for reform of the 1978 Constitution. The review process of the Solomon Islands Constitution began in unusual circumstances. During the peace talks leading to the 2000 Townsville Peace Agreement, the government agreed to the militias' demands to commence a constitutional review process, aimed at establishing a federal system of government. In 2002, a period of serious instability, Prime Minister Kemakeza signed an agreement to form a 'state government system' based on a 'homegrown' constitution.[136] This commitment led to a draft constitution bill in 2004, which was followed by a White Paper on constitutional reform in 2005. The White Paper committed the government to setting up a constitutional review process,[137] which was started in 2007 with the establishment of the Constitutional Reform Unit (CRU) in the Prime Minister's Office, the election of a Constitutional Congress and the nomination of an Eminent Persons Advisory Council. Also recruited were renowned constitutional law experts Professors Yash Ghai and Ronald Watts. The First Joint Plenary Meeting for constitutional reform took place in 2009, and in the Fourth Joint Plenary Meeting in March 2014, a draft Federal Constitution for Solomon Islands was finally endorsed by the Constitutional Congress.[138]

Despite the appearance of progress, however, the government has repeatedly stymied the Federal Constitution's official adoption. It has yet to be ratified by Parliament and there is currently no clear timetable for its adoption, although nearly all politicians are on record as

[135] Mae 2010. [136] Corrin 2007: 156. [137] Corrin 2007: 144.
[138] CRU 2014.

endorsing constitutional reform. This stasis has led long-time expatriate resident and former CBSI Governor Tony Hughes to claim: 'The official response to my recent inquiry about progress with a Federal Constitution indicates that we shouldn't waste time waiting for it. The present national government doesn't want it, and most likely the next one won't either'.[139] A Solomon Islander involved in the constitutional review process explains that in backroom discussions there is political consensus among MPs that decentralisation is a bad idea, but they change their tune completely when speaking publicly. When elected, he says, they 'just drag [their] feet on it until [they] are out or parliament dissolves. And then at campaign they say, "look I tried my best", but the PM, god bless his soul, he would not let on. And it's a cycle over and over again'.[140] Adding to the difficulties of decentralisation's proponents is the fact that, unlike in our other case studies of Indonesia and Cambodia, donors share Solomon Islander politicians' lack of enthusiasm for federalism. RAMSI was viewed as 'hostile' to constitutional reform,[141] and the ADB has warned against the poor cost-benefit ratio of decentralisation as early as 2004.[142]

Irrespective, however, of whether a federal system will eventually be established, which is possible because of its exceptional popularity among voters, the recent exponential expansion of CDFs is seen, even by the Solomon Islands Parliament's review of the 2013 Constituency Development Bill, as aiming to 'pre-emptively undermine the proposed state gov't system' by channelling vast resources away from lower level governments.[143]

Indeed, the expansion of CDFs has been directly aimed at undermining calls for deeper localisation. Their arrival in the 1990s coincided with the abolition of the Area Councils, thus 'severing ... formal linkages between the administrative centre and local levels'.[144] The Area Councils at the time played a key role in service delivery and public works, 'a function that was made largely redundant by the introduction of constituency development funds for national Members of Parliament'.[145] This was followed by the increasing marginalisation

[139] Hughes 2014.
[140] Shahar Hameiri's interview with a Solomon Islander involved in the constitutional review process (name withheld), Honiara, 5 December 2014.
[141] Fraenkel et al. 2014: 89. [142] ADB 2004: 3.
[143] Solomon Islands National Parliament 2013: 9.
[144] Dinnen and Allen 2013: 225. [145] Scales 2003: 9.

of provinces from service delivery activities, which according to the 1981 Provincial Government Act they were meant to be responsible for, via budgetary allocations from the centre. A 2004 report stated: 'Provinces are left managing little more than the payroll of their direct employees and are not able to execute their basic responsibilities'.[146] The same report also notes that, unlike national politics, provincial assemblies and political oppositions are basically inactive, since there are no resources to fight over. Indeed, provincial administrations are so underfunded that officials routinely cannot get funds to travel within the province, purchase basic office supplies, or even buy a sparkplug to fix a faulty motor.[147]

Meanwhile, CDFs are presented by proponents as making MPs directly responsible for service delivery in their constituencies and thus as a form of decentralisation and better representation. Former government minister Fred Fono, for example, said: 'The rationale behind this system of service delivery was that MPs should not only talk on the floor of parliament but they must be seen as directly responsible for delivering services to their people'.[148] Likewise, Rick 'Hou' Houenipwela, former CBSI Governor and the Finance Minister responsible for the 2013 Constituency Development Act, said in defence of the legislation when it was before Parliament: 'The Bill is a clear manifestation of the government's seriousness for service delivery'. Hou added that MPs should be directly responsible for economic development in their constituencies because they represent the people.[149] That Rick Hou, formerly a donor favourite in his role as CBSI Governor, was the one to triple the size of CDFs in one year is somewhat ironic, since he was previously an outspoken critic of government misuse of revenue for electioneering. It conclusively demonstrates, however, that the expansion of CDFs is not primarily motivated by cultural beliefs and norms of *wantokism* and reciprocity; Hou's volte-face clearly reflects his shift from the top echelons of a rescaled part of the bureaucracy into politics. Notwithstanding politicians' rhetoric, however, there is little indication that CDFs are used for service delivery or development projects. Available evidence, which is limited, suggests that the funds are primarily used to purchase and distribute in-demand goods in rural communities, such as roofing

[146] Cox and Morrison 2004: 8. [147] McDougall 2014: 3–4.
[148] Fono 2007: 128. [149] Dawea 2013.

sheets, cookers, and outboard motors, as well as consumables like beer and cigarettes, especially before elections.[150]

Despite the rapid enlargement of CDFs, the government has been slow to release regulations and guidelines on how they are to be spent, and auditing has been difficult and highly fraught.[151] Although Constituency Development Plans and Constituency Development Committees are mandated by the 2013 legislation, MPs are still essentially at liberty to select a Committee and Plan at will. The heavily rescaled OAG has attempted to conduct audits of the CDFs, starting an investigation in 2010. After many delays relating to lack of cooperation, audits were due to be tabled in Parliament's PAC in March 2013, but were repeatedly delayed. The reports were not released, however, as the Auditor-General, Edward Ronia, was forced by the Public Service Commission (PSC) to step down in November 2013.[152] The official reason cited was that Ronia was past the public service retirement age of 55; however, he was already older than 55 when first appointed to Auditor-General. The widely accepted view, also voiced by Ronia himself, is that he was forced to resign because of his insistence upon auditing the CDFs. Ronia subsequently sued the PSC in the High Court, claiming his dismissal was a matter of public interest.[153] His successor, Robert Cohen, an Australian, continued with the CDFs' audit, but said that he expected he would be asked to leave Solomon Islands once they were made public.[154] Despite his efforts to have the reports published, Ronia, when interviewed in late 2014, said, 'The reports published won't make a big difference. Our leaders aren't ashamed of what they're doing ... PAC isn't actioning the reports because of MPs' involvement with this much money – they're part of the process'.[155]

Indeed, PAC's record of following up on OAG recommendations is poor.[156] A report containing a random sample audit of CDFs in the period 2012–13 was finally publicly released in January 2015, though not tabled in Parliament, revealing SI$54.1 million were unaccounted

150 Cox 2015; McDougall 2014: 6. 151 Clark and Levy 2012: 54–55.
152 Transparency Solomon Islands 2013. 153 *Solomon Star* 2014.
154 Shahar Hameiri's interview with Robert Cohen, Solomon Islands Auditor-General, Honiara, 24 July 2014.
155 Shahar Hameiri's interview with Edward Ronia, former Solomon Islands Auditor-General, Honiara, 10 December 2014.
156 Clark and Levy 2012: 57.

for. As this was only a small sample, Cohen said he expected the real amount missing was much larger.[157] It is perhaps no coincidence that shortly after the report was released, the OAG began looking for a new Auditor-General. The Solomon Islands chapter of Transparency International, under the leadership of its new chief executive, the same Edward Ronia, has also launched its own investigation into how CDFs are used in February 2015, seeking grassroots evidence from constituents, with funding from the UN Democracy Fund. But this initiative is a sure sign of the impotence of the formal auditing processes. It is not surprising that attempts to regulate and audit CDFs are resisted so vigorously, since their discretionary distribution at the local level is an important means for reinforcing the centrality of the national scale over localist agendas.

The results of the 2014 national election clearly reflect the extent to which the Solomon Islands government's scalar strategies have succeeded in preventing significant challenges from above and below to the primacy of the national scale and the interests dominating it. Although Gordon Darcy Lilo – Prime Minister from 2011 to 2014 – surprisingly lost his seat, many long-term patterns have been maintained. For example, 32 of 50 seats were won by independents, once again demonstrating the insignificance of cross-cutting ideological or party allegiances – as opposed to access to resources – for electoral success. Indeed, Lilo lost his seat to his nephew and former campaign manager, Jimson Tanangada, by about 200 votes, reflecting shifting allegiances within the electorate, not substantive political change. Crucially, in 2014, 35 of 50 MPs managed to keep their seats, whereas historically 50 per cent of incumbents are replaced.[158] Solomon Islander academic Tarcisius Tara Kabutaulaka attributes this to the role of discretionary MP spending,[159] a view reinforced by one available case study of the Western Province constituency of North Vella Lavella. Milner Tozaka, who won the seat for the third time with 43 per cent of the vote, made extensive use of the CDF monies at his disposal to secure victory, especially in the form of small cash payments to individuals and the purchasing of in-demand items for supporters. In fact, the entire pre-election debate in the constituency was focused on whether Tozaka or his challengers would better manage petty disbursements to households.[160]

[157] Garrett 2015. [158] Tamsitt 2014. [159] Kando 2014. [160] Cox 2015.

The results of the 2014 election appear to reinforce the view that CDFs could herald a shift towards established oligarchy in Solomon Islands from a situation in which elite membership is more fluid and contested.[161] Irrespective of whether we will see less individual fluidity at the top, the analysis here suggests that more significant is that the structural primacy of the national scale is being maintained and that donor PAR programmes have played an important part in supporting this. Nonetheless, as the benefits from economic development continue to accrue unevenly, and negative externalities also accrue unevenly, the capacity of national elites to use redistribution to quell resentment indefinitely is increasingly uncertain. This is especially so since logging and aid levels have begun to decline. Furthermore, many respondents have voiced concerns that elites could only stall decentralisation for so long before real tensions, possibly violence, will resurface.

Conclusion

The case of Solomon Islands is instructive for our argument in this book. Although extensive international intervention has made Solomon Islands one of the world's most aid-dependent countries, RAMSI and its successors have struggled to implement programmes and projects that truly challenge the power of elites dominating the national scale. In fact, their interventions have only served to strengthen these elites, providing them with more resources with which to defeat alternative political agendas, especially localisation through constitutional reform.

The cohesiveness of national elites has meant that they have been able to use the state's scale management capacities coherently to strengthen their collective hold on the dominance of national scale over other scales. This argument supports Craig and Porter's claim that a relatively stable political settlement among elites has emerged in Solomon Islands.[162] But as we have seen, this accommodation is a product of long-term processes of uneven development and state formation, especially of the encroachment of logging on customary land since the early 1980s, which was itself a response to the fragmenting pressures of uneven development. As such, the cohesion of national

[161] Devesi 2013: 5; Craig and Porter 2014. [162] Craig and Porter 2014.

elites could be undermined if the political economy were to change significantly. Such a change is perhaps in the offing with the long-anticipated exhaustion of large-scale logging over the coming few years. Should mining development partly replace logging in Solomon Islands, as many predict, it would introduce new pressures, probably fracturing the elite group dominating the national scale into competing factions. In particular, since mining is far more geographically concentrated than logging operations, it could introduce greater local resistance, as well as give greater purchase to demands for the localisation of benefits in resource-rich areas, as we have seen, for example, in neighbouring Papua New Guinea.

4 *Public Administration Reform and the Politics of Scale in Post-Conflict Cambodia*

Successive crises of state institutions since Cambodia attained independence in 1953 have prompted a series of internationally assisted state-building initiatives in the country. These include initial post-colonial state-building efforts in the late 1950s and 1960s, a Chinese-backed programme of violent total collectivisation from 1975–78, a Vietnamese-led decade-long reconstruction programme in the 1980s, and a Western donor-assisted liberal peace-building programme from the 1990s to the present, precipitated by a UN peacekeeping mission in 1992–93. The most recent twenty-five years of Peace- and State-Building Initiatives (PSBIs) have incorporated good governance as a key theme for promoting political stability and liberal market property relations, seen as fundamental to successfully integrating Cambodia into a booming regional economy.

The present Cambodian elite emerged from the ruins of the Khmer Rouge revolution in the early 1980s, and has worked consistently under the cover of, first, Vietnamese and then broader international intervention to promote its own class interests through selective co-operation with internationally directed state-building initiatives. As Cambodia's economy has transformed, these interests have changed, entailing radical shifts in the way that governance strategies connect space, territory and power. This chapter shows how scalar strategies for controlling resources have varied over time in response to structural changes in constellations of local and international power, and the impact of this on elite perceptions of threats to their interests.

All of this forms the context for public administration reform. In the 1990s, a powerful centralisation process undermined provincial elites linked to local level business interests, awarding control over natural resources to the Phnom Penh-based government. This strategy was facilitated by selective elite co-operation with donor-funded reforms, particularly in the field of forestry administration. The ending of the war allowed the Phnom Penh-based elite to use control of natural resources, particularly timber and land, to win the allegiances of defecting insurgents, producing a powerful faction within the Cambodian military that was loyal to the centre and, increasingly, to Prime Minister Hun Sen in person. This section of the Cambodian military is widely believed to be the only section capable of serious fighting, and therefore represents a considerable boost to the centre at the expense of decentralised and business-oriented provincial elite-military networks.

At the same time, concern about the persistent popularity of opponent parties led Cambodia's dominant party, the Cambodian People's Party (CPP), to pay significant attention to mobilising local networks of village and commune chiefs to fend off electoral challenges. Elections were brought into Cambodia by the United Nations peacekeeping operation in 1993. Although the CPP lost the UN-organised election, it has subsequently placed a high priority on winning elections for the purposes of local and international legitimacy. This has prompted a significant drive to localisation, particularly to ensure that elections are fought at a scale favourable to the CPP – namely, at village level.

The simultaneous promotion by CPP leaders of the national scale as the appropriate one for governing lucrative resources and the local scale as the appropriate one for mobilising the population around issues of democracy and development has increasingly produced tension. A flurry of recent activity in public administration and public financial management reform has been welcomed by donors after years of slow and unpromising progress. But this momentum is driven by the Party's need to direct more significant levels of resources to the local level in an attempt to retain electoral dominance there in a rapidly changing landscape featuring better infrastructure, a younger and more mobile population and spreading urbanisation. At the same time, the Party's perception of the need to retain strong central networks of political loyalty within the key ministries of state in Phnom Penh make negotiating transfers of resources away from the central civil service difficult. This is currently driving efficiency reforms at the centre that have been long advocated by Western donors as well as prompting a drawing back from the localisation approach of the early 2000s.

Western Peace- and State-Building Interventions in Cambodia

The UN and aid agencies entering Cambodia for the first time in sixteen years in 1991 saw liberalisation and democratisation as the keys to peace. Development policy focused on boosting private sector agricultural and industrial activity, integration of Cambodia's economy into the then-booming Southeast Asian region and promotion of a technocratic policy agenda centrally focused on the reduction of violence, establishment of the rule of law and promotion of democratic accountability. The latter was to be achieved through regular multi-party elections and the proliferation of civil society organisations, particularly NGOs.

Over the course of the 1990s, however, electoral democracy developed rather differently than expected. The refusal of the Khmer Rouge armies to disarm under the UN peace process entailed that the war continued throughout the 1990s, paid for by unregulated logging of Cambodia's forests.[1] Similarly, natural resource revenues were used to fund competing party patronage projects, such as the building of schools, across the country. By the early 2000s, the difficulty of separating the state's administrative agencies – including both central ministries and local authorities – and the judicial system from politicised and personalised networks of control organised through the CPP, had become evident.

In 1997, fighting broke out between the main parties of the coalition government, and the CPP emerged victorious. Leading members of the other parties fled from Cambodia, and CPP leader Hun Sen emerged as a self-proclaimed 'strongman',[2] largely on the basis of the loyalty of former Khmer Rouge troops. Hun Sen has worked consistently to promote his control over these elite troops through strategic appointments in the chain of command and through the formation in 1994 of his own bodyguard unit – essentially a 7,000-strong private army permanently stationed in Phnom Penh.[3]

In response to US pressure, new elections were held in 1998, which the CPP won, although the integrity of these elections was disputed locally and internationally. After the 1998 elections, international donors pragmatically recognised the CPP's dominance of the political scene and accepted the elections' validity.[4] However, at the same time,

[1] Global Witness 1998; Le Billon 2000; Cock 2016. [2] Associated Press 1998.
[3] HRW 2015. [4] Hughes 2003: 108.

a critique emerged of the informal patronage systems organised through personal networks associated with the party, but penetrating the state and sucking in resources.[5] Such networks were funded to a significant extent out of the profits from Cambodia's reintegration into the regional economy. The state handed out licences to export logs; to import liquor, petroleum, and pharmaceuticals; to establish banks; and to build schools, roads and clinics to companies run by Cambodian tycoons who were party insiders and who made large profits from these licences.[6] Meanwhile, large tracts of land were given to key generals in return for their loyalty, and these in turn were leased to both Cambodian and foreign property and plantation developers.[7] Stability was achieved as a commodities boom provided a ready international market for Cambodia's natural resources.

After the attacks on the World Trade Center in 2001, international concern about Southeast Asia as a potential 'second front' in the War on Terror[8] prompted greater Western sympathy for Cambodia's ruling party, particularly as the government could show consistently high rates of GDP growth and apparent success in reducing poverty.[9] Rather than attempting further democratic reform, donors focused more intently on public administration reform (PAR), including public financial management reform, adopting both internationalisation and localisation as key rescaling strategies intended to address the issue of the problematic relationship between party and state at the national level.[10] These issues continue to centrally occupy Cambodia's donors today.

The CPP's response has been selective adoption of rescaling reforms, to manage tensions between a political strategy of inexorable centralisation of control of natural resources and armed violence. It has also created a highly decentralised and locally embedded network for imposing surveillance and control over the Cambodian electorate. However, this response has been implemented in a context in which the nature of space has been transformed by massive infrastructure projects, changes in land governance and the emergence of an increasingly literate and mobile population.

[5] Leuprecht 2001; Hughes and Conway 2003. [6] *Phnom Penh Post* 2000.
[7] World Bank 2004: 75. [8] Gershman 2002. [9] World Bank 2013.
[10] World Bank 2004.

Uneven Development in Cambodia

Before discussing these strategies and the contestation they have engendered, it is necessary to examine the way capitalist development in Cambodia has occurred from the colonial era onwards. The spatial distribution of different types of economic resource and activity and the way that state-building efforts have mapped on to them, particularly after the fall of the Khmer Rouge in 1979, is decisive for understanding the contemporary politics of scale affecting donor efforts at PAR in Cambodia.

The central and southern territory of Cambodia mostly comprises the flood plains of the Mekong River and the Tonle Sap lake. These extend to the Gulf of Thailand to the south and an arc of hills and mountains bordering Vietnam to the east. Laos lies to the north and Thailand to the west. Pre-colonial economies were heavily based on the management of flood waters to produce wet rice in the lowlands, while in the periphery hill-tribes harvested forest products. The arrival of French colonisers brought the beginnings of agro-industry, particularly in the eastern provinces where substantial rubber plantations were established, covering 70,000 hectares by 1970 (Royal Government of Cambodia Ministry of Commerce 2012). Plantation agriculture expanded further in the 1950s and 1960s in the northwest of the country, but elsewhere, Cambodia remained heavily dependent upon subsistence agriculture organised at household level, particularly wet-rice cultivation in the central floodplains. In the late 1960s, the country was overtaken by the devastating violence of the Vietnam War and the subsequent Khmer Rouge regime from 1975 to 1979.

Following the invasion of the Vietnamese army in 1979 which overthrew the Khmer Rouge, new political and economic systems were introduced. The primary concern was assisting the new political leadership in Phnom Penh to fend off a continuing insurgency by the remnant Khmer Rouge, which regrouped on the Thai border with direct support and assistance from Thailand and China. The Phnom Penh-based government was not recognised internationally, and the country was subjected to a Western trade and aid embargo, rendering the new government heavily dependent upon Vietnam and the Soviet bloc throughout the 1980s. In this context, the government began the task of rebuilding state structures, appointing local governments, staffing central ministries, re-establishing basic services, repairing infrastructure, and re-starting the economy. Vietnamese advisors were pervasive in this effort, situated within Cambodian ministries with significant powers of oversight. The systems that were introduced were heavily based on Vietnamese models.[11]

The key state-building success of this era was creating a system of local government that could maintain a basic level of order and stability in the rice-growing heartland. The power of the post-war state was largely achieved from the bottom up. Khmer Rouge insurgents were mainly confined to the remote jungles of the western border and the northernmost provinces, while the Phnom Penh-based government controlled the densely populated central lowlands. Insurgents were unable to make inroads into the lowlands, largely because of intense vigilance by local government chiefs. The establishment of a network of loyal local chiefs was a significant achievement. In the immediate aftermath of the Vietnamese invasion that overthrew the Khmer Rouge regime, Cambodia was in a state of chaos. Many village and commune chiefs associated with the Khmer Rouge fled or were killed; the country was in a state of upheaval as hundreds of thousands of families that had been forcibly relocated or separated under the Democratic Kampuchea regime sought to return home or find loved ones. Hundreds of thousands more Cambodians attempted to cross the border into Thailand.[12] In this context, and without a large base of loyal party members to draw upon, the incoming regime at first allowed villages to elect or appoint their own leaders.

However, as time went on and the armed insurgency became organised in the west, the regime increasingly tried to cement control of local government positions to ensure the loyalty of local leaders. In doing so, they relied heavily on Minister of Interior Chea Sim, a former Khmer Rouge party leader from the Eastern Zone's Region 20. Chea Sim had used his position in the Eastern Zone to develop a large network of personally loyal contacts, and many of these were given leadership positions centrally and locally following the Vietnamese invasion. According to Gottesman, 'the PRK [People's Republic of Kampuchea – the country's name in the 1980s] was extremely reluctant to remove former Khmer Rouge cadres from positions of responsibility'.[13] Vietnamese advisors feared that if former Khmer

[11] Gottesman 2003. [12] Gottesman 2003; Stuart-Fox and Ung 1998.
[13] Gottesman 2003: 68.

Rouge leaders were removed from power, they would shift their allegiance back to the insurgent movement. Meanwhile, the PRK leaders were themselves former Khmer Rouge and resisted the idea that those who had killed under the Khmer Rouge regime owed 'blood debts'. The personal connections between local former Khmer Rouge leaders and Interior Minister Chea Sim awarded protection to these local leaders while entrenching the power of Chea Sim himself and in the party, and only indirectly in the state apparatus.[14] The power of Chea Sim and his Interior Ministry to gate-keep relations between the centre and the local level persisted into the 1990s and underpinned his long-standing rivalry with Prime Minister Hun Sen, who, emerging from the 1980s Foreign Ministry, lacked local-level contacts and compensated for this initially by developing a support-base in the military.

Local governments played an enormously important role in stabilising the new regime, in the context of continued insurgency. They sustained armed militias comprising volunteers organised at the commune level[15] to patrol and maintain order. Throughout the 1980s, there was a general ban on individuals travelling outside their home villages without a permit, and this was actively policed by local authorities and militias. Anyone caught on the road without such a permit was assumed to be Khmer Rouge and arrested or killed.[16]

The personal loyalties underpinning local government were replicated in the central ministries in Phnom Penh. Initially, the Vietnamese and the PRK leaders appointed any individuals they could find who had a basic level of education; these newly appointed officials then sought opportunities for their friends and families, and the civil service burgeoned uncontrollably. This allowed the emergence of strong personal and hierarchical relationships within the state at both central and local level. Although this to an extent constrained the power of Vietnamese advisors, it also ensured cohesion and loyalty in an extremely insecure situation, where ideological commitment to the Vietnamese programme of socialist state-building was weak.

Civil servants in the central government were rewarded for their loyalty by being granted accommodation within the capital and

[14] Gottesman 2003.

[15] A commune is an administrative unit comprising six or seven villages.

[16] Gottesman 2003.

perquisites such as food and kerosene rations on top of their salary. In rural areas, local authorities benefited from their discretionary control over the implementation of unpopular national projects such as state rice purchasing and compulsory conscription into the army, as well as from greater freedom of movement and opportunities to profit from smuggling, cross-border trade and corruption. Over time, these benefits gave rise to a significant sense of corporate loyalty, even though this continued to be mediated by hierarchical relationships with particular 'big men' in government. In an atmosphere where the Vietnamese struggled to retain legitimacy, due to both their continued use of socialist rhetoric that the Khmer Rouge had thoroughly discredited and to their status as a 'historic enemy' of the Khmer people, these benefits were significant in allowing the state-building process to gain traction.[17]

The great achievement of the 1980s, then, was the construction of a state that was able to maintain control of 80 per cent of the territory and 90 per cent of the population, despite the border refugee crisis and the ongoing externally backed insurgency. Key policies, however, were never able to be implemented. The Vietnamese approach to collectivisation, for example, was much looser than that attempted by the Khmer Rouge, but it was unsuccessful, and over the course of the 1980s, land use gradually reverted back to subsistence farming on a household basis.[18] In part because of this, state rice purchasing targets were rarely met, leaving the urban population dependent upon food imported from Vietnam.[19] In the Cold War context, this was regarded as evidence of the heavily internationalised nature of the Phnom Penh regime, and its lack of local legitimacy.[20] Arguably, this had less to do with legitimacy and more to do with the level at which resources were available for wielding power, and in the early post-Khmer Rouge years, this was certainly the local level.

Similarly, conscription into the army was haphazardly implemented. For rural households, evading these policies required developing protective relationships with local officials and often entailed outright bribery.[21] This laid the foundation for a system whereby maintaining the loyalty of public servants required turning a blind eye to activities

[17] Stuart-Fox and Ung 1998. [18] Vickery 1984; Frings 1994.
[19] Hughes 2003: 27. [20] Economist Intelligence Unit 1989–90: 55.
[21] HRW 2015.

that promoted their self-interest but undermined the government's policy aspirations. The tension between a concern to retain personal and political relationships with local officials as a foundation for stability and the need to discipline local officials into providing a more effective public service as a foundation for legitimacy emerged very soon after the ouster of the Khmer Rouge and continues to be a significant problem for PAR programmes today.

As the Cold War wound down, external powers lost interest in supporting the Khmer Rouge insurgency, and Vietnam became increasingly eager to withdraw from Cambodia in order to improve relations with China. An international peace deal was brokered, which was largely dictated to local parties who continued to view one another with the utmost suspicion. The deal involved a UN peacekeeping mission, with a mandate to oversee a ceasefire between the various warring parties – CPP [which replaced the PRK-era Kampuchean People's Revolutionary Party], Khmer Rouge, royalist and republican – and to hold an election in which all these parties would compete. In this context, and aware of the massive popularity of the returning Cambodian king, the CPP looked to their network of local government officials as a key asset to defend their pre-eminent political status in Cambodia.[22] This tactic again flagged the liminal status of the national state in Cambodia, suspended between co-optation into international intervention agendas, on the one hand, and embedding into a deep-rooted local politics of resource extraction and population control, on the other.

Localisation as a Strategy for Dominance: Rescaling Democratic Legitimacy

Since elections became integral to Cambodian politics in 1993, the CPP has conflated the goals of maintaining national security and assuring its own political pre-eminence. The loyalty of local officials is central to its strategy for achieving these goals. This prompted, in the early 2000s, enthusiastic initial engagement with donor plans for decentralisation, which dovetailed neatly with CPP localisation strategies designed to undermine opposition parties whose popularity was mainly urban.

[22] Frieson 1996: 189.

Control at the local level was the key to the CPP's electoral strategy in 1993 and ever since. Indeed, intertwined personal, party and state networks extending from the central to the local level have been constitutive of the CPP's vision of the state itself.[23] The CPP's identity as the party that ousted the Khmer Rouge and which gets things done has been central to its electoral campaign platform.[24] Both of these achievements relied on the loyalty of local officials and their stake in the political dominance of the party. Just as this was used to contain the Khmer Rouge insurgency in the 1980s, so the CPP, despite losing the UN-organised 1993 election to the royalist party, was subsequently able to oust most other parties from the rural heartland since the early 1990s, reasserting itself as the dominant party and winning successive elections. This strategy succeeded until around 2010, when massive expansion of Cambodia's transportation and information infrastructure fundamentally transformed the nature of the country's rural–urban divide.

Although general elections were heavily monitored by international agencies, the CPP used the intimate relationships between villagers and village and commune chiefs that had been in place largely unchanged since the early 1980s to dominate key processes such as voter registration and education, election campaigning and the organisation of polling.[25] Local authorities openly joined election campaigns with the CPP and oversaw ceremonies to enrol villagers in the Party, employing a range of rituals from collecting thumbprints to requiring villagers to take oaths of loyalty to the Party. CPP dominance of the authorities organising election registration and polling ensured that opposition party supporters widely reported their fear of venturing into these spaces. Although balloting was secret, the close relationships between local authorities and villagers and decades of surveillance of the population to ensure political loyalty entailed that local authorities expressed great confidence in their ability to assess the loyalty of people living in their constituencies.[26]

Surveillance was backed by partisan distribution of the goods of development through heavily politicised patronage schemes overseen by CPP District Working Groups. Throughout the 1990s and early 2000s, the profits reaped from international aid, close relationships

[23] Hughes 2003; Pak 2011. [24] Hughes 2006: 476. [25] Hughes 2003, 2006.
[26] Hughes and Kim 2004: 26–27.

with increasingly wealthy business tycoons and rampant natural resource exploitation were used to fund wide-ranging patronage schemes that varied from provision of individual 'gifts' to every party member before elections to the funding of massive school- and road-building projects and irrigation schemes.[27] These development projects were routinely channelled towards party supporters, and designed to exclude as far as possible households identified as pro-opposition, relying upon the knowledge of local authorities to make this distinction. For poor households, who were dependent upon local village and commune chiefs for support and protection in times of austerity or conflict, being identified in this way was perceived as highly threatening. Frequent reports from opposition supporters in the 1990s and early 2000s that local authorities had threatened to take away their land, in a context where land conflicts were widespread, reflect the significance of local authorities to ordinary people.[28]

In 2002, the Cambodian government introduced commune-level elections in a move celebrated by international donors as a first step in a decentralisation programme, designed to promote better democratic oversight of governance by ordinary citizens. However, for the CPP, local elections represented an opportunity to boost the legitimacy both of local level government and of the party nationally and internationally, while cementing their dominance of the countryside at the expense of opposition parties. The opposition parties found it difficult to make inroads into the rural areas for a number of reasons. They lacked sufficient numbers to field thousands of credible candidates in commune council elections, and the candidates that they did put up had to campaign against incumbents backed by the huge resources of the CPP. In addition, rural voters routinely invested quite heavily over a number of years in friendly relations with their commune and village chiefs. For those voters who had succeeded in establishing themselves as loyal supporters of the chief, there was little incentive to vote for somebody new.[29]

Furthermore, the CPP's claim to be the only party that could get things done clearly resonated with voters at the local level: The opposition parties were notable by their absence from Cambodia's rural villages, whereas CPP local authorities had strong links with central power holders in the party and the ministries who

[27] Hughes 2006. [28] Hughes 2006. [29] Thon et al. 2009.

regularly visited 'the base' on weekends to distribute gifts and oversee development projects. The Party invested enormous effort in linking high-level patrons from Phnom Penh with designated provinces and districts in which they were responsible for ensuring political loyalty and public satisfaction.[30] This has been a tremendously successful strategy: the CPP won 1,598 out of 1,621 commune chief positions in the first elections in 2002, 1,591 out of 1,621 in 2007 and 1,592 out of 1,633 in 2012.[31] This has also undercut the fragile emergence of multi-party competition at the national level by entrenching relationships between local authorities and voters, enhancing party discipline over local officials and further isolating opposition parties in the capital. The introduction of local elections has effectively rescaled democratic legitimacy in Cambodia to a level at which the CPP leadership was sure of the party's dominance, reducing the significance of national elections internationally and locally.

Indeed, once local elections had been introduced, the decentralisation drive quickly stalled, revealing its limits as a strategy for promoting more genuine democratic accountability with respect to day-to-day decision-making over local affairs. Donor visions for decentralisation incorporated not just the election of local councils but also the transfer of significant responsibilities and resources to them, in a second phase of 'deconcentration' to be negotiated by the central ministries in Phnom Penh.[32] However, fourteen years after the first commune elections, significant deconcentration of resources or functions has still not occurred. Commune councils have been starved of state resources, receiving only on average less than $10,000 a year from central funding, which has frequently been uncertain or delayed and often attracts a 'service charge' from the Treasury before communes can access it. Such obstacles reflect unwillingness by specific elite groups in particular ministries in Phnom Penh to significantly sacrifice their own power and resources in the interests of localisation, even where this aids the Party's overall electoral strategy.

Commune councils do not have powers of local taxation but are expected to raise local 'contributions' in money and labour from their

[30] Pak 2011.
[31] Figures comprised from various reports by the Committee for Free and Fair Elections in Cambodia (COMFREL): www.comfrel.org/eng/index.php%3Foption=com_mypublications&view=list&catid=121&Itemid=1143
[32] World Bank 2015b.

citizens for local development projects, which has reportedly been a difficult task. This state of affairs renders communes heavily dependent upon the central administration and upon party patronage projects in order to complete the development projects that their constituents demand. One survey in 2011 suggested that commune councils receive two to three times more funding from the CPP than from the Commune/Sangkhat fund.[33]

This has tied the commune councils, CPP and central state apparatus into a political economy of relationships which was initially successful in mobilising popular support for the Party but has become increasingly problematic of late. Dependence of local officials on the Party nationally is exacerbated by the fact that formal state agencies continued well into the 2000s to operate poorly in Cambodia, largely due to the low salaries of civil servants. Below-poverty wages entrenched absenteeism and corruption into the state apparatus, and the informal and highly politicised patronage networks that had existed in every state agency since the early 1980s facilitated this by protecting civil servants from disciplinary measures and engaging them in extra-legal systems of reward. The result was a conundrum whereby the loyalty of civil servants became inextricably bound up with their access to informal and often illegal collective scams for making money. A percentage of the money raised from these scams was always passed on to the Party, linking, almost ritually, low pay and corruption to the politicisation of the state apparatus. In these circumstances, the loyalty of civil servants could be cultivated, but reforms of the public service itself to a more meritocratic and efficiency-oriented model, as attempted by donors, was effectively ruled out. This in turn meant that local authorities responsible for mobilising public support for the Party would have to rely not on the formal state, but on the Party's own increasingly elaborate structures for funding development.

Selective Adoption: Centralising Funding for Development

The funds that have been used to pay for party projects come from a variety of sources, but heavily feature the proceeds from deals between party leaders and business figures, both Cambodian and

[33] Craig and Pak 2011.

foreign. Particularly prominent have been deals whereby companies are awarded large tracts of land either for logging or for establishing plantations. In the 1990s, Cambodia still possessed large areas of pristine forest that were only just being opened up after the war by de-mining operations and infrastructure development. These forests tended to be in peripheral areas of the country, including the north and west, which are less populated than the rice-growing plains and feature a heavy military presence as a legacy of the war. As such, they were relatively easily brought under centralised control, and this occurred with the assistance of selectively adopted donor good governance programmes.[34]

Throughout the 1990s, logging for valuable hardwoods in these forests was a key source of finance for both the CPP, other political parties and the remnant Khmer Rouge insurgents. The funds gained from these practices could be spent on cultivating the loyalties of voters in the plains, while the number of voters directly affected by logging activities was relatively small. However, as the war wound down, alarm by local and international NGOs over the government's failure to subject logging activities to basic environmental and social safeguards combined with concern from donors that Cambodia's natural resource assets were being unsustainably stripped and the money disappearing into party campaign funds. These concerns prompted the IMF and World Bank to refuse to renew the government's Enhanced Structural Adjustment Facility loans in 1997, placing intense pressure on the government to do something about its forestry governance regime.[35]

This pressure was effective in the particular circumstances of the late 1990s to prompt new forms of control over logging, and represented a successful rescaling of forestry governance for a time. By 1997, the Khmer Rouge insurgency, which had continued following the Khmer Rouge's withdrawal from the UN peace process in 1992–93, finally began to abate. After a military battle in Phnom Penh in 1997 between pro-CPP and pro-royalist forces swung power back to the CPP, and after its disastrous defeat in the 1993 elections, the CPP, desperate to bolster international legitimacy and to secure sources of aid, was prompted to make rare concessions to world opinion.

[34] Cock 2016. [35] *Phnom Penh Post* 1997; Cock 2016.

This was particularly notable in the field of forest governance. Following a new election in 1998, which featured large numbers of irregularities and protracted post-election demonstrations by opposition parties, the new CPP-led government was desperate to promote its legitimacy internationally and to regain access to IMF and World Bank funds. Following a difficult meeting with the Consultative Group of Cambodia's donors in Tokyo in December 1999, the government allowed an international monitoring regime to be established in forestry. Donor agencies became much more prominent in forest governance, and officials from agencies such as GIZ were to be found ensconced in offices in the notoriously corrupt Department of Forestry and Wildlife (DFW) in the Ministry of Agriculture, Forestry and Fisheries in Phnom Penh, right at the heart of the CPP's money-making system. The DFW was led by CPP loyalist Ty Sokhun and was widely believed to be the main conduit by which millions of dollars in revenues from illegal logging and kickbacks from logging companies made their way into CPP party coffers. In addition to a more intrusive donor presence in the ministry, Forest Crimes Monitoring Units were created throughout the country, and an International Forest Monitor was appointed to report on illegal logging. The International Forest Monitor initially appointed was Global Witness, a UK-based NGO, which had campaigned on forestry governance issues in Cambodia since 1995 and had been instrumental in persuading the IMF to freeze funding because of these concerns. The appointment of an activist NGO that had been openly critical of government policy in this key area of finance for the CPP represented a significant concession to international demands for reform of Cambodian forestry practices.[36]

However, it quickly became clear that the government was more than capable of both undermining the new regime and selectively harnessing aspects to its own agenda, and it did so in several ways. First, the Forest Crimes Monitoring Units worked for the Department of Forestry and Wildlife. As such, they operated within the political economy of the Cambodian civil service, characterised by below-poverty wages, nepotism and personal and political connections. The units proved to be inadequate in stopping forest crimes. However, Andrew Cock argues that their deployment across the country with donor funding allowed the Party centre to get a much

[36] Hughes and Conway 2003.

better sense of the illegal forestry deals going on at local level between provincial civilian and military officials.[37] Thus the units did not necessarily reduce the amount of illegal logging, but they did allow the top echelons of the Party to more effectively monitor the situation and use both the units themselves and political and military pressure to ensure that they collected their share of the proceeds, through a system funded by Western donors.

This state of affairs was soon exposed by Global Witness, and its relationship with the government swiftly cooled. By 2002, Global Witness activists were being threatened, beaten and forced into hiding.[38] In 2003, the government cancelled Global Witness's contract as the independent forest monitor, and appointed a private Swiss company in its place. The new company took a much more limited approach to forest monitoring, but by this time, the CPP's concerns about its international legitimacy were largely moot because of the advent of the War on Terror. Furthermore, the People's Republic of China was emerging as a key donor, and by 2003 was regularly matching the pledges of Western donors.[39] Finally, the overwhelming victory of the CPP in the first commune elections of 2002 allowed the Party to rest its legitimacy on unreserved electoral credentials for the first time. In 2006, the CPP ended the Independent Forest Monitor programme claiming lack of funding and donors did not insist on its reinstatement.

A further strategy for using selective adoption to undermine the internationalised forest governance regime became evident in 2001 when the Land Law was amended to allow for the establishment of 'economic land concessions' – essentially plantations – on designated areas of degraded forest.[40] By this time much of the most valuable hardwood was gone. Increased stability in peripheral areas and the beginnings of the commodities boom made the establishment of plantations for palm oil, rubber, cassava, sugar and other goods a more lucrative strategy with regional investors prepared to partner with military and Party loyalists. Contributions to Party funds began to be formalised through a system whereby business tycoons making donations of certain amounts were awarded honours and medals, culminating in the prestigious title of Okhna, traditionally a noble honorific bestowed by the king, awarded

[37] Cock 2016. [38] Global Witness 2002. [39] Jeldres 2003. [40] Hap 2010.

to anyone donating more than US$100,000.[41] Since 2007, the amount of domestic private investment has exceeded foreign direct investment,[42] and Cambodian business tycoons became regular attendees at Party ceremonies to unveil new development projects across the country.

Importantly, however, local-level officials had no control over the land concession process, which was orchestrated entirely at the national scale. The award of a land concession was often signalled locally only by the arrival of a company that walled off a large area of land.[43] Almost invariably, this area of land would have been the source of common resources for local people, such as firewood and building materials. Sometimes it incorporated cultivated areas, such as orchards or resin trees, subject to customary household ownership rules. In the north-eastern tribal regions, concessions sometimes covered areas of traditional land ownership by ethnic minority communities practising nomadic agriculture. Although the customary rights of communities were formally recognised by law, in practice where villagers protested exclusion from these resources, security guards– sometimes from the Cambodian military – were frequently deployed to prevent them from entering. In some places, subsequent plantation development sometimes provided new sources of employment. In other places, companies appeared to be holding concessions either as a cover for clear-cut logging operations or for purely speculative purposes and no further development took place. In either case, the result was disastrous both for Cambodia's remaining forests and for local livelihoods.[44]

Initially, land concessions were confined to peripheral areas with low population densities, but as time passed, more and more concessions were awarded, with a significant impact on an increasing proportion of the population. This began to have electoral implications, particularly as NGOs began to advocate on human rights issues, and a specifically nationalist discourse began to emerge about a 'country for sale'.[45] In 2015, it was reported that three large land concessions covering 40,000 hectares in Ratanakiri province on the northeastern border

[41] Oldham and Delahunt 2004; Ear 2011: 72–3. [42] Hughes 2008: 72.
[43] Thon et al. 2009.
[44] Hughes and Conway 2003; Leprecht 2004; Licadho 2005, 2009; Global Witness 2007; Hughes 2008; CCHR 2013.
[45] Global Witness 2009; Vrieze and Kuch 2012; Pye and Pech 2015.

were controlled by the Vietnamese army, raising long-standing concerns about Vietnamese annexation of Cambodian land.[46]

According to the human rights NGO Licadho, between 1993 and 2012, 2.1 million hectares of land were leased out in land concessions.[47] In part because of this policy, Cambodia has gone from having one of the most equal distributions of land in 1989, when private landholdings were first reintroduced, to a highly skewed distribution, with 20 to 30 per cent of the land held by 1 per cent of the population, in a context where 70 per cent of the population rely on agriculture as their main livelihood.[48] The land concessions policy also began to cause tensions between the national and local level of the party as commune chiefs came under pressure from local constituents to more effectively protect them from the threat of lost livelihoods. In some places, opposition commune chiefs were elected, but they proved no more effective at dealing with the local socio-economic fallout of a land concession than the CPP chiefs were.[49] Concern by the CPP to maintain relationships between central and local officials in the context of a massive transformation of Cambodia's land resources to agro-industry put significant strains on the strategy of localising electoral politics, even while it provided the resources for central Party patrons to fund their weekend development programmes in their rural districts.[50]

Rising tension prompted Hun Sen to declare a moratorium on land concessions in the lead-up to the 2013 elections. The Party also initiated a land titling scheme, under the leadership of the Prime Minister's son, which involved teams of young urban Cambodians travelling to rural areas to measure land and award titles to poor families. The scheme was intended to galvanise the CPP's 2013 election campaign and contribute to a programme of 'grassroots strengthening', thereby regaining the Prime Minister's credibility with the rural poor by veering again towards a strategy of localisation. However, this scheme attracted criticism from human rights groups, which were concerned about the martial characteristics of the young recruits, who wore military-style uniforms and were transported in army vehicles. There were even reports that some youth leaders made threats of arrest and imprisonment against dissenting villagers. Hun Sen

[46] Blomberg and Van 2015. [47] Licadho 2013. [48] Neef 2016.
[49] Hughes et al. 2011. [50] Craig and Pak 2011.

announced that villagers who had already sought assistance from opposition parties or NGOs would be excluded. Another concern was that the scheme was quickly captured by local elites who used it to grab more land for themselves and to pressure poor villagers to make payments in return for inclusion.

These criticisms were covered in local media.[51] The experience of the land titling campaign suggests that the tension between maintaining relations with local elites and widening the Party's popularity with the poor has become more acute as inequality widens and the price of land rises. The interests of speculative investors and the interests of subsistence farmers have frequently been opposed in Cambodia, but the Party has been able to use a combination of gifts, threats and promises to reconcile their differences. The experience of the land titling scheme suggests that this may be becoming much more difficult, opening opportunities for opposition parties to become more assertive in local politics.

Demographic Change and Infrastructure Development: Unravelling the Local Scale in Cambodia?

Arguably, increased problems in managing the tension between centralised control of resources and local level approaches to electoral politics have emerged because the nature of the local – i.e. the Cambodian village – has transformed dramatically in large parts of the country. From 1993 to 2013, an emerging young landless generation increasingly found job opportunities in urban areas, particularly in the burgeoning garment industry. Cambodians who reached adulthood before 1989 generally participated in subsistence agriculture as customary land distribution practices were replaced by collectivisation and then by a distribution of land to the tillers. However, the 2001 Land Law outlawed distribution of land by local officials, and consequently, there was no local-level mechanism for allocating land to young families. Rural–urban migration offered a solution for hundreds of thousands of young people who moved to work in Phnom Penh factories or across the border to Thailand (legally or illegally) or even further afield, to places like South Korea via government-organised labour export schemes. Factory work offered an important supplement

[51] HRW 2013.

to rural household incomes, and many Cambodian households consider it a significant factor in improving incomes.[52]

However, rural–urban migration presented a significant problem for the CPP's political strategy. Young, mobile urban workers are much more difficult to control than rural subsistence farmers. The CPP's strategy of using local authorities to mobilise support relied upon local chiefs' close, long-standing and personal knowledge of a population that was pretty well settled, and upon farmers' need of local authority support to ensure their continued land tenure and access to scarce development resources. This strategy could not work with urban workers, whose livelihoods and lifestyles in an urban cash economy allowed them freedom from dependence upon local officials. From an early stage, opposition parties saw the factories of Phnom Penh as fertile recruiting grounds, and supported the formation of unions which were highly successful in organising strikes to raise minimum wages.[53]

Violence against unions, including the assassination of union leaders and heavy-handed policing of picket lines and beatings of striking workers, indicate that the CPP leadership regarded organised young workers as a significant threat to their political control. Election registration rules were passed which imposed localisation on urban factory workers, dictating they return to their home provinces to vote, rather than voting in Phnom Penh. This made voting costly through lost wages and travel costs, and split up the workers' vote, spreading it across several central provinces.

The post-civil war baby boom from the 1980s to the early 1990s has increased the number of mobile, landless young people dramatically. By 2013, people under the age of 25 constituted about half the population and in the 2013 election, 1.5 million out of 9.5 million voters were eligible to vote for the first time. For these people, their primary experience of the CPP was not historic liberation from the Khmer Rouge, but a contemporary politics of land-grabbing, widening inequality, poor services and rampant corruption.

For a time, arguably, the rural–urban divide safeguarded the CPP's localisation strategy for tackling elections by ensuring that the militancy of workers in the cities did not significantly affect the rural population. However, the rural–urban divide has been eroded by

[52] Babovic and Vukovic 2015: 23–27. [53] Hughes 2003.

infrastructure developments, considerably reducing dependence of villagers on local authorities for economic security and, crucially, information.

Research into rural–urban migration in Cambodia shows that contacts with home villages are important to urban workers. For example, networks of migrants based on village of origin are important in the success of migration – new migrants rely on contacts from home to assist in establishing themselves in the city and finding a job. Some rural communes are identified as 'sending communes' that provide large numbers of young people to the garment industry. In these urban-networked communes, the atmosphere of isolation, insecurity and dependence on local armed officials for protection, which characterised rural communes in the 1980s and 1990s, has been transformed.

Radical change can also be seen in the development of telecommunication infrastructure, which has better connected rural and urban areas. Cambodia's first fibre-optic cable was laid between 1997 and 1999, crossing the country from Vietnam to Thailand. Since 2007, the fibre-optic network has been much expanded, enhancing the possibilities for rural areas to connect to the internet.[54] Since 2007, also, 4G technology was introduced to Cambodia, allowing Cambodians to access the internet from mobile phones. A recent report suggests that 34 per cent of rural Cambodians now own at least one smartphone.[55] One industry report suggests that smartphone ownership amongst 15- to 24-year-olds increased from 24 per cent in 2013 to 33 per cent in 2014. This has significantly expanded opportunities for getting online, and cafés in rural centres are increasingly offering free Wi-Fi in order to attract the custom of young people.[56] Although estimates of social media use vary, a 2014 report estimated that 1.4 million Cambodians were Facebook users, with 5 out of 6 of those aged between 15 and 30 being members.[57] A 2015 industry report estimated 2.4 million active social media users, out of a total population of 15 million.[58]

This has transformed the information available to rural people. In the 1990s and early 2000s, survey data suggested that rural Cambodians were heavily reliant on local authorities for information about elections, development programming and other matters.[59] Social

[54] Hor 2009. [55] Everett 2015. [56] Hughes and Eng 2015. [57] Hai 2014.
[58] Baliga 2015. [59] Hughes and Kim 2004.

media appears to be transforming this situation: the 2013 elections saw increased political party use of Facebook to campaign and organise rallies.[60] The return of previously exiled opposition leader Sam Rainsy to Cambodia just before the election was not publicised in mainstream media, but the news spread via Facebook, and tens of thousands of people lined the streets of Phnom Penh to greet him. A small-scale qualitative survey conducted in two garment industry 'sending communes' in 2014 suggested that families containing migrant workers use mobile phones and social media frequently to stay in touch and also to get information online that they consider to be reliable.[61] This has significantly undermined the control strategies that the CPP has relied upon to mobilise voters in elections since 1993.

The 2013 election results were disappointing for the CPP. New opportunities to contact and mobilise supporters have arguably galvanised Cambodia's opposition parties, which united successfully for the first time under one electoral banner in 2013, presenting a much more coherent threat to CPP dominance than ever before. In response, the CPP has searched for a new strategy to cement its hold on power, in the context of a more critical, better educated, more mobile and better informed population and a territory that can no longer be governed through strategies of surveillance organised around settled patterns of household landholdings. Demographic change, infrastructure development and the dramatic expansion in social media use has disrupted the previous distinction between national level and local level politics, and in so doing, has made the CPP's network of local authorities less effective in mobilising electoral victories.

These developments have to some extent rendered commune officials less significant to the CPP's overall political dominance. There are some signs that, for their part, commune chiefs may be embracing a more democratic mode of relationship with villagers in response. The pressures exerted on commune chiefs by the need to stand for direct elections every five years appear to be increasing, as commune chiefs report a new assertiveness on the part of villagers and emerging tensions between their party and democratic roles.[62] Although there are no clear examples of CPP commune chiefs publicly defying the party in order to promote the interests of their constituents, anecdotal

[60] Hughes and Eng 2015. [61] Hughes and Eng 2015.
[62] Öjendal and Kim 2006; Hughes and Eng 2015.

reports from party insiders suggest that internal party structures are struggling to deal with these tensions.

The 2013 election raised a number of concerns for the government that are potentially in conflict with one another. The first issue was that corruption and poor quality service delivery was costing the government votes in the country as a whole, particularly among younger voters. The second concern was that the loyalty of the civil service itself was in question. The third concern was that dealing with these first two issues by promoting more rational-legal modes of governance would have spill-over effects for the central relationship between the Party, big business and the military, undermining the Party's access to big money and its monopoly on military power.

One response on the part of the CPP has been to backtrack from its localisation strategy, attempting to rescale local governance to the higher level of the District. For the Party, the District has long been the most significant level of operation, with District Working Groups responsible for linking high level patrons with communes. Aligning state functions at this level would allow a more effective interplay between party and state activities at a level where opposition party intervention and scrutiny is weak and democratic pressures only indirect. The District offers the advantage of being the level of government at which line ministries are organised and where technical officers work, whose loyalties can be presumed to align with the ministry that provides them with opportunities and perquisites, rather than with local people with whom their relationship is indirect. District-level governance is overseen by a District Governor, appointed by the Ministry of Interior, accountable to a District Council elected by commune chiefs and councillors in the area. District Councils were created in 2007; although they do contain opposition party representatives, their ranks are largely filled with retired CPP cadres and civil servants who earned a place on the party list, either because they paid the party for it or were owed a reward.

However, in attempting to rescale to the District level, the CPP has faced considerable opposition from within the ranks of the highly centralised civil service. As with the communes, there is reluctance among the central line ministries to delegate significant powers and resources to the District level, because this implies a surrender of their own status. As of 2016, after eight years of internal discussion, the only real deconcentration of function has been in waste collection under the

Ministry of the Environment. Other ministries have been successful in stalling the reform, with the powerful Ministry of Economy and Finance (MEF) reportedly amongst the most sceptical. The attitude of the MEF and the line ministries reflects the logic of their role in the system established by the Party for maintaining control. Hierarchical and personalised networks for hiring, firing and supervising the work of officials in the ministry operate on a ministry-by-ministry basis. Consequently, line ministry staff at local level tend to look upwards to their superiors within the central ministry for support and instructions, rather than engaging at local level with counterparts from other ministries, rendering local-level planning difficult. Where local-level politics has brought commune councillors from different parties into the mix, the problems appear insuperable. A senior Ministry of Interior official commented: 'We need to make more opportunities at local level and find people with good capacities. But it is hard to call them to attend training if they come from a different party. This is a political reform – the parties must reform, it's not an administrative reform'.[63] Furthermore, at local level, nepotism is a significant factor in hiring decisions, undermining the potential for promoting greater meritocracy.[64]

In addition, all the line ministries to varying degrees operate as conduits of money and resources from various sources – international aid, locally derived revenues, bribes related to procurement and so on – to the Party at central level. Central civil servants have benefited personally from this system, and so has the Party. Serious deconcentration in the interests of an electoral strategy focused on more effective planning and implementation of development projects at District level brings the Party's local level strategies for vote winning directly into conflict with established mechanisms for rewarding loyal civil servants in Phnom Penh. This is particularly problematic since Phnom Penh bureaucrats are required to spend their weekends and their own money financing election campaigns in their districts. This system was highly effective for much of the 1990s and 2000s, but has foundered on the rising expectations and greater sophistication of voters whose demands are increasingly expensive to meet.

63 Interview with Caroline Hughes, Phnom Penh, 16 June 2015, name withheld.
64 Eng and Craig 2009.

National Loyalties Versus Local Demands After the 2013 Elections

The CPP heard the warnings of the 2013 election clearly. According to officials interviewed for this project, the CPP interpreted the results as a shocking blow to its power and prestige, and attributed this to the CPP's failures to tackle corruption and poor quality service delivery. This prompted early attention on the part of the government to PAR initiatives. One official working for a donor agency in Phnom Penh commented:

> In Public Administration Reform, before the government just left it to the donors to do it. Now they are doing it by themselves. Existing work that was pioneered by donors has now been finalised and achieved. We have seen big results fast ... In civil service salary reform, the achievement in the last year has been bigger than in the past ten years.[65]

Reform of the civil service has been on the government's agenda for many years, but saw little effective action for two main reasons. First, as indicated earlier, the civil service had been created through the construction of personal networks of patronage formed primarily around considerations of loyalty in the context of the Khmer Rouge insurgency. These networks were found to be equally useful, initially, in combatting the threat of multi-party politics. When the royalist political party *Front Uni National pour un Cambodge Indépendant, Neutre, Pacifique et Coopératif* (FUNCINPEC) won the 1993 UN-held elections, the CPP effectively mobilised its loyalists in the civil service to exclude FUNCINPEC-appointed ministers and staff from having genuine access to decision-making within government agencies[66] and this significantly undermined the credibility of the FUNCINPEC party, opening the way for the CPP to claim the mantle of effectiveness in election campaigning.

As described earlier, the key means of preserving the integrity of these networks, as central government became more professional and complex with the arrival of Western donors in the 1990s, was the continuation of below-subsistence pay. This made sources of extra revenue – including discretionary awards of overtime, tolerance of absenteeism to pursue second jobs, or access to informal and illegal

[65] Interview with Caroline Hughes, Phnom Penh, 18 June 2015, name withheld.
[66] Hughes 2003.

sources of funds – vital for civil servants' ability to provide for their families. All such revenue sources were dependent upon loyalty to the CPP; and all came with the requirement that a certain proportion of the money gained be donated to the Party, thus effectively tying civil servants to the Party.

This modus operandi has blocked donor efficiency reforms through such strategies as performance management, merit-based pay or even basic anti-corruption initiatives. Donor efforts to introduce a Merit-Based Pay Initiative (MBPI) in the Cambodian civil service that would link pay increases to a widespread functional review of all ministries, leading to the creation of proper job descriptions and performance management for all civil servants, and opening the way for performance-related pay increases for those who were most effective, were ultimately rejected outright by the government, foundering on these problems. The MBPI was abruptly cancelled by the government in 2009, on the grounds that it unfairly excluded the Cambodian military, who have customarily received the same pay as civilian civil servants. While concerns about the military might well have been genuine, the MBPI also clearly created a direct conflict between, on the one hand, a concern to fulfil the Party's claim to be effective in development and to get things done and, on the other, the priority of maintaining the political loyalty of civil servants through maintenance of hierarchies of patronage and favour within the civil service.

Political loyalties and opportunities for money-making within the civil service continue to be entangled with personal and kinship-based networks of mutual support. Attempts to impose discipline or introduce a merit-based scheme within the civil service, even by the Party itself, are thus problematic, since individual civil servants have networks of powerful patrons and protectors. Managers within public sector agencies report that they have to deal with subordinates who are effectively untouchable because of their high-level connections.

From the perspective of Western donors, rooting out these networks of protection and patronage is essential to a more rational-legal and efficient civil service, and to an extent, this line of thought is accepted by CPP leaders. However, it directly conflicts with deeper and more longstanding concern stretching back to the immediate post–Khmer Rouge era of state-building, which is that without these personal and familial networks, which make up for a distinct lack of ideological conviction, maintaining loyalty and therefore control will be impossible and the state will crumble and chaos will return.

Similarly, the CPP's efforts on anti-corruption reforms have been extraordinarily weak. An Anti-Corruption Law passed in 2010 took 14 years to draft and contained articles apparently specifically designed to undermine the credibility of any serious anti-corruption activity. These included provisions for jailing whistle-blowers who made accusations that were not subsequently proved to be true in court, and a highly opaque system for declaring assets whereby officials placed their own estimate of their wealth in a sealed envelope that would not be opened unless there was an accusation made against them. These provisions appear explicitly designed to ensure that anti-corruption efforts remain ineffective and that the government can act to protect its loyal supporters. The Anti-Corruption Unit established by the law is closely controlled by the executive branch, raising concerns that it may be used primarily against the government's internal or external opponents.[67]

The 2013 election result appears to have shifted the government's thinking somewhat on PAR, although it has not freed the government of the constraints of its erstwhile strategy. Soon after the election, the government also created a new Ministry of Civil Service with three goals: enhancing the quality of service delivery, improving human resources policies, and reforming compensation practices. According to the first Secretary of State of the new Ministry, compensation reform was a central principle for the government's response to the elections, and the core principle underlying the reform was promoting equity within the civil service and between the civilian, police and military branches of the state:

> The government emphasises fairness: we have to look at remuneration for all, the police, the military and the civil service. We are trying to narrow the gap between the highest and the lowest and to get more financial support to those civil servants, military and police who get low payments.[68]

Improved performance in the key service delivery areas of education and health was to be achieved through financial incentives, but these were framed within the overall principles of 'affordability, fairness and productivity':

[67] Girishankar et al. 2011: 12.
[68] Interview with Caroline Hughes, Phnom Penh, 17 June 2015, name withheld.

First the government tried to introduce fairness among the civil service. Now what we are doing under Public Administration Reform is trying to look at priority sectors and performance. Now we are starting to discuss performance with the line ministry. It's not just narrowing the gap, but also providing motivation to perform better. But we try to be very simple about it – we can't apply a very complicated system.[69]

Initial discussions about performance management suggested that departments achieving particular targets would receive a financial reward, but significantly, one that is shared between high-performing individuals and their agency or department: 'It will depend on the criteria in the regulation: this percentage will be to motivate staff and this percentage for agency capacity to be in line with social capacity. One part for individual performance and one part for agency development'.[70] The emphasis on collective reward fits with the CPP strategy of promoting close personal networks within agencies that can foster loyalty on the part of civil servants to their team.

In line with these goals, the government announced a large increase across the board in civil servants' pay and a change in the structure of the pay spine, so that civil servants could expect faster promotion through a steeper salary gradient over the course of their careers. The government also brought in a system of electronic payments for civil servants, replacing the previous cash-based system. The cash-based system was notoriously slow and leaky, with wages frequently arriving weeks late, and civil servants reporting that their pay packets were regularly missing a certain proportion of the money owed, a result of docking pay by a certain percentage as a contribution to the Party. Electronic bank transfers have now been introduced across the board, ensuring that civil servants are paid in full and on time, even though anecdotal reports suggest civil servants are still being asked to pay back Party contributions in cash after they have been paid.

To some extent these initiatives represent too little too late. The civil service pay rise was expensive for the government, at a time when Cambodia is approaching middle income status and international commitment to provide aid is weakening. Yet it barely increased public servant salaries to subsistence level, and is therefore unlikely to significantly reduce corruption and improve the government's standing with voters. Since 2013, despite these efforts, the government appears

[69] Ibid. [70] Ibid.

politically stalled between the intransigence of its own ministries, which refuse either to agree on significant devolution of functions or on a significant upgrading of their own efficiency, and the demand of voters for a better claim on their vote.

Faced with this situation, the government has tried different strategies to promote its own electoral prospects. One focus is public financial management (PFM) reform. This has long been pushed by Cambodia's international donors, but progress has been inconsistent, and usually associated with financial crises within the government. The current public financial management reform programme was agreed between donors, particularly the World Bank, and a caretaker CPP government in 2004, during a twelve-month period when the opposition parties were boycotting parliament in protest at election irregularities.[71] During this period, when the party's need for international backing and funding was high, progress was made on a public financial management reform plan, and initial implementation began. However, once the political crisis ended and the government began receiving large amounts of Chinese aid, as well as funding from business tycoons in the context of the economic boom, progress on PFM slowed.

The need to raise civil service salaries has prompted new attention to PFM reform in the government. According to the Secretary of State for the Ministry of Civil Service, 'compensation reform cannot be achieved alone without reform in other sectors, especially public financial management in the Ministry of Economy and Finance. PFM reform and compensation reform depend upon one another'.[72]

One marker of progress is the shift to electronic financial management systems that streamline procedures for making payments and render them more transparent than the current manual, paper-based system. The implementation of electronic financial management in the Ministry of Economy and Finance was characterised, however, by a degree of foot-dragging within the Ministry, since it challenged not only traditional hierarchies of power but also systems by which informal fees and bribes could be extracted by different departments and individuals in return for processing invoices and payments. According to one donor official:

[71] Taliercio 2009.
[72] Interview with Caroline Hughes, Phnom Penh, 17 June 2015, name withheld.

> In the MEF, the old system involved so many people in different stages of the process. So the first step in reform is to get people off the transaction. Get them to do something else. But then what do we do with these people? The perception is that they want to be attached to the MEF because it is a powerful and prestigious ministry. And then there is the patronage network – they don't want to upset people in there. They need to retrain and redeploy people, but they haven't made any plans for that.[73]

Retraining and redeploying is difficult for the Cambodian civil service because it significantly disrupts the personal relationships that are considered central to ensuring bureaucratic loyalty. The imperative of increasing the efficiency of financial management to fund increased pay for civil servants thus conflicts directly with two long-standing practices: that of using the civil service as a vehicle for personal connections used to channel money from the state to the Party, and that of allowing civil servants to reward themselves in return for their loyalty.

The government is also experimenting with a more managerialist approach to the civil service, focusing on delegation of powers to discrete service delivery units with contractual requirements to meet particular targets. In the context of the Cambodian civil service, where a culture of conformity, loyalty and deference to hierarchy has been specifically promoted as a strategy for control, this represents a considerable shift in emphasis. Consistently rewarding performance potentially conflicts with a longstanding policy of rewarding loyalty equally, and those interviewed for this project expressed some concerns over the potential problems. For example, one senior MEF official commented:

> Before managers just try to follow the instructions from the ministries, but now they are the head. They have to make decisions, develop strategies and action plans. Not just stay there and get instructions, they have changed from being followers to being leaders. Before they were not accountable for results. Now they are accountable not just for the financial recording of what they have spent, but also for their results. But it is very hard to change minds, it is a change in organisational culture, you can't build it in just one day.[74]

For senior state and party officials, this creates new pressing problems of control. One solution is to establish a new auditing and inspection culture to promote accountability, but this clashes with longstanding

[73] Interview with Caroline Hughes, Phnom Penh, 18 June 2015, name withheld.
[74] Interview with Caroline Hughes, Phnom Penh, 20 July 2014, name withheld.

resistance within the state and party to public transparency. Although auditing can boost the image of officials and promote central control, publicly available audit reports also represent a hostage to fortune in a context where the opposition is increasingly vocal, well organised, and able to circulate information via social media.

A possible solution to this problem is to focus on the establishment of local user groups as primary mechanisms for accountability, resolving the problem of accountability at a scale at which the CPP dominates. Technical auditing agencies tend to be based in capital cities where the opposition party and critical NGOs are strongest; but in rural villages and communes, the government can still rely on commune authorities to control public deliberative decision-making spaces.

In education, for example, plans by reformist education minister Hang Chuon Narong to delegate greater power to school directors hinge on two factors: first, the political loyalty of school directors who have long been political appointees; and second, the particular relations of power between school directors, teachers and parents in rural Cambodia. The education ministry is the most decentralised ministry in Cambodia with by far the largest workforce. Teachers have long been a somewhat unruly constituency within the civil service, since their relatively high level of professional training and their limited opportunities for making money encourage a tendency to criticise the patronage system. The main supplements to teachers' salaries are providing private tutoring lessons, selling items such as cakes to students and accepting bribes. However, rural schools in poor areas have limited opportunities for enrichment, and teachers are heavily dependent on school directors who allocate overtime activities such as examination marking. School directors have long been appointed on the basis of their political loyalty, specifically to ensure that teachers who do not support the Party are punished by exclusion from overtime.

Parents, for their part, are disempowered in their relationship both with school directors and with teachers. Because teachers rely on bribes from students to supplement their wages, the practice of failing or excluding children whose parents do not pay is widespread in Cambodia. Primary school enrolment rates are close to 100 per cent in Cambodia, but dropout rates are also very high, reflecting the difficulty of keeping a child in school and ensuring their progress through the different grades. Parents and students cannot afford to antagonise teachers in a situation where teachers routinely and effectively wield the threat of exam failure.[75]

Awarding more power to school directors through reforms that promote school autonomy thus does not constitute a significant risk in terms of the directors' own political allegiance. However, it does raise the risk that school directors and teachers might abuse their powers in a manner that confounds the aim of improving government legitimacy in the eyes of parents. The Ministry of Education's plan for dealing with this is to promote School Support Committees (SSCs) among parents, who can engage with school directors, assist in developing the school plan and help raise money for the school.[76] However, this represents a very weak form of accountability in a situation where parents are easy and customary targets for retaliation by teachers. According to an Education Ministry official in charge of the SSC project, the committees were not functioning particularly well in the early stages: 'Some of them take a passive role, not an active role. There is a lack of motivation, confidence and capacity. We have a School-Based Management Initiative to try to empower them to perform their function'.[77]

In theory, SSCs are elected from parents and work alongside 'elders: those who have educational background and experience in helping the community'.[78] In practice, that usually means that they are chaired by the commune chief. Furthermore, most SSCs stick to the minimum requirement of meeting only three times a year, limiting the degree of oversight they can exercise. The powers of the SSC are limited to complaining to the commune chief if any shortcomings are noted. In theory, the commune chief can take tough action against teachers, including, for example, stopping a teacher's pay for not attending class. If this happens, according to the Ministry, 'then the teacher will come to meet the Commune Chief and they will decide on an agreement'.[79] A further aspect of school-based management is the proposal that school directors will have hiring and firing power over teachers. This is intended to resolve the problem of teacher absenteeism, in particular, quickly and effectively.

[75] Eng et al, 2015.

[76] MOEYS official's interview with Caroline Hughes, Phnom Penh, 21 June 2015, name withheld.

[77] Ibid. [78] Ibid. [79] Ibid.

It remains to be seen how far this reform will be implemented, but its intent is to rescale governance of education to the local level in a manner which stitches education more firmly into CPP-dominated commune- and district-level politics, rather than significantly challenging hierarchies of power embedded in relations between schools and families. Although the Ministry has not conducted a comprehensive review of the functioning of SSCs, anecdotal evidence cited by a Ministry official supports the view that SSCs reflect power relations at the local level rather than challenging them. The official remarked that in general SSCs were not effective in imposing accountability; however, 'In Preah Vihear there is a very effective SSC: that is a military area on the border, so the members of the SSC and the village chief are all military. If the teacher is absent, the SSC members will use the military leadership – the military leaders will make a call to the school director and that is very effective'.[80]

Conclusion

The CPP has dominated Cambodian politics through a strategy of intensive local control by local authorities stitched into long-standing personal networks of loyalty and patronage. This is fostered by the flow of resources gained from a highly centralised system of taking bribes and donations in return for awarding opportunities for the exploitation of Cambodia's natural resource-base to foreign investors and rich Cambodian tycoons. In large areas of the rice-growing heartlands where land ownership is largely settled, this works effectively. However, in more remote areas where natural resource exploitation directly affects livelihoods of poor families, it has long given rise to contestation. In the past 25 years, there are a number of instances of the CPP selectively adopting reform programmes advocated by international donors in order to manage this tension.

Recently, the rapid increase in the mobility of people and information technology in Cambodia has exacerbated this contestation, as news about the destruction of forests and the crushing of protests circulates widely and quickly on social media, transforming the scale over which individual citizens are capable of evaluating government

[80] Ibid.

and prompting a disappointing outcome for the CPP in the 2013 elections. This has created a problem for the party's continued dominance because its decentralisation strategy, initiated with the commune elections of 2002, was intended to boost the accountability and popularity of local authorities and render them more effective as agents of legitimation. This initially worked well, with reports of strengthened relationships between local government and villagers. However, as voters begin to look beyond their own village and make larger demands, the commune is unable to respond and the party needs the cooperation of line ministries to improve services and make a difference in voters' lives.

This has been hugely problematic for the Party, since the ministries themselves largely comprise complex hierarchies designed to extract resources from state budgets and citizens. Making the central civil service more effective requires root and branch reform in hiring and firing practices, anti-corruption measures, increased pay, promotion policies, performance reviews and financial management, among others. Yet implementing these reforms risks disrupting the personalist networks within the ministries that are still required to maintain civil service loyalty and to ensure continued flows of money from the state to the Party.

The election results of 2013 prompted the CPP to rethink its approach to public administration so that a number of reforms have been introduced, including salary increases and efforts to promote efficiency and quality of service delivery that selectively adopt international good governance plans. However, the problem remains that each of these reforms has to be negotiated with the set of party insiders that constitute the civil service itself. This has proved a significant problem, such that progress on issues like performance management, introduction of electronic financial management and deconcentration of functions to the local level has been exceptionally slow.

Shortcuts borrowed from New Public Management practices have been imported into this programme, including the practice of creating autonomous agencies accountable to local user-groups. In part, this is genuinely intended to put pressure on school directors to improve their performance in a way that will boost the legitimacy of the party. But this is also, in part, going ahead because it is a safe move that puts power back in the hands of the commune chiefs, who are the bedrock of

CPP power. Whether this compromise proves sufficient to deliver a CPP victory in the forthcoming elections, scheduled for 2018, remains to be seen. Current levels of political intimidation and violence against opposition activists and politicians in Phnom Penh suggest the CPP leadership might think not.

5 The Politics of Scale and the Aceh Government Transformation Programme

The Aceh Government Transformation Programme (AGTP) was the most ambitious project to rescale the provincial government of the post-disaster and post-conflict province of Aceh. Aceh became the recipient of considerable international aid in the aftermath of the 2004 earthquake and tsunami that killed about 167,000 Acehnese and destroyed or damaged large swathes of the coastline.[1] A second tragedy followed in March 2005 when an earthquake shook the nearby island of Nias, leaving another trail of destruction and deaths behind. The unprecedented disasters were met with an equally unprecedented response. International donors and the Indonesian government quickly pledged about US$7.2 billion, and 93 per cent of it was later committed to funding the reconstruction under the leadership of the Agency for the Rehabilitation and Reconstruction of Aceh and Nias (BRR, or *Badan Rehabilitasi dan Rekonstruksi NAD-Nias*).[2]

Indonesia's President, Susilo Bambang Yudhoyono, established the BRR in April 2005 in what was, essentially, a scalar strategy to centre decision-making on the new agency and bypass the notoriously slow and corrupt central and local government agencies. The BRR operated outside the Indonesian civil service system, and Kuntoro Mangkusubroto, the BRR head, had ministerial-level rank. The agency coordinated some 60 bilateral donors, several multilateral agencies, and around 700 NGOs, while supervising and implementing over 12,500 projects.[3] Donors supported the BRR with technical assistance,

[1] Bappenas 2005.

[2] This chapter uses a simplified foreign exchange rate of IDR 10,000 = USD 1.00. This constant conversion facilitates highlighting the magnitude of the fluctuations discussed. The exchange rate has varied over the decades, though. Past exchange rates can be retrieved via a tool of Bank Indonesia: www.bi.go.id /en/moneter/kalkulator-kurs/Default.aspx. The work title of the sources cited in this chapter relates to their positions during the lifespan of the AGTP and not their position when interviewed.

[3] BRR 2009; Nicol 2013.

often embedded in the various branches of the agency. This included management consultancy by McKinsey & Company, which prepared the BRR's early organisational strategy, and the Asian Development Bank (ADB) and Ernst & Young, which assisted in developing a fiduciary management structure.[4] However, as the May 2009 closure of the BRR approached, donors progressively focused on the Aceh administrations. The provincial government was slated to take over the bulk of the BRR's responsibilities, while the district and city administrations were to play an important role in completing the rehabilitation and manage what had been built. The AGTP was established in this context in early 2007.

Indonesia's bureaucracy is viewed as politicised, corrupt and inefficient – problems partly rooted in the country's authoritarian past.[5] These problems were augmented in Aceh by a pro-independence war that erupted in the mid-1970s and ended in August 2005, when the tsunami's devastation overwhelmed the political ambitions of both Jakarta and the Free Aceh Movement (GAM, or *Gerakan Aceh Merdeka*) rebels. The AGTP was designed to support the administration of Irwandi Yusuf, a former senior member of GAM who won the 2006 gubernatorial election after the 2005 peace agreement allowed independent candidates to contest for office, an exception in the archipelago at that time.

A US$17 million project, the AGTP was funded by the Multi-Donor Trust Fund for Aceh and Nias (MDF), managed by the World Bank and implemented by the provincial government in partnership with the United Nations Development Programme (UNDP). The project had four outputs.[6] The first was to support the provincial government to take over the responsibilities of projects and assets inherited from the BRR. The second extended support to coordinate and implement reconstruction work beyond the transition. The third aimed at strengthening the capacity of the Provincial Personnel, Training and Education Agency (BKPP) to 'retain, manage and transfer to provincial and district government agencies the knowledge and skills required for successful transition and sustainable recovery'. The fourth, which was added in 2011, was to support the provincial government in

[4] Scarpello 2009: 32. [5] Emmerson 1983; Gaus et al. 2016: 6.

[6] We use the term 'output' here because this is how they are referred to by the project. This does not necessarily mean that each was implemented successfully or as planned.

completing the assets transfer from the BRR.[7] Beyond the transition imperative, these outputs came to include scalar strategies intended at making the provincial government more responsive to the international 'good governance' agenda, thus bypassing the Acehnese socio-political context, viewed by donors as corrupt and hindering development. Results have been mixed.

The project, which closed on 30 June 2012, was successful in supporting the Irwandi administration in its immediate needs, largely via *Tim Asistensi* – a group of 60 advisors hand-picked by the governor. It was also successful in institutionalising a transparent ad hoc monitoring system of provincial government units' budget expenditures, and in introducing predefined guidelines for the allocation and use of some budget resource streams. The AGTP, however, failed both to establish the BKPP as a 'centre of excellence' and to institutionalise a merit-based recruitment system for bureaucrats.

Two sets of analyses have looked at the AGTP. The first, technocratic in orientation, explained the project's mixed results against a list of outputs and outcomes framed within the 'aid effectiveness' agenda introduced in the Paris Declaration.[8] Overall, these analyses have focused on 'measurements' and 'impact' and have neglected the political nature of AGTP. Against AGTP's first output, for example, one report lists a series of documents produced by *Tim Asistensi* and assessed whether these were converted into laws or government policies.[9] Against AGTP's second output, the report lists the capacity-building activities AGTP has provided and assesses whether these have translated into changes in how the target agencies operate.[10] These reports view AGTP's shortcomings as due to insufficient engagement. Their suggested solutions include further and deeper donor engagement and a focus on technical assistance and capacity building.[11] In line with neo-liberal praxis, 'capacity' here emphasises technical-managerial skills that challenge the 'notion that a doctor should manage the government's health department, or a forestry expert lead the forestry agency'.[12]

The second set of analyses focuses on AGTP's political aspects.[13] Instructively, these studies have explained the shortcomings of the

[7] UNDP 2012b: 17. [8] OECD High-Level Forum on Aid Effectiveness 2005.
[9] UNDP 2012a: 19–20. [10] UNDP 2012a: 20–25.
[11] UNDP 2012a: 38–41. [12] UNDP 2012b: 25.
[13] Aspinall et al. 2012; Hillman 2011, 2013.

project by pointing out that donors failed to grasp Irwandi's intention to use the AGTP to consolidate his power within the local bureaucracy, predominately recruited during the war and aligned with Jakarta, and that donors failed to gain the necessary support with key individuals and agencies. These studies argue that the way forward is to establish alliances with reform-minded individuals who understand the local context. They thus manifest the liberal-pluralist approach of engaging politically, especially in regard to what the UK Department for International Development calls 'drivers of change'[14] that was discussed in Chapter 1. Hillman suggests that in Aceh 'time must be invested in identifying and cultivating political champions, especially at the political centre ... Without political champions, donor efforts to bring about institutional change are doomed to fail'.[15] He adds that 'strong expertise in foreign systems of public administration must be combined with a deep understanding of local institutions, political actors, opportunities and constraints'.

While both sets of analyses add to our understanding of AGTP's successes and failures, the analytical and conceptual premises upon which they are based prevent them from fully explaining why *some* elements of the project were successful and others were not. In other words, they fail to explain the inherent unevenness of public administration reform (PAR) programmes.

As shown in earlier chapters, this unevenness is better addressed by our approach which incorporates the politics of scale within a broader social conflict analysis. This allows us to explain how donors' rescaling efforts have been *selectively* resisted or embraced by various actors. Importantly, our approach also demonstrates that 'donors' and the 'provincial government' are not monolithic because actors within these groups were engaged in fluid, transversal alliances to further their own interests. Such alliances were important in shaping the AGTP's mixed results.

The following section explains the 'plight and riches' of the provincial and district administrations in Aceh, and positions the AGTP within the main post-tsunami PAR initiatives. We will then look at Aceh's historical trajectory to explain, in particular, the uneven development that characterises the province's capitalist development since the 1970s and how this sowed the seeds of rebellion. This

[14] DFID 2004. [15] Hillman 2013: 13.

historical-sociological analysis continues by explaining how peace changed the strategic selectivity of the state in Aceh to favour groups associated with GAM, but how it also led to intra-elite struggles for political and economic dominance. This analytical background subsequently allows us to explain the selective adoption of the AGTP by the provincial government in a context also shaped by intra-donor competition and tension between the national, provincial and district scales.

The Plight and Riches of the Aceh Government and Post-Tsunami PAR Initiatives

The structural problems of Indonesia's public administration were hugely amplified in Aceh by the effects of the thirty-year war, the tsunami, and the 2005 peace agreement. Donors have made PAR a key area of intervention since Indonesia returned to democracy in 1998.[16] But attempts to rescale departments by introducing mechanisms for auditing, accounting, reporting, punishing and rewarding have been stifled by obstructionism or unresponsiveness.[17]

Indonesia's bureaucracy remains structurally resistant to reforms. For example, employment conditions and pay policies are bypassed by a flawed recruitment system and the lack of procedures to deal with corruption.[18] Bribes are paid to enter the system and to move up the ladder,[19] and service to the public often depends on the payment of informal fees. Another problem is the inflexible hierarchical structure of the bureaucracy, reflecting the military's once-dominant influence in the state.[20] The apparatus also suffers from lack of job descriptions so staff positions are based on management decisions, not competency and job skills, as well as the lack of professional development opportunities and the inability to relocate staff or dismiss them for poor performance.[21] The process of decentralisation, which started in 2001, has possibly made a bad situation worse, allocating significant

[16] Edi and Setianingtias 2007: 10.
[17] Brinkerhoff and Wetterberg 2013; Buehler 2011; Gaus et al. 2016; Harun et al. 2013; Turner et al. 2009.
[18] World Bank 2005: 1. [19] *The Jakarta Globe* 2013.
[20] Aspinall et al. 2012: 17. [21] Aspinall et al. 2012: 18–19.

fiscal and administrative responsibilities to ill-trained district and provincial civil servants.[22]

In Aceh, these problems were compounded by the province's tormented history. Until 2006 the governor was appointed by Jakarta, but the war meant that decisions required authorisation from the Indonesian military (TNI, or *Tentara Nasional Indonesia*). Thus, the provincial administration never developed adequate organisational or decision-making skills. The interference of GAM, which at its peak controlled up to 70 per cent of the province, stifled the development of district administrations.[23] The conflict increased corruption, prevented checks and balances on the government from operating, and restricted civil society and the media.[24] It also kept the province sealed off and donors away.

No important PAR initiative targeted Aceh before 2006. The tsunami crippled the public administration further, destroying 20 per cent of public buildings, 19 per cent of equipment and 27 per cent of public records, as well as killing 5,266 civil servants.[25] The peace agreement ended the war but paved the way for many former rebels, including Irwandi, to occupy senior positions in various administrations without any relevant skills.[26] This was the situation when the provincial government was called to take over from the BRR, and, together with the districts, tasked with reintegrating former combatants and improving the lives of the many living in poverty. By then, Aceh had one of the largest government revenues in the country thanks to windfalls associated with the process of decentralisation, the 2005 peace agreement and the post-tsunami reconstruction projects.

Aceh's revenue had first increased considerably in 2001 when decentralisation allocated to provinces and districts 26 per cent of the central government's revenue base via the general purpose central–provincial–local transfers (DAU, or *Dana Alokasi Umum*). Aceh was one of the main beneficiaries of this reallocation and also benefitted from the peace agreement of 2005. The Law on Governing Aceh (LoGA) – the legislation that enshrined some of the principles of the peace accord – allocated an additional 2 per cent of the DAU for 15 years starting in 2008, and 1 per cent for the five subsequent years.

22 Aspinall et al. 2012: 17. 23 World Bank 2006: 90.
24 Barron and Clark 2006: 17.
25 Bappenas 2005: II-8; Bappenas and International Donor Community 2005: 64.
26 Ansori 2012; Hillman 2012; ICG 2007b.

Between 2008 and 2015 this Special Autonomy Fund (OTSUS, or *Dana Otonomi Khusus*) added IDR 41.49 trillion (US$ 41.4 billion) to Aceh's coffers, accounting for about half of the region's overall revenue.[27] Among other resource streams, the LoGA maintained Aceh's 70 per cent share of the locally produced oil and gas revenue (MIGAS, or *Minyak dan Gas Bumi*), first granted with the 2001 special autonomy status, and allowed the province to raise taxes.[28]

Donors and the central government allocated more money and assets to Aceh for the post-tsunami reconstruction. In 2006, for example, this resources stream totalled IDR 17 trillion, or US$ 1.7 billion.[29] In 2008, as the AGTP started operating in earnest, Aceh's overall revenue of IDR16 trillion (US$1.6 billion) was the third highest per capita in Indonesia and twice the national average.[30]

The Post-Tsunami PAR Initiatives and the AGTP

The United States Agency for International Development (USAID), the Australian Agency for International Development (AusAID), UNDP, the European Union (EU) and the World Bank were among the many donors supporting every administrative layer in Aceh from 2007. Some of the projects rescaled governance via embedding consultants or introducing international best practices, among other strategies. The AGTP was the most ambitious.

Various programmes rescaled development planning and execution at the village level, as part of a broader mission of establishing a new institutional framework of governance. These localisation strategies, inherent in the donors' broader decentralisation agenda in Indonesia, were prominent in the World Bank's large-scale *Kecamatan* Development Programme (KDP) and AusAID's Local Governance and Infrastructure for Communities in Aceh (LOGICA I and II). Their aims were to 'foster the creation of village-level development committees, or support existing village-level institutions, to oversee reconstruction and development projects according to strict guidelines of community involvement, accountability and transparency'.[31] In so doing, they rescaled the planning and monitoring of projects to the

[27] Pusat Pengembangan Keuangan Daerah 2016: 9.
[28] Morgan et al. 2012: 13.
[29] World Bank 2006: 45.
[30] Morgan et al. 2012: 13.
[31] Thorburn and Bryan 2014: 10.

village level and away from the existing bureaucracy. The implementation of these projects included 'capacity building training and mentoring of individual community members to inculcate standards of value and practice akin to the governance ideals of these programs'.[32]

Similarly, the Support for Poor and Disadvantaged Areas Projects (SPADA), another World Bank-MDF project, rescaled planning downward by establishing and training sub-district committees in participatory planning. The plan was to link these committees to Bappeda, the regional branch of the Ministry of Development and Planning (Bappenas), and to other agencies responsible for Public Works, Education and Health so that 'real people's needs' were included in the district planning process.[33] The good governance aims of this scalar strategy were to strengthen 'local participation in development planning; promote private investment and job creation; and increase the utilisation of effective education, health and dispute resolution services'.[34]

The Canada/Aceh Local Government Assistance Programme (CALGAP) wanted to strengthen relations between the province and district administrations to improve efficiency in their development programmes. The main output was the establishment of the Communication Forum of Local Governments and Legislatures (FKKA, or *Forum Komunikasi Pemerintahan Kabupaten dan Kota se-Aceh*) in March 2008, which gathered representatives of districts and cities. The FKKA became an advocacy tool for the districts in their attempts to rescale the management of OTSUS funds to the district level. CALGAP supported FKKA with technical assistance and workshops to build its capacity to formulate recommendations to the provincial government and legislature.[35]

USAID's Local Governance Support Programme (LGSP) operated at the national, provincial and district levels. LGSP was a national programme to 'support both sides of the good governance equation' through 'support[ing] local governments to become more democratic, more competent at the core task of governance and more capable of supporting improved service delivery and management of resources' while also 'strengthen[ing] the capacity of local legislatures and civil

[32] Thorburn and Bryan 2014: 10. [33] World Bank 2012: 16.
[34] World Bank 2012: viii. [35] FCM and VNG International 2010: 12–13.

society to perform their legitimate roles of legislative representation and oversight, and citizen participation in the decision-making process'.[36] In practice, this US$61.8 million project, one of largest USAID projects worldwide, provided policy support to key national ministries dealing with local governments, and technical assistance and training to 62 district governments in nine provinces of Indonesia, and two provincial governments, including Aceh.[37] In Aceh, LGSP first funded initiatives to support the 2006 election, and then an Executive Development Programme to provide training and information to newly elected officials of the provincial and district governments. This marked a shift in the programme's orientation from a 'recovery initiative' – the original title of the Aceh programme – to one of more broad-based good governance within decentralised systems.[38] In line with New Public Management priorities, LGSP's primary focus became providing technical assistance and capacity development programmes for integrated participatory planning and budgeting.[39] Beside attempts to introduce international best practices and performance-based budgeting, LGSP embedded an advisor in Governor Irwandi's office to provide policy advice and two planning and finance specialists in the planning/finance service office.[40]

As we shall elaborate later, Aceh was an important test case for the EU's foreign policy, and Brussels was active in funding several PAR projects. These included the Aceh Local Governance Action Programme (ALGAP and ALGAP II), the Aceh Governance Stabilisation Initiative (AGSI) and Aceh District Response Facility (ACDF). These projects aimed at supporting the drafting of bylaws necessary to implement the LoGA. Each project included important capacity building and technical assistance components.[41] Noteworthy, the European Commission (EC), the executive arm of the EU, established a European House in Aceh to maximise the effectiveness of its operations. The House became an important player in interacting with the provincial government where the EC also embedded a consultant in the early years of Irwandi's administration.

Recipients welcomed some of the activities of the projects outlined above, while others were resisted, though we lack the scope in this

[36] RTI International 2007: 1.
[37] RTI International 2009: 1.
[38] RTI International 2009: 1–8.
[39] Daly et al. 2016: 188.
[40] RTI International 2009: 1–9.
[41] Daly et al. 2016: 189.

chapter to discuss them in detail. This unevenness was evident in the AGTP as well, which was the only project developed to support exclusively the provincial government.

The AGTP was the MDF's main PAR project, and part of the UNDP's country programme to strengthen the institutional capacity of provincial governance.[42] The project was framed by the MDF as 'essential' to develop the capacity of the Aceh provincial government to take on some of the responsibilities that had been the BRR's.[43] The UNDP stated that it would 'strengthen sustainable and equitable governance capacity for ongoing reconstruction – an aspect of disaster response of equal importance to the refurbishment of physical infrastructure'.[44] Within this, as noted, the AGTP's four outputs were aimed at: (1) supporting the provincial government to take over the responsibilities of projects from the BRR; (2) supporting the coordination and implementation of reconstruction work beyond the transition; (3) strengthening the capacity of the BKPP; and (4) supporting assets transfer from the BRR.[45] However, donors saw the AGTP *also* as a vehicle to introduce reforms to make the provincial government more responsive to international standards and bypass the corrosive local socio-political context.

Outputs 1 and 2 included strategies to introduce a 'fit-and-proper' test to internationalise recruitment towards a merit-based approach. This was paired with an attempt to rescale the training of civil servants to 'international standards' by turning the BKPP into what Williams calls a 'good governance enclave' to discipline other government units (output 3).[46] A capacity needs assessment in output 2 led to the AGTP supporting two ad hoc agencies, which operated largely independently from the bureaucratic apparatus, and were tasked, respectively, with rationalising and disciplining access and spending of the OTSUS and MIGAS funds, and with accelerating and monitoring budget expenditure by provincial units. The best practices, processes and systems these agencies introduced rescaled some functions of government agencies, most prominently the monitoring of project disbursements, to meet donor good governance expectations. As later elaborated, the internationalisation of the recruitment and training of civil servants was resisted, while the rescaling via the ad hoc agencies was adopted.

[42] UNDP 2010: 5. [43] MDF Secretariat 2009: 65. [44] UNDP 2008: 4.
[45] UNDP 2008: 4. [46] Williams 2003.

To explain this unevenness – and indeed the contested genesis of the AGTP, and the struggle over the controversial *Tim Asistensi* – we need to situate the project within Aceh's capitalist development trajectory. In particular, we need to explain the uneven development that characterised the province's relations with Jakarta, planting the seeds of distrust and war, and the societal and political struggles that emerged in the province following the 2005 peace agreement. It is to this historical-sociological analysis we now turn.

Uneven Development and the Strategic Selectivity of the State in Aceh

Aceh's early capitalist development was shaped by its geostrategic position, facing the Andaman Sea and the Indian Ocean, and by the contacts it had with foreign traders and powers.[47] The capitulation of the Aceh Sultanate to the Dutch intertwined the future of the region with that of Indonesia, leading to highly problematic centre–periphery relations.

At its peak, in the seventeenth century, the Sultanate was an important trading port, exporting mainly pepper and gold. Political power was contested by various rulers and often resided with the one that secured the trade routes.[48] The societal groups contesting for state power changed as Aceh fought the Dutch and eventually fell to the colonial power in 1906, after a 35-year war. The Islamic scholars, or *ulama*, emerged as the leaders of the anti-Dutch resistance, while the traditional chiefs, the *uleebalang*, became the middlemen for the Dutch and later for the Japanese occupiers.[49] The Japanese defeat in 1945 invigorated the *ulama*, which subsequently gained control of the region.[50]

The *uleebalang–ulama* conflict was also framed within the broader trajectory of the nascent Indonesian state. After the Japanese defeat, the *uleebalang* supported the return of the Dutch, while the *ulama* sided with the pro-independence movement that had emerged in the archipelago. The victory of the *ulama* meant that Aceh played an important role in this movement, and Sukarno, Indonesia's first president, rewarded the province with a 'special status' within the Indonesian

[47] Feener et al. 2011; Reid 2006. [48] Özay 2012: 60.
[49] Aspinall 2007: 248; Sulistiyanto 2001. [50] Sulistiyanto 2001: 438.

state, which was established in 1945 and recognised by the Dutch in 1949. Sukarno also promised the *ulama* that they would be allowed to implement Islamic law in Aceh.[51] This was important to the *ulama* to cement their place in the local socio-political order. However, tensions arose from the early days of Indonesian independence, sowing the seeds for the difficult centre–periphery relations that have endured since.

The initial contention was about the nature of the Indonesian state. The anti-Dutch war had brought together groups with different ideologies. After independence, these groups attempted to impose their ideology on the newly formed state. The core conflict emerged between an Islamic and a secular camp. The Acehnese *ulama* sided with them first, and supported the inclusion of the Jakarta Charter into the 1945 constitution. This contained a clause obliging Muslims to follow sharia law. Once Sukarno sided with secular forces and blocked the insertion of the Jakarta Charter,[52] the *ulama* felt betrayed. Amid the tensions that ensued, Aceh's special status was abolished in 1951 and Aceh was incorporated into the neighbouring North Sumatra province.[53] The amalgamation shifted part of the power to Medan, North Sumatra's capital, and affected the *ulama*'s control of Aceh's political and economic resources.[54] The change of status was quickly politicised, and in 1953 Daud Beureuh'eh, a charismatic *ulama*, joined the Darul Islam movement and declared Aceh to be part of an Indonesian Islamic state.[55] The conflict ended in 1962 after Sukarno awarded Aceh separate province status in 1959, and upgraded this to 'special region' status with autonomy in the areas of religion, customary law and education in 1961.[56] The *ulama*'s privileged position within Aceh did not last long, though, and Aceh's special status was revoked soon after General Suharto rose to power in 1965.

Suharto's rise followed a coup attempt on 30 September 1965 blamed on the Communist Party of Indonesia (PKI, or *Partai Komunis Indonesia*).[57] He quickly centralised power with a combination of coercive force and state patronage, partly via the Golkar Party. The support of the TNI was essential for Suharto's rise. Suharto granted the military political representation and allowed it, as an institution and via its officers, to engage in income-generating activities

[51] Sulistiyanto 2001: 439.
[52] Hefner 2000: 42.
[53] Barron and Clark 2006: 3.
[54] Aspinall 2007: 249.
[55] Barron and Clark 2006: 3.
[56] Sulistiyanto 2001: 439.
[57] Hughes 2003; Hunter 2007.

throughout the territory on the condition that a share of the revenue made its way up to the top.[58] This idiosyncrasy, based on the fact that the government only funds part of the TNI budget, persists to this day.[59] In 1974, Suharto produced a law that granted the president the prerogative to appoint and sack governors.[60] This strategy consolidated the national scale as the dominant one in centre–province relations and strengthened Suharto's control over the political economy of the archipelago.

The rise of Suharto greatly affected Aceh. He supported technocratic elites to operate as regime proxies in collaboration with the military. The *ulama* put up a fight and won important victories at the 1977 and 1982 elections under the banner of the United Development Party (PPP, or *Partai Persatuan Pembangunan*), a Muslim party tolerated by the regime. They eventually capitulated at the 1987 vote, after years of the regime implementing hard and soft measures to ostracise them. The last nail in the *ulama*'s coffin was the extension of Suharto's Golkar Party patronage to Islamic institutions. This led to several influential *ulama* joining Golkar and to the demise of the *ulama* as a political force.[61]

Suharto's efforts to control Aceh reflected the growing economic importance of the province. Indeed, from the mid-1970s until the 1980s Aceh developed from being irrelevant to the national economy to being a key source of income for the regime and a driver of Indonesia's capitalist development.[62] The relationship was skewed in favour of Jakarta and this uneven development sowed the seeds of war.

At the core of the transformation was the discovery by Mobil Oil of huge deposits of liquid natural gas and oil near the town of Lhokseumawe in 1971. Once production started in 1977, Aceh's contribution to the national coffers ballooned to between US$2 and $3 billion annually.[63] In 1989 Aceh's oil and gas accounted for 30 per cent of Indonesia's overall oil and gas exports.[64] But Aceh saw little benefit from this boom. The province received about US$82 million annually from what it contributed to Jakarta, and Acehnese were prevented from getting jobs in the industry and gaining

[58] McLeod 2011: 56.

[59] EIA and Telepak 2005; HRW 2010; Kontras 2004; Rieffel and Pramodhawardani 2007.

[60] Kell 2010 [1995]: 58. [61] Aspinall 2007: 254.

[62] Sulistiyanto 2001: 439. [63] Sulistiyanto 2001: 440.

[64] Kell 2010 [1995]: 14.

contracts to build infrastructure.[65] The exploitation of the reserves was carried out by a joint venture that included Mobil Oil, Pertamina (Indonesia's national oil and gas company) and Jilco, a Japanese consortium. Pertamina preferred employing Javanese, while ancillary contracts were routinely awarded to businesspeople connected to the political or military elites in Jakarta, or to Mobil Oil.[66] The benefits of the oil boom did not extend to the community either. Indeed, the New Order implemented a scalar strategy developing Lhokseumawe into a major economic enclave – the Lhokseumawe Industrial Zone (ZILS, or *Zona Industri Lhokseumawe*) – that was controlled from Jakarta, operated by non-Acehnese and detached from the surrounding societal context.[67]

The oil boom led to an increase in poverty, inequality and social tensions instead. In the late 1970s, oil and gas accounted for less than 17 per cent of Aceh's GDP.[68] The province had a low level of poverty and inequality with only 1.8 per cent of the rural population, and 1.7 per cent of the urban population below the poverty line in 1980.[69] Only two out of 26 Indonesian provinces had lower poverty rates.[70] By 1998, however, as more than 40 per cent of Aceh's GDP was due to oil, poverty had increased by a staggering 239 per cent.[71] This was most astounding considering that 'over the same period, poverty in Indonesia as a whole fell by 47 per cent'.[72] There are two plausible explanations for this. The focus on the extractive industry meant that the regime neglected the rural economy, setting the province on a path to reverse-development. Moreover, the secessionist conflict that erupted in 1976 had turned some of the rural zones into no-go areas for the government, increasing the power of the military, paralysing civilian administrations and making life very hard for farmers.

Inequality worsened as well. In 1990, more than half the Javanese employed in the urban areas of Aceh held jobs in the top strata of their profession, compared with only a third of Acehnese, while in the rural areas, Javanese had larger land-holdings than Acehnese.[73] Many Javanese were relocated through the bureaucracy; others were moved by the government through the transmigration scheme that relocated millions of people from overpopulated Java and Bali to the more

[65] Sulistiyanto 2001: 439. [66] Sulistiyanto 2001: 440.
[67] Emmerson 1983: 1234. [68] Kell 2010 [1995]: 14. [69] Ross 2005: 38.
[70] Brown 2005: 4. [71] Brown 2005: 4. [72] Brown 2005: 4.
[73] Brown 2005: 5–7.

sparsely populated outer regions; and some 50,000 had come to Aceh because of the oil and gas boom.[74] The inequality fostered Acehnese hostility against the Javanese. It is in this context that GAM was established and rose to challenge Jakarta.

From Rebels to Leaders

GAM's trajectory has shaped Aceh's contemporary history. The group emerged in reaction to Jakarta's exploitation of local resources, but after the 2005 peace agreement, the rebel movement has transformed itself into a dominant, yet fragmented political force.

In 1974 an Acehnese businessman, Hasan di Tiro, applied to construct an oil pipeline for Mobil Oil. His application was rejected, and the contract awarded to an American company.[75] On 4 December 1976 Hasan di Tiro established GAM and declared Aceh independent. Tiro framed the GAM insurgency as a reaction to the uneven development strategy implemented by Jakarta, stating in the declaration of independence that 'during the last thirty years, the people of Acheh [*sic*], Sumatra, have witnessed how our fatherland has been exploited and driven into ruinous conditions by the Javanese neo-colonialists'.[76] The declaration was an extreme example of a strategy meant to shift power towards the local scale.

Over the years, GAM successfully sought the support of the international community for its struggle, with Tiro claiming that 'it had a moral duty to support Aceh's self-determination as it had colluded with the illegal transfer of sovereignty from the Dutch'.[77] Libya trained GAM rebels in the mid-1980s. Sweden gave exile to GAM leaders, including Tiro, from the early 1980s and mediated peace talks in the late 1990s. The Henry Dunant Centre for Humanitarian Dialogue, a Swiss NGO, brokered a peace deal in 2002, which collapsed soon after, and the Crisis Management Initiative, headed by former Finnish president Martti Ahtisaari, mediated the peace talks that culminated with the 2005 Helsinki Memorandum of Understanding (MoU). In 1976, however, Jakarta responded to the declaration by launching military operations in Aceh. It was the beginning of a bloody 30-year war.

[74] Ross 2005: 42. [75] Rist 2010: 112. [76] Quoted in Rist 2010: 113.
[77] Quoted in Reid 2006: 239.

The Jakarta–GAM conflict is conventionally divided into three periods. The first, from 1976 to about 1979 saw a small GAM quickly repressed; the second, from 1989 until 1998, saw the movement gaining public support and launching attacks. This phase also saw Jakarta stationing up to 12,000 soldiers in the province and declaring it a Military Operations Area.[78] It was to keep this status until August 1998. The third period, from the fall of Suharto in May 1998 till the 2005 peace agreement, saw GAM growing to control much of Aceh's countryside, and the government placing the province under martial law and launching its largest ever military operation in 2003.[79] There is an extensive literature on GAM and the conflict.[80] A few points are nonetheless important to reiterate here.

The conflict was tainted by widespread human rights abuses committed predominantly, but not exclusively, by the TNI.[81] It was also punctuated by the failure of two peace negotiations and the poor implementation of two different 'special statuses'.[82] One of the main reasons for lack of success was the TNI's economic interests. Aceh provided the TNI with the perfect environment to build a thriving illicit logging business and other illegal and legal activities.[83] War also allowed GAM to trade in marijuana and extort protection money.

The tsunami struck as Indonesia's largest-ever military campaigns was unfolding, distrust between the Acehnese and the Javanese was at its highest, and TNI and GAM businesses were thriving. Nevertheless, on 15 August 2005, representatives of the Indonesian government and GAM reached a peace settlement.

The catalyst for peace was the sheer magnitude of the disaster that forced GAM to drop its call for independence, and Jakarta to concede a large autonomy to the province and withdraw most of the TNI.[84] The TNI's compliance was ensured via compensatory inflated budgets for troop withdrawal (IDR 526 billion, or US$526 million), funds to rebuild barracks (IDR 400 billion, or US$400 million) and, in 2007, substantial financing for its non-combat activities in Aceh (IDR225 billion, or US$225 million).[85] The LoGA, adopted by the Indonesian House of Representatives on 11 July 2006, laid the

78 Sulistiyanto 2001: 440. 79 Aspinall 2009a.

80 Aspinall 2007; Kingsbury 2007; Schulze 2004; Sukma 2005; Ziegenhain 2010.

81 HRW 2004. 82 Aspinall and Couch 2003.

83 Aspinall and Couch 2003: 3; Rist 2010: 114–15.

84 Gaillard et al. 2008; Klitzsch 2014. 85 Mietzner 2009: 301–2.

foundation for lasting peace by dealing with some of the grievances of uneven development. Two sets of decisions were particularly significant. First, the national government compensated and supported Aceh with the OTSUS and MIGAS resource streams, among others. Second, the LoGA allowed GAM members to partake in electoral politics as independent candidates at first, and then via the establishment of local political parties later on. Both were exceptions in the Indonesian context at that time.[86]

GAM became Partai Aceh (PA) in 2008, but, as detailed below, those associated with the rebel group swept to power even before. GAM's political control of the province was instrumental in avoiding a relapse into war, but it has not ended societal and political conflicts. To the contrary, 'the transitional period has produced a new social arena for competition and created particular patterns of conflict'.[87] Among the fissures are: (1) centre-periphery tension over the implementation of the LoGA;[88] (2) rifts between pro-GAM Acehnese ethnic groups and the anti-GAM non-Acehnese ethnic groups living in the province;[89] and (3) disputes between former GAM leaders and foot soldiers over who gets what of the spoils of peace.[90]

In the next section, the focus is on the struggles for political and economic supremacy among GAM elites. Indeed, GAM proved far from monolithic; it fragmented and soon deteriorated into little more than an umbrella name under which individuals and groups contest to further their own political and economic interests. These struggles are closely linked to the control of the provincial government and of the bureaucracy and have critically affected the uneven results of the AGTP.

Elite Political Struggles in Post-Conflict Aceh

The peace agreement affected the strategic selectivity of the state in Aceh where – as the International Crisis Group puts it – 'loyalty to GAM replaced good connections to Jakarta or local army commanders as the key to political and business opportunities'.[91] As GAM fragmented, however, the relationship between political power and patronage

[86] Barron and Clark 2006: 7. [87] Ansori 2012: 33.
[88] ICG 2007a, 2009, 2013; Jafaruddin 2013. [89] Ansori 2012; ICG 2013.
[90] Aspinall 2009b. [91] ICG 2007a: 1.

became particularly pronounced, and electoral politics turned into a 'zero-sum' game with 'politically motivated killings, kidnapping, vandalism, and widespread intimidation and threats to voters' widespread in each post-Helsinki vote.[92] The provincial government, the most prominent scale vis-à-vis the national and the district scales, was the hardest fought administrative level.

Many former rebels benefited from the spoils of peace. Most senior GAM members gained important positions and lucrative contracts. Ansori,[93] for example, notes that Nur Djuli, the senior GAM negotiator at the Helsinki peace talks, was awarded the chair of the Aceh Reintegration Agency; Nurdin Abdur Rahman, another GAM negotiator and the former GAM leader in Malaysia and Australia, became the director of Aceh World Trade Center; Muzakkir Manaf, the former supreme commander of the armed wing of GAM and the vice-governor from 2012, became the CEO of Pulo Gadeng, a major contracting company; and Sofyan Dawood, the former military commander in North Aceh and GAM's spokesperson, won several high-value contracts.[94]

Less senior former GAM members became active in business. Aspinall explains how they were favoured in gaining government-funded construction contracts, but also how this patronage extended to trade, mineral exploration and mining, electricity production, and agriculture and plantations. Former rebels used their connections in government to win supplier contracts with government departments; help mining companies acquire government licences, becoming partners in the exploitation of natural resources; or act as brokers for national companies or foreign investors that wanted to enter the Acehnese market.[95] Political connections were instrumental for those seeking to enter the oil-palm plantation sector too. They did so 'by seeking access to government-organised land grants or licenses, or by attaining money provided to KPA-linked community cooperatives'.[96] The KPA, or the Aceh Transition Committee (*Komite Peralihan Aceh*), is a civilian organisation established after the peace agreement to represent the former GAM's military wing. It has become very powerful in post-conflict Aceh as it maintains control of the territory and guarantees a reservoir of votes for the political elite.

[92] Zyad 2014. [93] Ansori 2012: 36. [94] Ansori 2012: 36.
[95] Aspinall 2009b: 15–16. [96] Aspinall 2009b: 15–16.

In such a context, control of the provincial government and of its public administration has become essential for elites to establish and maintain the patronage network needed for political and economic supremacy. A key role in this process is that of the so-called echelon II, bureaucrats in charge of provincial government units. Indeed, as fissures within the GAM elite deepened, struggles over control of the provincial government and administration intensified.

Various intra-GAM rifts have developed since peace was signed. The first emerged at the 2006 gubernatorial election, won by Irwandi, a former senior GAM member. However, he ran as an independent paired with vice-governor candidate Muhammad Nazar, a former NGO leader. The senior GAM leadership, headed by former exiles Malik Mahmud and Zaini Abdullah, supported Ahmad Humam Hamid and Hasbi Abdullah, two uncontroversial local academics, who ran as candidates of the Islamic PPP. GAM's rebuff of Irwandi was a strategy by Malik to prevent Irwandi from gaining too much power while GAM was turning itself into a political party. Most GAM military commanders and the young Acehnese supported Irwandi, though, and portrayed GAM leaders as being out of touch. This was made possible as the KPA adopted a neutral stance.[97]

Hamid's lack of GAM credentials and his association with the Jakarta-based PPP proved costly. He won in Pidie, the birthplace of Hasan di Tiro and a stronghold of the old GAM, and garnered some support amongst the urban, educated middle class and the religious establishment, enticed by his PPP connections.[98] But Irwandi won comfortably with 38.20 per cent versus Hamid's 16.62 per cent, in a contest that saw six other pairs trailing further behind.

The intra-GAM split meant that Irwandi's priorities after taking office were to control the pro-Jakarta bureaucracy by replacing several echelon II officers and strengthening his network of supporters within GAM. Patronage politics, supported by access to government funds was instrumental for both objectives. Irwandi is generally considered personally 'clean' and many believe he did not directly interfere in the bidding process for government projects. He did not need to do so, though, as the reshuffle of echelon II put in place the conditions for his supporters to be favoured. In addition, control of the provincial government allowed Irwandi to direct allocation of OTSUS-funded

[97] Santoso 2006. [98] Otto 2007.

project to districts and cities headed by friendly administrations, opening another window to patronage politics.[99]

The intra-GAM split deepened. Over time the balance of power shifted in favour of the old GAM as, once established, PA tightened its alliance with the KPA, developing overlapping memberships and structures. A key example is Muzzakir Manaf, the former head of GAM's military wing that rose to lead both the KPA and PA. Many other PA cadres held positions also in the KPA. This facilitated a mutually beneficial relationship between PA and the KPA members, most of which had become active in business. In short, KPA's patronage machinery provided party cadres, while PA provided KPA with the purpose for continued existence and provided favoured access to valuable government provisions to KPA members.[100]

This became clear at the 2009 legislative elections when KPA members mobilised in favour of PA. The election was marred by particularly high levels of violence and intimidation and culminated with PA wining 47 per cent of the vote and 33 of 69 seats in the provincial legislature. PA also gained 237 of 645 district and municipality-level seats across the province, including a majority of seats in seven district legislatures and a plurality in nine others.[101]

Political conflict continued during the build-up to the 2012 gubernatorial election as the competing GAM factions took their grievances to the national Constitutional Court. The core dispute related to Irwandi's intention to run again as an independent candidate, while the LoGA specified that this was possible only in the first post-conflict election. Irwandi appealed to the Court, which backed up his position because, by then, independent candidates were allowed to compete in elections nationwide.[102] PA responded by renewing the threat to boycott the vote, and lobbying President Yudhoyono.

Yudhoyono saw PA's boycott as a serious risk for the peace process. Jakarta responded by delaying the election enough for Irwandi to be replaced by an interim governor, thus missing out on government funds with which to build his campaign.[103] PA consolidated and registered its candidates – Zaini Abdullah, GAM's former foreign minister, and Muzakkir, KPA and Partai Aceh's head. The pairing further

[99] Cahyono 2016: 7–8. The regulations for the allocation of the OTSUS fund are dealt with later in this chapter.

[100] Sindre 2016. [101] Thorburn and Bryan 2014: 15.

[102] Arbas et al. 2015. [103] Aspinall 2011.

institutionalised the PA–KPA alliance and overpowered Irwandi, winning 55.75 per cent of the votes, while Irwandi and Muhyan Yunan, his running mate, garnered 29.18 per cent. Irwandi filed for the nullification of the election at the Constitutional Court for, among other reasons, 27 recorded acts of violence against his supporters during the campaign, but the case was dismissed.

Once he gained office, Zaini moved fast to replace a number of echelon II and III officers. As we shall see, he reshuffled the public administration several times, even placing family members in key positions, including his brother, two brothers-in-law and several other relatives. The appointment of his wife's cousin as an 'expert' in Bapedda, the regional development agency, was particularly instrumental in facilitating many of Zaini's associates gaining lucrative government contracts, according to an anti-corruption activist.[104]

Zaini's zeal in cementing control of the bureaucracy became particularly pressing as the governor soon became engulfed in a rift with his vice-governor Muzakkir, who has used his position to broaden the political base of PA by including younger, better educated cadres, and relying less on ex-combatants.[105] Muzakkir has also reached out to the *ulama*, promising to strengthen the role of Islam in everyday life.[106] Aceh is the only province in Indonesia where sharia law can be applied in some spheres of social life. Jakarta had granted this exception during the height of the conflict in an attempt to win the support of the *ulama*.

From the above it is clear that provincial government has become a turf for political struggles among GAM elites keen to control state resources to strengthen their political and economic position. As we shall see in the next section, the AGTP became engulfed in these power struggles with outputs of the project co-opted, rejected or selectively adopted by Irwandi and Zaini.

Transversal Alliances, Political Struggles and the Selective Adoption of the AGTP Outputs

The AGTP was undoubtedly innovative in its form and some of its outputs. A representative of the European Commission, the main

[104] Fabio Scarpello's personal communication with Alfian, Coordinator of Masyarakat Transparansi Aceh, 20 September 2016.

[105] IPAC 2015: 1. [106] IPAC 2015: 1.

donor of the MDF, said that the project was 'all about reform', meaning moves towards liberal good or 'good enough' governance.[107] He rated the project a success, but acknowledged that there were problems and challenges. In this section, we explain what these were through the lens of our framework, paying particular attention to how the AGTP outputs were selectively adopted in a contest affected by not only intra-elite struggle but also competing donor interests, as well as tensions between the national and the provincial scales and between the provincial and the district scales. We start by explaining how intra-donor competitions shaped the AGTP outputs, setting the project on its path of selective adoption; we then investigate the nature of *Tim Asistensi*, its function for Irwandi and how donors tried and failed to assert control over it by tightening the purse. We then focus on the key scalar strategies donors attempted: the internationalisation of the recruitment and training of civil servants, the introduction of predetermined objectives and rules on how to access and spend OTSUS and MIGAS funds, and the establishing of an ad hoc monitoring system for provincial budgetary expenditures.

International Politics, Transversal Alliances and the AGTP

The AGTP is the result of a close alliance between the UNDP and Irwandi that brought de facto decision-making to the provincial level in Aceh, forcing the MDF to accept the AGTP and its various components as a fait accompli.

The exit of the BRR concerned donors, worried about the legacy of the post-disaster reconstruction. Particularly nervous was the EC – the MDF's co-chair and largest donor with a US$240 million contribution.[108] The EC had invested enormous political capital in Aceh, which it saw as a test case in its foreign policy approach. The EU is the world's largest provider of aid and a strong supporter of the multilateral approach, but Brussels has often lamented that it rarely receives due recognition at the international level. In political terms, visibility often translates into influence, and the predicament bothered the EU for two decades. A possible way forward was

[107] Fabio Scarpello's interview with senior EC representative, Jakarta, 22 January 2016.

[108] MDF Secretariat 2005: 14.

identified after the tsunami hit Aceh. Brussels was quick with humanitarian help, and later, its strong support for the MDF confirmed its commitment to the multilateral approach. But as donor consultation about establishing the MDF progressed in Jakarta throughout January 2005, the EC 'demanded' to be co-chair.[109] When the EC had its wish granted, the MDF's strategic relationship with the BRR added to the EC profile in the region, and this was further boosted by Brussels' leading role in monitoring the implementation of the 2005 peace agreement.

The EU-led Aceh Monitoring Mission (AMM) was instrumental in ensuring the smooth disarming of GAM and withdrawing of TNI troops. Pieter Feith, the EU diplomat in charge of the AMM, called the operation a quantum leap for European efforts to build a common foreign policy.[110] By the end of 2005 many agreed that the EU's post-conflict and post-disaster activities in Aceh were the best example of its 'soft power' policy potential.[111] Aceh was heralded as a major political achievement within the corridors of Brussels too. This, for example, transpired in a 2008 report of the European Courts of Auditors where the EC stated: 'The Commission in its role of co-chair of the Steering Committee has enhanced the visibility of the EU in Indonesia through its *strategic influence* in the MDTF, as well in linking the reconstruction to the complementary initiatives in support of the Aceh peace process'.[112] The sustainability of the post-conflict and post-disaster success of Aceh thus mattered a lot to Brussels. It follows that the EC was keen to support Irwandi; the question was how and through which implementing partner.

Two potential partners emerged in late 2016: the German federally owned international cooperation enterprise GTZ, with whom the EU was collaborating on several projects, and the UNDP. The EC and World Bank preferred GTZ as they saw UNDP as too accommodating to the demands of recipients, to the detriment of careful monitoring.[113] But UNDP had a good relationship with Irwandi and moved fast. Immediately after Irwandi was elected, UNDP proposed to develop a project to support his administration.[114] Irwandi agreed and laid out

109 Scarpello 2009. 110 Quoted in Minder 2005.
111 Bivar 2005; Schulze 2007.
112 European Court of Auditors 2008: 37, emphasis in original.
113 Fabio Scarpello's interview with EC representative, Jakarta 22 January 2016.
114 UNDP 2012b: 11.

some requirements. UNDP developed the AGTP to fit Irwandi's desires, including the establishment of *Tim Asistensi* (about 60 'advisors' hand-picked by Irwandi). The agreement between Irwandi and the UNDP, which was also supported by the BRR's head Kuntoro, made it politically impossible for the EC and World Bank to consider a different implementing partner or project.[115] The UNDP–Irwandi–Kuntoro's transversal alliance de facto rescaled decision-making to Aceh, and away from the MDF offices where the EC and the Bank would have had more power.

The MDF was sidelined during the process of developing the project too. In August 2007 the provincial government and the BRR jointly presented policy papers to the MDF outlining their strategy for the transition process. These documents incorporated the outline of the AGTP, including *Tim Asistensi*. The EC and World Bank vehemently opposed *Tim Asistensi*, but they were reminded by Kuntoro that 'they needed to give Irwandi the support he required, not what they thought he required'.[116] Soon after, Irwandi issued a decree creating *Tim Asistensi*, and UNDP responded to his request for initial funding.[117] The establishment of *Tim Asistensi* once again rescaled decision-making to the provincial level, bypassing the MDF process. By the time the AGTP Project Concept Note was approved by the MDF Steering Committee in December 2007, the project was truly underway.

Intra-donor differences never subsided.[118] The EC, in particular, maintained a critical view of UNDP. This culminated with the EC commissioning in 2010 an independent audit report on nine UNDP projects funded under MDF. This prerogative of the EC, stipulated in the MDF Operational Manual, coincided with the AGTP requesting an extra US$13 million to consolidate asset transfer from the BRR.[119] The EC and World Bank blocked the request and forced UNDP to redraft the proposal, adhering to specific guidelines. To the disappointment of Irwandi and UNDP, the MDF eventually released only US$3 million for output 4.

This example demonstrates that donors are far from monolithic, and intra-donor contestation is, at times, capitalised upon by recipients to

[115] Fabio Scarpello's interview with EC representative, Jakarta 22 January 2016.
[116] Fabio Scarpello's interview with senior UNDP staff, Jakarta, 1 January 2016.
[117] UNDP 2008: 3. [118] Scarpello 2009. [119] UNDP 2012a.

further their interests or defeat political rivals. In this case, Irwandi was able to capitalise on the competition between UNDP and GTZ over funds to insist on the establishment of *Tim Asistensi*, while UNDP was able to impose this on the MDF thanks to its alliance with Irwandi and Kuntoro, despite the reservations of the World Bank and EC. The example also shows the importance of scalar strategies. Irwandi and the UNDP first rescaled decision-making in Aceh, largely bypassing the MDF process, but the MDF later reasserted its own scale in deciding the detail of output 4.

Tim Asistensi

Tim Asistensi was a successful rescaling attempt by Irwandi that shifted policymaking away from the bureaucracy he distrusted and towards 60 advisors he hand-picked. *Tim Asistensi*, though, was a conundrum for donors, who unsuccessfully tried to assert control over the advisors with the introduction of a reimbursement procedure.

Tim Asistensi consisted of seven clusters: human resources, economy, anti-corruption, transition, law, communication and information systems. Their primary responsibility was to help the governor formulate policies and strategies. The clusters were meant to liaise with the various provincial government units in developing policy, but the relationship with the bureaucracy varied greatly and depended on the policy and the personal relationship between the *Tim* member and the bureaucrats involved.[120] In general terms, *Tim Asistensi* sat uneasily within the governance structure, and civil servants looked at the advisors with suspicion. The *Tim*'s most daring initiatives were stalled by the bureaucracy, showing that Irwandi's rescaling was resisted. One such initiative was the Aceh Green paradigm.

This was first conceptualised by an American consultant embedded in Irwandi's office[121] and then developed by the information systems *Tim Asistensi*, headed by Ilarius Wibisono.[122] The policy was thus

[120] Fabio Scarpello's interview with a member of MIS Tim Asistensi, Jakarta, 22 January 2016.

[121] Aspinall et al. 2012: 112–3.

[122] Wibisono personified the rescaling of *Tim Asistensi*. A Javanese with experience in government and international organisations, he was considered Irwandi's right-hand man and was respected and feared among the civil servants, who labelled him the de facto vice-governor. Notably, once *Tim Asistensi* closed, Wibisono took over the management of the AGTP.

a clear rescaling of policymaking with senior civil servants not involved in the process, but informed of its detail afterward.[123]

The Aceh Green plan was ambitious and called for the development of renewable energy (especially geothermal and hydropower), sustainable agro-forestry, carbon trading, fisheries and aquaculture, and waste management.[124] As a first step Irwandi imposed a moratorium on logging. Donors welcomed this and supported some ad hoc projects, but the Aceh Green paradigm and the moratorium clashed with the entrenched interests of many political and societal forces, including the military. Resistance took the shape of stalling the initiative, with several of the government departments supposed to play a role, and failing to do so. According to an independent evaluator of the AGTP, civil servants in the Forestry Department saw the Aceh Green 'as the pet project of Irwandi's *Tim Asistensi*', and decided to weather the storm because 'it will go away with *Tim Asistensi*'[125] Aceh Green never took off.[126]

Tim Asistensi produced some legal documents,[127] although several bills were never passed into law by the Aceh House of Representative, staffed by members of national parties until 2009 and controlled by PA afterward. *Tim Asistensi also* drafted job descriptions and competencies that constituted the basis for the 'fit-and-proper' test of public servants and was involved in the establishment of Unit P2 K, both discussed below. Overall, the *Tim* was a successful scalar strategy implemented by Irwandi: the various clusters contributed in devising policy initiatives that would have been difficult to pursue through the bureaucratic apparatus at that time. But the political nature of *Tim Asistensi* was a thorny matter for donors.

Donors were aware from the outset that Irwandi needed technical advice, but that he also wanted to strengthen his patronage base and assert control over the pro-Jakarta bureaucracy.[128] Irwandi addressed these priorities by recruiting advisors from academia and international organisations; but also many from GAM and SIRA, a pro-GAM NGO

[123] Fabio Scarpello's interview with a member of *Tim Asistensi*'s information systems, Jakarta, 22 January 2016.
[124] Minas 2010.
[125] Fabio Scarpello's interview with AGTP independent evaluator, Jakarta, 27 January 2016.
[126] Aspinall et al. 2012: 112–13. [127] UNDP 2010: 9.
[128] Fabio Scarpello's interviews with EC and senior UNDP representatives, Jakarta, 22 and 28 January 2016.

active during the conflict and headed by Irwandi's vice-governor, Nazir.[129] The executive branch of the Indonesian government, both at the national and provincial level, is allowed to recruit advisors. This notwithstanding, donors struggled to justify Irwandi's appointments as 'technical in nature' or as processed through 'best practice'. The EC and World Bank pressured UNDP on several occasions to cancel *Tim Asistensi.*[130] But UNDP resisted this because the output represented an essential part of the overall project negotiated with Irwandi. Donors thus attempted to reassert control over the advisors by holding the purse tight. This took place through a rescaling of responsibilities downwards.

Relations between the World Bank and UNDP within the MDF were marred by competition over funds and by inter-agency rules that prevented the Bank from auditing other UN agencies. The Bank argued that its role as a trustee should grant it the right to peruse UNDP accounts to better explain to donors how money was spent.[131] The problem extended to UNDP monitoring, which the Bank and the EC considered inadequate.[132] Ironically, however, the Bank and EC capitalised on what were normally sources of frustration, making it clear that UNDP was responsible for ensuring *Tim Asistensi* was monitored and accountable.[133] UNDP did not want to jeopardise its relationship with Irwandi and rescaled the monitoring downwards by putting in place a management unit at Banda Aceh's Syiah Kuala University to implement a reimbursement procedure, which called for advisors to be compensated for 'costs' only after they submitted relevant documentation that proved they had provided a service. However, the staff at Syiah Kuala University were embedded in Aceh's broader socio-political context and found it tough to meaningfully implement the system. While some advisors duly submitted reports of their activities, others submitted only one-line justifications, and a few threatened the managers when asked to comply.[134] Reimbursement reached up to IDR60 million a month (US$6,000) for some of the recalcitrant

[129] Fabio Scarpello's interview with a senior AGTP staff, Banda Aceh, 9 February 2016.
[130] Fabio Scarpello's interview with senior UNDP staff, Jakarta, 28 January 2016.
[131] Scarpello 2009.
[132] Fabio Scarpello's interview with EC representative, Jakarta 22 January 2016.
[133] Ibid.
[134] Fabio Scarpello's interview with a member of Syiah Kuala University management unit, Banda Aceh, 4 February 2016.

advisors.[135] At the end, the process represented a thin layer of accountability behind which donors hid their discomfort.

The example of *Tim Asistensi* is instructive to elucidate how targeted agencies can co-opt segments of a project and implement rescaling strategies that, although useful for the recipient, run against the very principles of accountability, transparency, and capacity building that permeate the good governance agenda underpinning donors' interventions.

The Failed Rescaling of the Recruiting and Training of Civil Servants

The key rescaling strategies implemented in outputs 1, 2 and 3 aimed at internationalising the recruitment and training of civil servants to limit patronage and corruption and improve service delivery. As discussed in Chapter 1, improved service delivery is often seen by donors as the key to state legitimacy and hence as important for long-term stabilisation. Specifically, the AGTP introduced a merit-based, 'fit-and-proper' test in the recruitment of mid-level civil servants, and attempted to rescale the agency in charge of training and supervising the transfer of staff, the BKPP, into a 'Centre of Excellence' that would progressively introduce good governance principles into other units. Neither scalar strategy was successful in altering the institutional behaviour of the targeted institutions.

The fit-and-proper test was the result of a 'tactical alliance' between the UNDP and Irwandi to advance 'particular and well-defined goals in areas where a convergence of interest is possible'.[136] Though the UNDP had reservations regarding Irwandi's reform credentials, the agency saw the governor's concerns over the dependability of civil servants as an opening to promote reforms aimed at rationalising and disciplining recruitment.[137] The aim was to introduce a merit-based approach to recruiting civil servants, or what Kaufman calls 'new rules of the game' to alter the institutional behaviour of the government.[138] In this case, the merit-based approach wanted to make recruiting more responsive to international standards, and less prone to politicisation and corruption.

[135] Ibid. [136] Hutchison et al. 2014.
[137] Fabio Scarpello's interview with senior UNDP staff, Jakarta, 28 January 2016.
[138] Kaufman 2003: 36.

The fit-and-proper test was implemented in 2008 for the recruitment of 42 middle-level civil servants (echelon II), the heads of provincial government departments.[139] It was the culmination of a process that included various elements of AGTP's output 1 and 2. For the first time in Aceh, and probably Indonesia, positions were open to both echelon II and echelon III civil servants that fit the criteria. The process was managed by an assessment centre established by the AGTP and staffed with Indonesian academics and experts trained in interview techniques by consultants recruited in England and Malaysia.[140] The consultants also drafted a 'standardised scoring format' used during the assessment process, while the human resources cluster of *Tim Asistensi* drafted the job descriptions and competencies for echelon II staff that underpinned the entire process. Once the fit-and-proper test was implemented, and a number of echelon II staff were replaced, donors claimed to have successfully introduced best practice and merit-based recruitment.[141] The test, however, was constrained by the prominence of the national scale in setting the wages, measuring the performance and deciding on hiring and promotions of civil servants even at the provincial level.[142] It was also instrumentally executed by Irwandi for his short-term political gains.

Irwandi's initial concern was actually to replace the Provincial Secretary, the most senior local bureaucrat (echelon I). This position is filled via a process that allows a small provincial team, which includes the governor, to select candidates according to guidelines set by the national government. The national Ministry of Home Affairs (MoHA) assesses the candidates and makes the final decision. The selection guidelines proved too difficult for Irwandi, who was unable to find a suitable candidate. Only then did he decide to focus exclusively on the echelon II layer.[143] At this level of the bureaucracy, donors wanted to institutionalise an assessment process that placed primacy on managerial skills. This approach, favoured by neo-liberal development orthodoxy, meant that donors wanted to 'select the 40 candidates with the

139 The Indonesia civil service comprises of four echelons. Echelon I officials are the heads of national government departments and the Regional Secretary of a province; echelon II are followed by the more junior echelon III and IV.

140 UNDP 2012b: 26.

141 UNDP 2012a: 21; Fabio Scarpello's interviews with EC and senior UNDP representatives, Jakarta, 22 and 28 January 2016.

142 Harun et al. 2013: 386.

143 Fabio Scarpello's interview with senior UNDP staff, Jakarta, 28 January 2016.

best managerial skills and appoint them to manage the 40 provincial agencies'.[144] This proved unfeasible. The LoGA granted the provincial and district governments in Aceh authority over local civil servants. But the lack of specific bylaws to implement the LoGA, and lingering central government's requirements regarding seniority, qualifications and training of staff, limited donors' space for manoeuvre. The fit-and-proper test was in the end designed to evaluate mostly the criteria set by the central government, rather than the candidates' managerial skills.[145] The test would still have been an improvement on the murky modus operandi prevailing had Irwandi not implemented it to suit his political objectives.

The avowed commitment to international 'best practice' in recruitment was questioned from the outset as most reshuffled echelon II staff appeared to be GAM sympathisers. Civil servants and observers noted that the fit-and-proper test did not abolish patronage networks but legitimised Irwandi to dislodge the existing network and replace it with his own.[146] Any lingering best practice pretence dissolved as Irwandi dismissed 12 of the newly (re)appointed heads of agencies after less than 12 months in office. One of the governor's advisors said that 'this decision was made on the basis of a performance evaluation of all heads of department conducted six months after their appointments'.[147] But the arbitrariness of the sacking made it clear that appointments had little to do with merit. Aspinall and colleagues add that the fear of sackings 'was particularly pronounced among those without strong personal ties to the governor or former combatant networks'.[148] UNDP quietly acknowledged this bias later on.[149]

Irwandi never implemented the fit-and-proper test again and did not maintain the assessment centre that donors hoped could extend the test to echelon III and IV staff, for which *Tim Asistensi* had prepared job descriptions and competencies too.[150] This was the last nail in the

144 Ibid.
145 Fabio Scarpello's interview with senior UNDP staff, Jakarta, 28 January 2016.
146 This was the opinion of two civil servants of the provincial administration interviewed by Fabio Scarpello in Banda Aceh, on 3 February 2016 and what several sources said during informal conversations. Aspinall et al. (2012) and Hillman (2013) draw similar conclusions.
147 Quoted in Aspinall et al. 2012: 22. 148 Aspinall et al. 2012: 22.
149 Fabio Scarpello's interview with senior UNDP staff, Jakarta, 28 January 2016.
150 Aspinall et al. 2012: 22; Hillman 2013: 6.

coffin of the attempted rescaling toward a merit-based recruiting. Not much has changed post-Irwandi.

Zaini has repeatedly made calls for bureaucratic reform since taking office in June 2012.[151] Yet he has opted not to revive the fit-and-proper test or the assessment centre, and has frequently reshuffled the bureaucratic apparatus for his political ends. According to anti-corruption NGO GeRAK Aceh, Zaini has carried out nine major reshuffles involving at least 664 civil servants between June 2012 and June 2016, and echelon II staff have remained in their role for an average of only six to eight months.[152] Vice-Governor Mazukkir has allegedly not been consulted on the reshuffle, fuelling suggestions that Zaini is building his own patronage network to ward off the challenge of Muzakkir, the overwhelming favourite for the 2017 gubernatorial election. The failure to rescale recruitment to a merit-based approach is confirmed by ongoing accusations of corruption, with bribes paid to intermediaries that facilitate promotion,[153] of nepotism;[154] and of politicisation, with Zaini placing his loyalists in the top positions.[155]

Donors paired their attempt to rescale recruitment with a concerted effort to internationalise the training of civil servants via focusing on the BKPP (output 3), which had emerged from a recent structural reorganisation of provincial government units as the sole agency tasked with training Aceh civil servants. The first stage of the rescaling entailed, basically, training the trainers (the BKPP) according to 'international benchmarks'.[156] Donors expected that once the BKPP had internalised the benchmarks, the agency would pass them onto the other agencies when training civil servants.[157] The rescaling plan included a grand design or blueprint to strengthen the BKPP role in monitoring and assessing promotions and transfers of civil servants. To this end, the AGTP supported the establishment of a team of eight assessors, drawn mostly from the BKPP.[158] The internationalisation of the BKPP, donors hoped, would lead to a progressive improvement in the quality of the entire bureaucratic apparatus, limiting the detrimental effects of patronage and corruption. In other words, donors wanted to ensure the rolling of good governance principles beyond the lifespan

151 *Serambi Indonesia* 2015a, 2015b, 2016. 152 GeRAK Aceh 2016.
153 Askhalani 2013. 154 Askhalani 2013. 155 IPAC 2014: 3.
156 UNDP 2012a: 9. 157 UNDP 2012a: 28–29. 158 UNDP 2012a: 26.

of the AGTP in order to move beyond intervention and towards what scholars have termed 'ongoing, unceasing governance'.[159]

Irwandi's nominal support for bureaucratic reform did not extend to the BKPP, an institution unable to produce immediate political returns for the governor. BKPP staff perceived this lack of political interest, and stonewalled any attempt to internationalise the agency,[160] for example, by refusing to participate in the 'capacity needs assessments' that the AGTP had organised for all the provincial agencies (output 2). Senior BKPP staff argued that 'the agency did not need capacity development – that it was already capable of performing the functions it needed to perform and that the only problem it faced was 'political interference'.[161]

Senior BKPP staff also refused to take part in the workshops organised by the consultants and sent their junior delegates instead.[162] Junior staff interpreted this as sign that the workshops were not to be taken seriously.[163] Consultants engaged in the training explained that sometimes they convinced BKPP staff to participate by offering compensation for transportation, or similar costs.[164] Ironically, while the BKPP rhetorically still aims to become a 'Centre of Excellence',[165] the agency has never diverged from its modus operandi. As Aspinall et al. note: 'Training continues being supply-driven with the BKPP proposing the courses ... BKPP does not conduct needs assessments of the agencies for which it is supposed to provide training services ... and there has been no systematic assessment of BKPP staff competencies'.[166]

The resistance to the internationalisation of recruitment and training shows that political elites had no interest in supporting deep reform; the current rules of the game (patronage, corruption, frequent reshuffling) are instrumental in their jostle for power. Pluralist analyses suggested that the fiascos were due to donors failing to gain the support of reform-minded elites, and a lack of knowledge by the AGTP staff of the political context.[167] These seem only partly substantiated. As we

159 Pender 2001; Williams 2013.
160 Fabio Scarpello's interview with a BKPP staff, Banda Aceh, 5 February 2016.
161 Cited in Hillman 2013: 8.
162 Fabio Scarpello's interview with a consultant for the BKPP output, Banda Aceh, 4 February 2016.
163 Ibid. 164 Ibid.
165 http://bkpp.acehprov.go.id/visi-dan-misi/, accessed 8 September 2016.
166 Aspinall et al. 2012: 28. 167 Hillman 2013: 13.

have explained, the UNDP actively sought a tactical alliance with Irwandi, then considered the most reform-minded leader. But Irwandi proved only interested in reforms that benefitted him in the short term. Some of the non-Indonesian UNDP staff had a long experience in Indonesia, and several of the AGTP personnel were from Aceh. The UNDP was aware, and noted on several occasions, the risks associated with the political context,[168] but it was simply unable to overcome the structural forces that underpin provincial political power.

The Successful Rescaling via Tim Otsus Migas and Unit P2 K

The AGTP's support for the Special Autonomy and Oil and Gas Funds Team (*Tim Otsus Migas*) and the Activity Acceleration and Control Unit (Unit P2 K) was meant to improve how the provincial government drafted its budget and spent its money. The two ad hoc agencies rescaled some functions of Bappeda, the regional planning agency, and of the Provincial Inspectorate to predetermined objectives and rules, and to an ad hoc monitoring system. These were aimed at bypassing the risks of collusion, inefficiency and corruption in fund allocation and project implementation.[169] The ad hoc nature of the two agencies – a scalar strategy – appealed to donors because it insulated the agencies from the 'excessive political interest and bureaucratic controls which have greatly limited managerial flexibility' in Aceh.[170] Both Irwandi and Zaini supported the agencies, despite resistance from other government units.

Tim Otsus Migas was tasked to: (1) amend the allocation ratio of the OTSUS and MIGAS funds between the province and the districts, (2) draft guidelines for how to spend these funds, and (3) set-up a legal framework on the functions of an Otsus Migas Permanent Secretariat in the provincial government.[171] Aceh's long-term development depended, in no small amount, on whether the provincial and district

[168] E.g. see UNDP 2010: 18–19.

[169] The two units were established after a capacity needs assessment coordinated by UNDP in 2008 for all 42 provincial agencies identified the Provincial Finance Office and Bappeda as among those in need of support (output 2). Several other departments were supported by the AGTP, but these two received the bulk of the assistance.

[170] Aspinall et al. 2012: 52.

[171] Islahuddin 2010: 8.

governments made the most of the OTSUS fund, due to be halved in 2023 and extinguished in 2028. Donors thus saw these predetermined objectives and rules as essential to improving its efficient use.[172] Irwandi's strong support for *Tim Otsus Migas* was, however, also due to the growing tension between the province and the districts over the control of the OTSUS fund.[173]

The LoGA mandated the provincial government to regulate how the province and the districts shared and managed the OTSUS fund. A 2008 bylaw (*qanun* 2008/2) allocated 60 per cent of the OTSUS fund to the districts and 40 per cent to the province. The *qanun*, though, granted the province the power to manage the money, making the province the dominant scale in the province-district relations. For example, the provincial government: decided the maximum to be allocated to each district according to criteria such as the size of the territory, population, and Human Development Index; assessed the projects proposed by districts; and disbursed funds to districts several times a year.[174] This arrangement was contested as soon as it became effective in 2009.[175]

In the heated political debate that ensued, districts employed a localisation strategy claiming that the province lacked the local knowledge to make informed decisions, and this affected the quality of the projects. Reports commissioned by the Aceh House of Representatives in 2010 strengthened the localisation thesis highlighting the poor results of the projects despite the IDR11 trillion (US$ 1.1 billion) OTSUS funds allocated to Aceh between 2008 and 2010.[176] District heads sought the support of the national government arguing that the prominence of the provincial scale sanctioned in the 2008/2 *qanun* contravened Indonesia's 2001 decentralisation law that devolved most fiscal and administrative powers to the district level.[177]

On the other hand, Irwandi was unhappy with the ratio allocation and wanted to maintain control of the purse strings. His centralisation

[172] Fabio Scarpello's interviews with EC and senior UNDP representatives, Jakarta, 22 and 28 January 2016.
[173] The problem included the MIGAS fund too. Here we focus on the OTSUS as it was, by far, the most contested.
[174] Islahuddin 2010: 8–9.
[175] For the 2008 budget, the allocation of the OTSUS fund followed the LoGA that granted the province full control (Pusat Pengembangan Keuangan Daerah 2016: 15).
[176] Taqwaddin 2010. [177] Tryatmoko 2016.

strategy claimed that the province had the knowledge and capacity to provide a broad vision for the best use of the OTSUS fund, and argued that the 'special autonomy' is located at province level, and not at district or city levels.[178] Ironically, he also sought the support of the central government, the signatory to the Helsinki MoU. *Tim Otsus Migas* was called to mediate between these sets of interests.

The *Tim Otsus Migas* presented a draft for an amended *qanun* in late 2010, but to the disappointment of Irwandi, no agreement was reached during his term. Zaini retained *Tim Otsus Migas*, and in September 2012, he gained the support of a special Committee of the House of Representatives for a new allocation ratio that allotted the province 60 per cent and the districts 40 per cent of the OTSUS fund.[179] This infuriated district heads and risked weakening the support base of PA.[180] A compromise was eventually reached as Zaini conceded to the districts the financial management of their share of OTSUS funds.[181] This was ratified in a new in *qanun* 2013/2, which took effect in the 2014 budget year.

Tim Otsus Migas also helped to establish mechanisms and guidelines to ensure that OTSUS funds are allocated to four strategic sectors: infrastructure, health, education and economic development, as mandated by the LoGA.[182] These have been institutionalised and remain active. The establishment of a permanent *Otsus Migas* Secretariat within the governor's office, another of the original outputs of the *Tim*, was abandoned due to the opposition of Bappeda that claimed authority over linking OTSUS funds to the province's long-term development goals,[183] which discloses lingering national–provincial competition over the management of the resource stream.

The institutionalisation of the OTSUS rules seems to have improved the process of preparing the budget. In 2014, the provincial government managed to submit its budget by 20 December, the best result in eight years.[184] Indeed, since the end of the conflict, the Aceh provincial government had not once met the 31 January deadline. Local observers have also noted a shift toward more development spending, rather than routine.[185]

178 Cahyono 2016: 4. 179 *Serambi Indonesia* 2012d.
180 *Serambi Indonesia* 2012a–c. 181 *Serambi Indonesia* 2013.
182 UNDP 2012b: 29. 183 UNDP Monitoring Staff 2010.
184 Kantor Berita Radio Antero 2013.
185 Fabio Scarpello's personal communication with Harry Masyrafah, economist at Syiah Kuala University, 9 September 2016.

Unit P2 K was established to accelerate and monitor the budget disbursement of provincial government units. The Unit maintains a website that in January publishes the expected expenditure and completion date of every provincial government project for that year.[186] Throughout the budget cycle, it updates information on the procurement of goods and services, on disbursement, and on the progress in the physical realisation of the projects.[187] The Unit conducts field report and data analysis, and gives warnings to underperforming projects and reports them to the governor if they fall behind. The Unit also assists Bappeda in planning development projects, supports government units in monitoring and reporting, drafts monthly reports for the governor and performs other tasks related to accelerating budget implementation, such as facilitating the allocation of projects to suitable working units.[188]

The establishment of the Unit was a contested affair, though. Those that supported the Unit included Irwandi, Kuntoro, the anti-corruption *Tim Asistensi* and the donors. Irwandi was frustrated with the slow disbursement of the provincial budget. The appeal for the donors was clear. The Unit aimed at introducing best practices in monitoring budget expenditure by rescaling this function beyond the sole control of the Provincial Inspectorate and Bappeda, both considered underperforming and corrupt. The open access website allowed civil society organisations (CSOs) to play a watchdog role too. This is in line with the more liberal variant of New Public Management model that 'not only aims to insulate a technocratic form of authority from undesirable political and societal pressure but also to mobilise progressive social forces behind liberal development objectives'.[189]

Those opposing the establishment of the Unit were the Provincial Inspectorate, Bappeda and the Provincial Secretary – echelon I civil servants in charge of the provincial bureaucracy that Irwandi wanted to dislodge.[190] They claimed that the Unit would undermine Bappeda and the Inspectorate, the agencies tasked to coordinate, monitor and audit provincial government units. Instead, they called for further strengthening of the Inspectorate and better coordination with Bappeda.

186 http://p2k-apba.acehprov.go.id/v1/index.php, accessed 15 September 2016.

187 Rachman 2012: 26. 188 Rachman 2012: 37.

189 Hutchison et al. 2014: 42.

190 Fabio Scarpello's interview with member of AGTP M&E team, Banda Aceh, 3 February 2016.

The Irwandi, Kuntoro, *Tim Asistensi* and donors alliance suspected that their opposition was based on the realisation that the Unit would increase transparency and bypass the system.[191]

A turning point in the conflict was the eventual support of MoHA for the pro-Unit alliance. This came after Irwandi had requested the Inspectorate use the 'real time online payment system' for procurement developed by MoHA. The Inspectorate insisted on continuing using a manual system. This makes it harder to get a reconciliation of a project account until after the end of the financial year and enables project managers to manipulate how funding is used.[192] With the MoHA's green light, Irwandi established the Unit by decree in March 2010.

The AGTP provided the initial funding for the Unit to operate until it could be managed through the provincial budget. Irwandi was able to secure some local funding too. Some of the key staff were drawn from a similar unit that was operative within the BRR. The BRR gave some equipment and, when it closed, handed over all its computers.

Unit P2 K has been reproduced in other provinces[193] and is now institutionalised in Aceh. Zaini has retained it and now works as a tool for the governor to monitor the progress of provincial projects,[194] and for CSOs to question how the money is spent.[195] Donors claim that the Unit has introduced transparency and improved budget disbursements. Evidence suggests it has indeed improved budget absorption. In 2009 the provincial government absorbed 64 per cent of its budget, but in 2010, after the Unit started operating, it absorbed 93 per cent.[196] This high rate has been maintained in most years since. There is no evidence that it has put a significant dent in government corruption, though.[197]

Overall, the *Tim Otsus Migas* case study shows that competing interests between elite groups at different scales, in this case provincial and district, can open the door to institutionalising rule-based, pro-development objectives. The Unit P2 K case study shows the

[191] Fabio Scarpello's private correspondence with senior UNDP staff, 14 September 2016.
[192] Ibid.
[193] Antara 2014. A similar unit had been established at national level by Yudhyono in 2009 and headed by Kuntoro (Sabarini 2010).
[194] Atjehpost.co 2014b; klikkabar.com 2015; LintasGayo.co 2016.
[195] Acehterkini.com 2015; Atjehpost.co 2014a.
[196] Rachman 2012: 34.
[197] Fadillah 2016; Heriansyah 2015; *Serambi Indonesia* 2015c.

importance of short-lived, tactical alliances to pursue gradual reforms.[198] Irwandi and Zaini were willing to support progressive reforms because these did not threaten their power base. To the contrary, while Unit P2 K's monitoring enhanced transparency and efficiency of budget expenditure, it allowed the governor to assert authority over other government units while claiming reformer credentials.

Conclusion

The tsunami and the 2005 peace agreement turned Aceh into a target of international intervention, but donors have had mixed fortunes in pushing through meaningful public administration reforms. Peace affected the strategic selectivity of the state in Aceh, where individuals and groups associated with GAM are now favoured in accessing state resources. But GAM has fragmented, leading to heated intra-elite conflicts. The peace agreement, moreover, contributed in making the provincial scale the most prominent vis-à-vis the national and district scales. But the post-conflict landscape manifests lingering tension and conflicting interests between elite groups within and between each scale. In such a context, some of the AGTP's outputs were adopted and others rejected. This unevenness allows us to make several final considerations.

First of all, states are far from monolithic. Indeed, in Aceh political contestation interested different groups located within the state, whether at national, provincial or district level. We have also shown, though, that donors can be fragmented, as exemplified by the differences between the UNDP and the EC and World Bank. These differences facilitated Irwandi, who aligned with the UNDP and dictated many of the AGTP's components. The intra-donor politics demonstrated that the UNDP proved more willing than the EC and World Bank to establish tactical alliances with elite groups, and that alliances often transcend the local-international divide – a cherished notion in the hybrid literature.

The AGTP outputs have shown that donors' interventions have been useful for the provincial elites to cement their control of the political economy. This is evident in *Tim Asistensi*, in how Irwandi

[198] Hutchison et al. 2014.

hijacked the fit-and-proper test to legitimise the reshuffle that strengthened his patronage network, and in how Unit P2 K allowed the provincial government to assert some control over other government units.

However, this case study also demonstrates that when elite groups are fragmented, donors have better chances to establish pro-reform tactical alliances – an insight that contrasts with what we saw in Solomon Islands and Cambodia, where the cohesiveness of the national elites prevented donors from introducing meaningful reforms that were not directly beneficial to them. In Aceh, the conflict among provincial elites was one of the factors driving the tactical alliance between Irwandi and UNDP that led to the AGTP. Irwandi, we explained, needed to strengthen his patronage system and used the project to do so, but the AGTP also opened the door to limited, progressive reforms, as our focus on Unit P2 K, in particular, has shown. The Unit rescaled monitoring of government units' budget expenditure to an ad hoc system that speaks directly to the donors' good governance drive.

Our focus on the *Tim Otsus Migas*, on the other hand, demonstrates that reforms can be facilitated when inter-scalar conflict takes place in a context where no scale is overtly dominant. This also differs from what we saw especially in the Solomon Islands where the dominance of national elites is virtually unchallenged and leaves little space for donors to exploit inter-scalar conflict. In Aceh the provincial scale is the most prominent one, but provincial elite groups are reliant on the support of district elite groups for their political supremacy, and are challenged by national elites whose hold on the machinery of government remains important despite the extended 'special autonomy' granted to Aceh after the 2005 peace agreement. This high degree of inter-scalar conflict opened the door to compromise – hence reforms – once provincial and district elites fought over control of the OTSUS funds.

Finally, the chapter shows that PAR initiatives need to be targeted and limited in scope. This relates in particular to reforms aimed at altering the rules of the game or how power is contested. Aceh's political economy remains dominated by struggles to control the revenue streams of the provincial budget. This makes control of the bureaucracy an imperative for competing elite groups and limits the scope for deep reform such as those attempted by the AGTP. This could change should Aceh's economy develop and diversify in the future, especially in relation to the end of the OTSUS funds in 2028, which currently account for about half of the province revenue. In that case, the bureaucracy could be less pivotal in power struggles and donors may find more fertile terrain.

Conclusion

This book contributes to the debate spurred in the last decade by the apparent inability of many Peace- and State-Building Interventions (PSBIs) to attain their preferred governance and political outcomes. In this period, new approaches in the seldom-intersecting fields of peace-building and development studies have called for greater analytical attention to the precise ways in which international interventions and local politics interact.

Though this is overall a welcome shift from the earlier focus on interveners and their ideas and modalities, our initial contention has been that none of these approaches sufficiently engages with the spatial/scalar dimensions of struggles over the political outcomes of PSBIs. The peace-building scholarship has primarily advanced the related concepts of 'hybridity', 'friction' and 'the local turn', which view the outcomes of interventions as stemming from conflict and accommodation between the agendas, institutions and values of liberal internationals and non-liberal locals.[1] The hybridity literature implicitly recognises the importance of scales in its discussion of the local and the international. Yet, we explained that it is constrained by its inability to specify the local and its problematic tendency to assume that PSBI outcomes are produced along the lines separating local and international, Western and non-Western or modern and customary. We have argued that these binaries lead to narrow explanations of PSBI outcomes as located on a continuum between prototypical modern–international and traditional–local alternatives. This neglects, however, the consideration that ostensibly local–traditional or international–liberal modes of governance can be, and often are, advanced by alliances of both local and international actors. Also, locating intervention outcomes as hybrids on the local–international spectrum does not actually explain how particular modes of governance have

[1] Belloni 2012; Mac Ginty 2011; Richmond and Mitchell 2012.

emerged, how they operate in practice and which precise social and political groups benefit from this.

Approaches associated with the 'political economy turn' in development studies have instead investigated how domestic politics, political economies and elite 'political settlements' mediate the implementation of international aid programmes.[2] These approaches are almost entirely scale-blind, implicitly accepting that the spatial and social scope of their political economy analysis aligns with the territorial borders of states and the societies living within them. We have found this scholarship useful, especially the structural political economy approach, which, like our own, is based on Gramscian state theory and which views development programmes as interventions in ongoing struggles over the distribution of power and resources between groups operating on unequal institutional terrains shaped by earlier, similar struggles.[3] The state, or any institution, is viewed as 'strategically selective'[4] – structured to favour specific groups, ideologies and political strategies over others. This strategic selectivity emerges and changes through conflicts and compromises between historically specific socio-political coalitions rooted primarily in the political economy – classes, class fractions, distributional coalitions and other social groups, such as ethnic or religious organisations.[5] We have adopted this broad analytic perspective while arguing that, in the context of international intervention, it has to be coupled with an analysis of the politics of scale.

As our three case study chapters show, scalar strategies are crucial to both the ways donors attempt to implement their programmes and to recipient groups' responses. Donors often seek to rescale policymaking into the parts of the bureaucracy they control that are insulated from domestic political or popular interference, which is viewed as pernicious and a hindrance to good governance. Recipients respond to this in various ways, but especially through efforts to selectively admit or constrain particular programmes or aspects thereof, in a manner that promotes their own interests and marginalises their rivals. Especially important are the scalar strategies of national governments, given that donor interventions cannot usurp recipients' sovereignty and therefore

[2] Belloni 2012; Mac Ginty 2011; Richmond and Mitchell 2012.
[3] Hutchison et al. 2014. [4] Jessop 2008. [5] Hewison et al. 1993: 4–5.

must rely on some cooperation from recipients. Our main contribution in this book is to identify this politics of scale as a crucial aspect of struggles over the outcomes of international intervention programmes and develop an analytic framework for explaining how it affects the outcomes of international interventions in given contexts.

Borrowing from Brenner,[6] we have defined the politics of scale as the 'contestation over the construction of scales, as well as differentiation and ordering among various scales'. In political geography, 'scale' refers to vertically differentiated, hierarchised social, political and economic spaces, each denoting 'the arena and moment, both discursively and materially, where socio-spatial power relations are contested and compromises are negotiated and regulated'.[7] The scalar arrangement of political life is always contested because different scales afford different configurations of actors, power, resources and political opportunity structures.[8] Hence, rescaling – or the attempt to shift power to a specific scale and associated mode of governance – is frequently contested because it can alter the power balance on a given issue and potentially change political outcomes.[9]

Our grounding in Gramscian state theory allows us to identify the broader socio-political context in which the politics of scale takes place and pinpoint the structures favouring specific political and societal groups over others in particular moments in time. Indeed, as we have explained in our case studies, coalitions engaged in rescaling efforts – or in resisting these – reflect power relations in state and society and the position of political elites and bureaucracies within this. Overall, our approach allows us to explain: (1) how and why some donor initiatives are selectively supported or resisted by recipients, as well as the likelihood of either action to succeed; (2) the scalar strategies attempted by donors and recipients, as well as the emergence of alliances; (3) which societal and political groups benefit from the governance outcomes of given intervention programmes; and (4) how the structures that underpin power relations survive, transform or collapse in particular historical moments, specifically in the context of international intervention.

Below we compare the key findings from our case studies, we analyse and reflect on some cross-cutting conclusions and identify the potential policymaking implications.

[6] Brenner 2001: 599–600. [7] Swyngedouw 1997: 140.
[8] Hameiri and Jones 2015. [9] Gough 2004.

Key Findings

We provide three in-depth case study chapters in the book – Solomon Islands, Cambodia and the Indonesian province of Aceh – each focussing on donor-promoted public administration reform (PAR) programmes, a core aspect of most PSBIs. All three cases clearly demonstrate the significance of scalar strategies – especially the selective adoption and rejection of PAR projects – in shaping the outcomes of conflicts over the implementation and outcomes of particular interventions.

In Chapter 3 we look at the PAR programmes attempted in Solomon Islands via the Australian-led RAMSI and the subsequent SIGOV programme. Our findings show that donors have sought to rescale many core state functions beyond domestic political control, but that only programmes that benefit the elites dominating the national scale have been fully implemented. In other words, nationally dominant elites have successfully adopted or thwarted donor programmes, or aspects thereof, to suit their interests, despite the considerable resources at the donors' disposal relative to the size of the overall economy and the government's budget.

In Solomon Islands we identified the national scale as dominant, and explained that this dominance is perpetuated by a dual process of centralisation and redistribution of resources. A relatively cohesive group of nationally powerful elites has been able to centralise rents from extractive economic activities occurring in the provinces – mainly logging – then redistribute some of these resources back to electoral constituencies around the country – many of which are in remote areas – in discretionary ways that reinforce the dominance of the national scale. This socio-political structure, as well as its scalar manifestations, is rooted in the uneven development patterns cemented during the British colonial period and reinforced post-independence with the logging boom from the 1980s.

Most recently, the national scale's dominance has been strengthened via the use of Constituency Development Funds (CDFs): large amounts of money assigned to MPs to spend on development in their constituencies. As we have shown, the rapid growth of CDFs has ironically been enabled through the significant growth in state revenue, which itself is an outcome of a successful donor-led intervention that, in this case, national elites have allowed and supported. Indeed, the rapid growth of

CDFs has served to undermine the popular localisation strategy of weaker groups in Solomon Islands, who have attempted to shift control over resources down to the provincial scale via constitutional reform. In this context, unsurprisingly, donor rescaling efforts to improve the transparency of CDFs' management have been vigorously resisted and have so far failed.

In Cambodia, analysed in Chapter 4, the national scale is also dominant, a process beginning with the post-Khmer Rouge, Vietnamese-backed regime's attempts to maintain central control over the country's territory in the context of international isolation and an ongoing civil war in the borderlands. This period saw the ruling Kampuchean People's Revolutionary Party, later renamed the Cambodian People's Party (CPP), use patronage to develop a network of loyal local leaders who could maintain control over populations in many areas of the country. We have explained that, until recently, the CPP elites at the national scale perpetuated their dominance by selectively adopting donor reform programmes to support their related dual strategies: centralised control over lucrative economic sectors, especially natural resource exploitation, and localised support for ongoing control of village- or commune-level politics in order to secure electoral domination despite the growing popularity of opposition parties in the cities.

The two strategies, at least for a period, had been mutually supportive since money collected through natural resource exploitation and other developmental strategies was crucial for the patronage politics underpinning the CPP's rural domination. We have argued, however, that changes in Cambodia's political economy in recent years appear to have increased inter-scalar conflict, weakening the CPP's hold over the countryside.

Over the past decade, the increasing mobility of villagers, especially moving into cities to work in garment factories, along with significant improvements in transportation and communication technologies, have weakened the capacity of village heads to ensure that their communities continue to vote for the CPP. These changes have combined with growing popular discontent over the exploitation of natural resources, which has increasingly encroached on more populous regions, and corruption in government and public administration to produce a relatively underwhelming electoral performance for the CPP in the 2013 elections. The party is now under pressure to increase its popular legitimacy without losing its close relationship with the country's business elite and entrepreneurial military.

In this context, some in the party are advocating a turn to neoliberal PAR measures, focused on promoting efficiency in service delivery as a legitimation strategy. This has resulted in limited reform, along the lines donors had previously advocated unsuccessfully for years, accompanied by increasingly intense contestation within the national scale and across scales, which limits the reforms' efficacy. For example, although the CPP has implemented significant salary increases for civil servants, its programmes aimed at promoting efficiency and better service delivery have been contested and partly stymied by a public administration in which personal income-generating opportunities have long been a key benefit and where favouritism and nepotism are widely accepted.

In Chapter 5, we analysed the Aceh Government Transformation Programme (AGTP), the most ambitious programme to rescale the provincial government of the post-conflict and post-disaster Indonesian region of Aceh. We focused on four broad rescaling attempts: two aimed at internationalising the recruitment and training of civil servants via the introduction of a 'fit-and-proper' test, as well as the internationalisation of the agency tasked with training provincial civil servants; and two aimed at rationalising and disciplining access to, and the spending of, budget resource streams via two ad hoc units operating outside the usual bureaucratic apparatus. We explained that the first two rescaling attempts were rejected by provincial elite groups and therefore largely failed, while the latter two were adopted by provincial elites and were therefore broadly successful.

We have identified two key factors that shaped the outcome of these rescaling attempts. First, the provincial scale has emerged as the most prominent in a context in which inter-scalar conflict remains significant, with powerful societal and political interests dominating the national and district scales and seeking to redirect resources upwards or downwards. We have traced the rise of the provincial scale to the 2005 peace agreement signed between the national government in Jakarta and the Free Aceh Movement (GAM). This has rescaled control over resources to the Aceh provincial government, shattering the uneven, Jakarta-centric distribution of benefits from development that had characterised inter-scalar relations since the establishment of the Indonesian state in 1945. Second, GAM elites have turned on each other in their quest for political and economic control of the province. Indeed, provincial elites are fragmented and see the control of the provincial bureaucracy and budget as essential for establishing and maintaining patronage networks, which are necessary for holding political power. This is the context in which decisions whether to adopt or reject good governance reforms have been made by provincial elites.

We have shown, for example, that Aceh's first popularly elected governor, Irwandi, co-opted the 'fit-and-proper' test to install his trusted allies in the administration under the guise of reform, but he did not support the rescaling of the training of civil servants, as this brought him no immediate political benefits. On the other hand, both Irwandi and his successor, Zaini, supported two ad hoc agencies: the *Tim Otsus Migas*, which was an attempt to ease inter-scalar tensions with district elites over the control of budget resource streams, and Unit P2K – arguably the donors' most successful rescaling effort in Aceh – which focused on monitoring provincial government agencies and hence providing the leadership with a greater capacity to scrutinise the workings of a bureaucracy they did not trust.

Cross-Cutting Conclusions and Broader Reflections

The findings summarised above lead us to some cross-cutting conclusions and broader reflections of significance to the wider debate over the interaction between international interventions and local politics.

Our first conclusion is that s*calar strategies are inherent in PSBIs and pursued by both donors and recipients*. PSBIs' aims, in essence, entail strategies to rescale key governance institutions and processes in recipient states to make them more responsive to donors' good governance agenda. This transpired in our three case studies. In Solomon Islands, donors rescaled the Ministry of Finance and Treasury (MOFT) and established the Core Economic Working Group (CEWG), among other initiatives. Donors dominated the CEWG, which aimed at monitoring the Solomon Islands government's implementation of the Economic and Financial Reform Programme (EFRP) – a matrix of policy objectives and benchmarks relating to economic and financial policy, set by the IMF and adopted through the CEWG framework.

Our case studies have also shown, though, that groups in recipient states and societies often respond to donor scalar strategies with counter-scalar strategies. In Cambodia, partly in response to donors' democratisation and decentralisation drives, the CPP rescaled political contestations to the commune level, which it was effectively able to control. In Aceh, the provincial governor used the AGTP to rescale decision-making away from the Jakarta-friendly bureaucracy he distrusted, and towards 60 advisors he hand-picked.

Our second conclusion is that *PSBI outcomes are best analysed at project or programme level.* Analyses of how international interventions affect a sector (health, education, finance management) or, indeed, a recipient state miss the uneven ways through which different aspects of international programming affect power relations within recipient states and societies, and therefore the uneven ways in which recipients react to different aspects of the intervention, leading to variable outcomes. This analysis has to be grounded, however, in a broader analysis of the underlying power relations pertaining within given societies.

Observers have, for instance, claimed that donors have been unsuccessful in introducing significant good governance measures in Solomon Islands despite the substantial funds channelled there.[10] While we do not disagree with this overall assessment, our project-focused analysis offers more precise explanations of where donors have been successful and where they have not, and why. For example, a sector-level analysis of Solomon Islands' MOFT would struggle to appreciate the uneven results donors have achieved, and why reforms of the Custom and Excise division have partly failed, while those of the Internal Revenue Division have succeeded remarkably. Likewise in Aceh, although we agree with the consensus that corruption and patronage remain pervasive in public administration,[11] our study of the AGTP has shown that donors have been able to introduce an ad-hoc system to monitor the provincial budget's disbursement. This has rescaled monitoring beyond the sole reach of local agencies and introduced some of the 'transparency' and 'efficiency' sought by donors.[12]

Our third conclusion is that *recipient states maintain a crucial scale manager role*. This function is usually exercised by the national government, which can decide whether to accept an intervention in the first

[10] Fraenkel et al. 2014; Haque 2013; Hayward-Jones 2014.
[11] Fadillah 2016; Heriansyah 2015; *Serambi Indonesia* 2015c.
[12] Rachman 2012: 34.

place. It could also be exercised by other administrative layers of the state, if they are the target of the intervention. Similar to the findings of Hameiri and Jones,[13] who investigated the scalar strategies inherent in the governance arrangements to counter transnational security threats, our case studies have demonstrated that total rejection of international intervention is rare, but that recipients often mediate interventions via selectively adopting aspects of intervention programmes while rejecting others.

In Solomon Islands, the national government has maintained its scale manager function throughout the RAMSI and post-RAMSI intervention, despite its heavy dependency on aid. In Cambodia, following the end of the Vietnamese invasion in 1989, the CPP was in no position to reject international aid, but the party saw the UN peace plan – with its provisions for multi-party elections – as a threat to be negotiated rather than a binding solution. The CPP reluctantly adopted electoral democracy, but mediated this via its network at the village level, which harnessed a range of strategies, including coercion, to ensure electoral success. Later, when donors pushed for decentralisation, the CPP elite introduced commune-level elections, thus rescaling political contestation to a scale it could again comfortably control. In Aceh the scale manager function was first exercised by the Indonesian national government, which opened up Aceh to international intervention following the tsunami, lifting the ban that had been imposed because of the conflict on independent international observers, foreign correspondents, diplomats and international human rights organisations. The provincial government later negotiated the detail of the AGTP, with Irwandi dictating the partner organisation for the AGTP and the key components of the project, including the controversial *Tim Asistensi*.

Importantly, our case studies have also shown that the scale manager function is often a tool elites deploy predominately vis-à-vis other societal and political groups that threaten their political or economic interests. One constant finding that has emerged from our Solomon Islands study is, for example, that the selective adoption or rejection of PAR projects by national elites has been aimed at undermining localisation challenges. Similarly, in Cambodia, the CPP's rescaling of political competition to the commune level was, first and foremost, aimed

[13] Hameiri and Jones 2015.

at disempowering the opposition parties that emerged in the context of a new constitution enshrining a multi-party electoral system. In Aceh, *Tim Asistensi* was established to bypass the local bureaucracy, seen as pro-Jakarta, and to empower advisors hand-picked by Irwandi.

Our fourth conclusion, which follows from the one above, is that *elite groups, at the most dominant scale, almost invariably claim the benefits of PSBIs' initiatives*. In Solomon Islands and Cambodia we identified the national scale as the dominant one, while in Aceh the provincial scale was dominant. In each of the three case studies the elite groups at the dominant scale could harness most, if not all, of the benefits of reforms. In Solomon Islands, we have shown that international interventions have not only failed to alter the dominance of the national elite, but have rather contributed to strengthening its hold on power by providing more resources with which to defeat alternative political agendas. In Cambodia, donor-driven democratisation and decentralisation drives have been harnessed by the CPP in a manner that has added electoral legitimacy to its control of the political and economic landscape. In Aceh, provincial elites were able to harness the fit-and-proper test to their benefit, make full use of *Tim Asistensi* and benefit from the rescaling of the monitoring of government units' budget expenditure to an ad hoc system, as this allowed the provincial government to assert greater control over other government units. This finding underlines the difficulties in bypassing the existing power structures while pushing for meaningful reform, and the resulting need to pursue tactical alliances and limited, targeted reform. We shall elaborate this point in the policymaking implications section.

Our fifth conclusion is that the *cohesiveness of the elites at the targeted scale is often a decisive factor in the relative success or failure of PSBIs to attain their stated objectives*. This conclusion emerged from the different dynamics we examined in our case studies. Our findings in Solomon Islands show that interventions aimed at the national scale were rejected or co-opted by relatively cohesive national elites. To be sure, there are many apparent fractures and factionalism among Solomon Islands' national political elite, but given the overwhelming reliance of all national politicians on a system that centralises rents from extractive activities within Honiara and then redistributes some resources back to the periphery to win elections, this elite's *class* interests are remarkably cohesive. In Cambodia, we have shown that national elites are relatively fragmented, with opposition to the CPP located largely in Phnom Penh. But the CPP has been able to bypass the opposition, and co-opt donors' initiatives, by rescaling political contestation to the commune level. Important changes to the broad political economy of the country, though, have recently weakened the ability of the CPP to rely on commune chiefs to legitimise the party's hold on power, and have partly refocused political contestation at the national level. This is at core of the CPP's own PAR initiatives, which have included a lukewarm turn to donor-advocated PAR measures, focused on promoting efficiency in service delivery, as a legitimation strategy.

On the other hand, our case study in Aceh has demonstrated that fragmented elites can allow the introduction of limited reforms by donors. The division within GAM was one of the reasons that allowed the UNDP to forge the tactical alliance with Irwandi underpinning the AGTP. While the project did not deliver on all of its aims, it did introduce some important reforms, especially in monitoring the budget expenditure of provincial government units. In other words, this finding indicates that if elites are fragmented, they are potentially more amenable to compromises with donors' requests. If they are cohesive, they can easily thwart donor efforts.

Our sixth conclusion is that *inter-scalar conflict may facilitate reforms, especially if no scale is overtly dominant*. The Aceh case study is emblematic. The 2005 peace agreement led to the relative rise in prominence of the provincial scale in Aceh. However, provincial elites are dependent on the support of elite groups at the district level, and their power is constrained by restrictions imposed at the national level. We explained that these contested inter-scalar relations opened the door to political compromises and to the introduction of some reforms. The clearest example was the *Tim Otsus Migas*, an ad hoc team tasked with mediating the conflicting interests of provincial and district elite groups over the control of budget funds. As the provincial government could not afford to antagonise district elites, the AGTP was able to support the institutionalisation of predefined processes to access these funds and develop spending objectives. These have, to some extent, rescaled fund allocation beyond the local, patronage-ridden socio-political context. The degree of inter-scalar conflict in Aceh differs substantially from what we found in the Solomon Islands, where Honiara-based national elites are overtly dominant and have easily been able to co-opt and deflect any attempt to shift control over resources to the provincial level. Cambodia presented a different landscape altogether. Political opposition to the CPP is located at the national scale, while support is located at the village scale, which is largely subordinated to the national scale via the CPP's patronage-based political machine. There is thus no substantial interscalar conflict, though this could be in the process of changing.

Our seventh conclusion is that *states and donors are far from monolithic and alliances transcend the state–society divide*. In each of our case studies we have noted that struggles over rescaling attempts involve conflicts between different parts of the states, linked to different societal actors.[14] In Solomon Islands, the government's channelling of funds into CDFs is a strategy to weaken those calling for localisation via constitutional reform, and is pursued through an alliance that includes many sub-nationally based actors who are empowered via the same political-economic structures. Similarly, in Cambodia the localisation strategy of the CPP is aimed at weakening the political opposition located in the major cities, while benefiting from the links between the CPP and business elites exploiting natural resources. In Aceh, the provincial government and the district administrations struggled over control of budget funds, and both attempted to gain the support of the central government while mobilising their respective support-bases among the former rebels. Furthermore, donors are also on occasion far from monolithic and may partake in transversal alliances to further their interests and agendas. In Solomon Islands, the overwhelming dominance of Australia within RAMSI and subsequent aid programming has ensured considerable cohesion among donors. In Aceh, however, the AGTP resulted from a close, tactical alliance between Irwandi, the UNDP and Kuntoro, the head of the national ad hoc agency in charge of post-tsunami reconstruction until May 2009. This alliance rescaled decision-making to the provincial level, weakening the power of the World Bank, the EU and GTZ, which were pushing for a different project to support Irwandi.

Finally, our eighth conclusion is that *PSBIs are intrinsically neither good nor bad. Rather, we can only evaluate them normatively against the particular ways in which their various components end up advancing specific interests, agendas or ideologies.*[15] While it is common to assume that donor PAR programmes are normatively desirable because

[14] See also Hameiri and Jones 2014. [15] See also Hameiri and Jones 2014.

they advance laudable objectives such as transparency, accountability or efficiency, our findings show that outcomes often greatly diverge from those intended, given the crucial role of socio-political conflict and scalar strategies in shaping what actually happens to these programmes. Rather than evaluating PSBIs against what they set out to achieve, we argue that these interventions must be evaluated against what they actually achieve in terms of their effects on the distribution of power and resources among recipients. This should encourage greater caution and attention to political analysis in the design and implementation of reform.

Policymaking Implications

Our findings have considerable implications for planning and implementing PSBIs. In particular, we argue that interveners need to: (1) seek, wherever possible, tactical, instrumental alliances with elites or powerful groups to introduce limited, incremental reforms; (2) understand better the structures underpinning power relations, not only in the target states and societies as a whole but also around given institutions or policy areas; and (3) pay attention to the scalar dimension of interventions. While these obviously intertwine, we expand on each individually below.

Interveners should seek wherever possible tactical alliances with elites or powerful groups to advance limited, incremental reforms. Our case studies have shown that blueprints for grand reform fail to reach many of their objectives. This is indeed the sense provided by most large-scale reviews of PAR, as outlined in Chapter 1. In Solomon Islands, the rescaling of the MOFT was only selectively adopted. In Cambodia, the rescaling of forestry governance completely faltered. In Aceh, the internationalisation of the recruitment and training of the bureaucracy went nowhere. This is unsurprising, based on what we have shown: elites are unwilling to support reforms that challenge their hold on power and, when their positions are relatively coherent, tend to use scalar strategies effectively to deflect damaging reforms. We thus concur with Hutchison et al.,[16] who first suggested the need to pursue tactical alliances even with elites who are not necessarily reform-

[16] Hutchison et al. 2014: 130–45.

minded but with whom interveners may find a convergence of interest for a specific goal. Tactical alliances are by nature instrumental, volatile and short-lived. Thus, 'reform objectives need to be manageable as a series of limited steps, each of which delivers some concrete outcome'.[17] Below we argue that structural political economy analyses that also account for the politics of scale can help identify inter-elite conflicts and their scalar dimensions, and hence assist donors to recognise who to pursue tactical alliances with, when and how.

PBSIs have better chances of success if based on comprehensive structural political economy analyses, aimed not only at the macro-societal level, but specific to particular institutions and policy areas. Here we again build on Hutchison et al.'s insight that PSBIs are 'interventions into socio-economic realities and relations'[18] that will invariably be threatening to the interests of some groups, while advantageous to others. Structural political economy analyses help in explaining the emergence and transformations of the processes, practices and relationships through which power is exercised and resources distributed. In other words, they can help explain the strategic selectivity of the state or of institutions, which as we have argued invariably favours specific groups, interests and ideologies over others.[19] We accept that compromises are often unavoidable, and that donors do not have full control of project design. But we contend that structural political economy offers a better understanding of the terrain PSBIs enter and 'can enable donors to be more strategically informed in their decisions'.[20]

At its simplest, this political economy analysis can identify what not to do, which – as Hutchison et al. remark – 'is important'.[21] Indeed, it can prevent donors from strengthening particularly predatory elites, and help avoid wasting efforts and resources on projects that are doomed to fail. In our cases, a structural political economy analysis of Solomon Islands would have emphasised the high likelihood that initiatives aimed at curtailing the capacity of national elites to control and redistribute logging rents would be rejected. In Aceh, it would immediately have alerted donors to the fact that deep reforms of the bureaucracy were likely to be resisted.

[17] Hutchison et al. 2014: 147. [18] Hutchison et al. 2014: 72.
[19] Jessop 2008. [20] Hutchison et al. 2014: 151.
[21] Hutchison et al. 2014: 151.

But structural political economy analyses can also help identify structural changes in the target states and societies that may open the door to some reform. The key is to identify possible fissures in the elite constellation and what powerful groups, at the national, provincial or district level, may be amenable to support moderate reforms in such a changing landscape. We have hinted at such possible changes in each of our case studies. In Solomon Islands, we explain that the main hurdle to reform is the cohesiveness of the national elite. We have noted, though, that this could be undermined in the near future as mining is set to supplant large-scale logging as a key driver of the economy. This may displace the existing power relations and possibly lead to a fragmentation of the elite and to increasingly successful resistance from below. In Cambodia, we have argued that urbanisation and technological development are progressively weakening the ability of the CPP to control commune- and village-level politics. This has already led to increasing political competition at the national elections, with the CPP needing to engage more with other political and societal forces; and increasing resistance in the countryside, where the patronage links established by the CPP are no longer able to effectively control discontent. Here, a structural political economy analysis could help interveners map elite interests at various scales and tailor reform programmes that take advantage of the fissures.

In Aceh, we have explained that there are already significant fissures among elites at the national, provincial and district levels, and ongoing conflict among provincial elite groups. Interventions could exploit such divisions to advance limited, targeted reforms through tactical alliances. In addition, more fissures may emerge as the structures underpinning the power relations in the province are set to be shaken up in the next decade as the Otsus and Mingas funds expire in 2028. These funds currently account for about half of the region's revenue and have made control of the provincial administration, and through it of the budget, an imperative for provincial elites. If the Aceh economy grows and diversifies in the next decade, the exhaustion of the Otsus and Mingas funds may lessen provincial elites' eagerness to control the bureaucracy and usher opportunities for some public administration reforms. If the economy does not grow and diversify according to expectations, however, the end of the Otsus and Mingas funds may lead to increasing political conflict over the dwindling budget and possibly even violence. This could weaken GAM's stronghold on politics and broaden the spectrum of elite groups and possible tactical alliances.

Interveners must think in terms of scale, and not treat recipients as a spatially undifferentiated terrain. Thinking in terms of scale means, first and foremost, acknowledging that interventions take place in contested social, political and economic territorial spaces and that each space – or scale – is organised in ways that reinforce or challenge a particular distribution of power and resources. Scales are thus never value-neutral, and hence rescaling is not value-neutral either: PSBIs are interventions in the power relations within and *across* scales.

Scalar analyses, when combined with attention to the power relations associated with broader political economy structures, can help by identifying: (1) the dominant scale within a given context, and the power structures underpinning it; (2) the degree of inter-scalar conflict, and the issues driving it; and (3) the composition, interests and ideologies of the elite groups at different scales, and how they relate to each other. These assessments can provide useful information to develop reform initiatives that exploit inter-scalar conflicts to introduce reform. Scalar assessments are particularly relevant in the developing world where most states have pursued some kind of decentralisation, thus creating the conditions for conflicting interests between elites dominating different scales.[22]

This in practice means interrogating closely the socio-political bases of claims to national or local authority or legitimacy, as well as any claim to power and resources based on a scalar demarcation of political action. It also means paying close attention to how various reform programmes play out in terms of the politics of scale – how they reinforce or weaken claims made by different groups, which have a scalar dimension. In Cambodia, for instance, the CPP's reliance on control over the countryside for electoral domination has meant that the decentralisation programme promoted by donors was highly unlikely to advance the agenda of bringing governance closer to those being governed, in order to improve transparency, accountability and service delivery. So while donors welcomed the CPP's introduction of commune elections in 2002 as a positive step towards decentralisation, they failed to grasp that this had actually undermined the democratisation drive.

[22] Falleti 2010; Ichimura and Bahl 2009; Shah 2006.

In Indonesia, on the other hand, decentralisation took place in the midst of a deep crisis of the authoritarian New Order regime, which had seen long-term ruler Suharto removed from power in 1998. Suharto was especially adept at using centrally organised relations of patronage with business elites and the military to maintain a Jakarta-dominated political system that fully subjugated sub-national political units to demands from the centre. Yet, rather than fundamentally transform Indonesian politics, decentralisation has essentially involved the localisation of the same socio-political structures, which have supported the ascendancy of typically predatory politico-business networks.[23] In Aceh the situation has been complicated by the broadened special autonomy granted after the signing of the 2005 peace agreement that empowered the provincial government, while Indonesia's decentralisation process largely bypasses the province and empowers districts and cities. In Aceh, the inter-scalar tensions produced by these partly conflicting dynamics, as we have seen, provide opportunities for harnessing localisation and centralisation agendas towards limited reform.

Thinking in terms of scale also helps interveners identify, and possibly counter, the scalar strategies that elite groups may pursue to attain their own objectives. In Solomon Islands, for example, although it is highly unlikely, given the context described here, that RAMSI and SIGOV could overcome the united front presented by a cohesive national elite, the programmes could have pursued more limited reforms at sub-national scales that could have perhaps yielded better outcomes in terms of service delivery, rather than continuing to insist on central state-building in Honiara. Although such programmes would probably not have advanced good governance, they could have delivered limited tangible improvements in material conditions for people living in provincial areas often seen as excluded by the central state.

Concluding Comments

As we write this conclusion, the prevailing sentiment among many scholars and practitioners is that the age of highly intrusive international state-building is unwinding following its high point in the first

23 Hadiz 2010.

two decades of the post-Cold War era.[24] Indeed, the debates with which we have engaged are clear indications of the decline of the triumphalism that had accompanied the onset of the age of intervention in the early 1990s. Liberal peace-building, it has been argued for almost a decade now, is in crisis.[25] And just as we send this manuscript off to the publisher, the world is stunned by the unexpected news that Donald Trump has been elected United States President. Although his foreign policy agenda is currently largely unknown, his election appears to only reinforce the broader sentiment that liberal interventionism is in decline. Adding to this, the fiscal woes of many developed states have had a detrimental effect on overall aid spending. The rapid development of China and other rising powers has also been taken by many to suggest a growing challenge to the capacity and legitimacy of Western governments to undertake the kinds of interventions that became routine during the post-Cold War era. Yet, it would, in our view, be a mistake to conclude that international interventionism, designed to ensure that particular modes of governance and institutions emerge across borders, will dissipate as a result. There are several reasons to think the opposite is true and that there has never been a more important time to understand how international interventions and local politics interact.

First, our case studies have clearly shown that PSBIs can take subtle and complex forms, extending well beyond the headline-grabbing large-scale interventions of the earlier part of the post-Cold War era. Second, although 'saving strangers' is perhaps a declining priority for cash-strapped and increasingly populist governments, many of the interventions we see are driven by security considerations, which remain a priority. Indeed, PSBIs have arguably always been primarily concerned with making recipient states more resilient and able to deal with potentially transnational security issues than about supporting good governance and market-led development.[26] For example, though the United States and its allies are no longer engaged in attempted large-scale PAR in Iraq, they continue to be deeply entrenched there as part of the fight against the Islamic State. And although rising powers like China often profess their attachment to the principle of non-interference in the domestic affairs of other states, evidence shows

[24] E.g. Mazarr 2014; Wallis and Wesley 2016. [25] Hameiri 2014a.
[26] See Hameiri 2010.

that as elites in those countries have developed transnational interests, there has been a clear tendency to intervene across borders in various ways to support desired political outcomes.[27]

Crucially, as these interventions by rising powers tend to take place alongside, and often in contention with, ongoing interventions by traditional donors, this development appears to be introducing greater fragmentation among intervening actors, and hence provides both opportunities and challenges to recipients, which our framework can help analyse. This book hence ultimately aims to open up a range of research agendas dedicated to studying the changing and complex, yet crucial, relationship between international and domestic politics in a world that appears to be getting simultaneously smaller and more contested.

[27] Hameiri and Jones 2016.

Bibliography

ABC (2014), 'Floods Used as "Excuse" to Release Funds to MPs – TSI', Australian Broadcasting Corporation, 9 April, available at www.radioaustralia.net.au/international/radio/program/pacific-beat/floods-used-as-excuse-to-release-funds-to-mps-tsi/1292942, accessed 10 November 2016.

Abrahamsen, Rita and Williams, Michael C. (2011), *Security Beyond the State: Private Security in International Politics* (Cambridge: Cambridge University Press).

Acehterkini.com (2015), '28 Paket Proyek Otsus Aceh Belum Tanda-Tangan Kontrak [28 Aceh Special Autonomy Package not Complying with Contracts]'. www.acehterkini.com/2015/11/28-paket-proyek-otsus-aceh-belum-tanda.html, accessed 11 November 2016.

ADB (2004), 'Country Strategy and Program Update (2005–2006): Solomon Islands', (Manila: Asian Development Bank).

Airlangga Pribadi Kusman (2016), 'The Politics of Good Governance in Post-Authoritarian East Java: Intellectuals and Local Power in Indonesia', PhD thesis (Perth: Murdoch University).

Akin, David (2013), *Colonialism, Maasina Rule, and the Origins of Malaitan Kastom* (Honolulu: University of Hawai'i Press).

Alasia, Sam (1997), 'Party Politics and Government in Solomon Islands', *State, Society and Governance in Melanesia Project Discussion Paper 1997/7* (Canberra: Research School of Pacific and Asian Studies, Australian National University).

Allen, Matthew G. (2011), 'The Political Economy of Logging in Solomon Islands', in Ron Duncan and Stephen Pollard (eds.), *Strengthening Pacific Economic Analysis* (Manila and Canberra: Asian Development Bank and the Australian National University).

(2013), *Greed and Grievance: Ex-Militants' Perspectives on the Conflict in Solomon Islands, 1998–2003* (Honolulu: University of Hawai'i Press).

Allen, Matthew G. and Dinnen, Sinclair (2010), 'The North Down Under: Antinomies of Conflict and Intervention in Solomon Islands', *Conflict, Security & Development*, 10 (3), 299–327.

Andrews, Matt (2012), 'The Logical Limits of Best Practice Administrative Solutions in Developing Countries', *Public Administration and Development*, 32 (2), 137–53.

Ansori, M. H. (2012), 'From Insurgency to Bureaucracy: Free Aceh Movement, Aceh Party and the New Face of Conflict', *Stability: International Journal of Security and Development*, 1 (1), 31–44.

Antara (2014), 'Pejabat NTT Belajar Kendali P2 K Di Aceh [NTT Officials to Learn about P2 K Aceh]'. http://aceh.antaranews.com/berita/17182/pejabat-ntt-belajar-kendali-p2k-di-aceh, 25 September, accessed 11 November 2016.

Arbas, Cakra, Jalil, Husni and Suhadi, S. H. (2015), 'Independent Candidates of Regional-Head Election in Aceh', *IOSR Journal of Humanities and Social Science*, 20 (1), 35–42.

Asante, Augustine, Roberts, Graham and Hall, John (2012), 'A Review of Health Leadership and Management Capacity in the Solomon Islands', *Journal of Community Health and Clinical Medicine for the Pacific*, 18 (1), 166–77.

Askhalani, Oleh (2013), 'Birokrasi "Dagang Sap" ala Aceh [Bureaucratic "Horse-Trading" l à la Aceh]', *Serambi Indonesia*. http://aceh.tribunnews.com/2013/02/13/birokrasi-dagang-sap-ala-aceh, 13 February.

Aspinall, Edward (2007), 'From Islamism to Nationalism in Aceh, Indonesia', *Nations and Nationalism*, 13 (2), 245–63.

(2009a), *Islam and Nation: Separatist Rebellion in Aceh, Indonesia* (Stanford, CA: Stanford University Press).

(2009b), 'Combatants to Contractors: The Political Economy of Peace in Aceh', *Indonesia*, 87, 1–34.

(2011), 'Aceh's No Win Election', *Inside Indonesia*. www.insideindonesia.org/aceh-s-no-win-election, October–December.

Aspinall, Edward and Couch, Harold (2003), *The Aceh Peace Process: Why It Failed*, (Washington DC: East-West Center).

Aspinall, Edward, Hillman, Ben and McCawley, Peter (2012), *Governance and Capacity Building in Post-Crisis Aceh*, (Canberra: UNDP).

Associated Press (1998), 'Government Creates National Election Commission', Phnom Penh, 26 January 1998. *Camnews*, camnews@lists.best.com, accessed 27 January 1998.

Atjehpost.co (2014a), 'Masa Anggaran Berakhir, Realisasi APBA Dinas Pendidikan Aceh Masih di Bawah Target [End of Busget Period; Realisation Education Department below Target]'. http://atjehpost.co/berita2/read/Masa-Anggaran-Berakhir-Realisasi-APBA-Dinas-Pendidikan-Aceh-Masih-di-Bawah-Target-17306, 19 December.

Atjehpost.co (2014b), 'Pelabuhan Penyeberangan Meulaboh-Sinabang Terus Dipacu [Construction Meulaboh-Sinabang Bridge Still

Ongoing]'. http://atjehpost.co/berita2/read/Pelabuhan-Penyeberangan-Meulaboh-Sinabang-Terus-Dipacu-10849, 9 September.

Babovic, Marija and Vukovic, Danilo (2015), 'Cambodia: A Survey of Livelihood Strategies and Expectations for the Future', (Phnom Penh: Asia Foundation), http://asiafoundation.org/resources/pdfs/Cambodia LivelihoodsandFutureExpecationsSurvey.pdf, accessed 10 November 2016.

Baliga, Ananth (2015), 'Cambodians Flock to the Net', *Phnom Penh Post*, 12 March 2015, www.phnompenhpost.com/cambodians-flock-net, accessed 19 August 2015.

Bappenas (2005), *Master Plan for the Rehabilitation and Reconstruction of the Regions and Communities of the Province of Nanggroe Aceh Darussalam and the Islands of Nias, Province of North Sumatera*, (Jakarta: Republic of Indonesia).

Bappenas and International Donor Community (2005), *Indonesia: Preliminary Damage and Loss Assessment*, (Jakarta: Republic of Indonesia).

Barbara, Julien (2014), 'From Intervention to Partnership – Prospects for Development Partnership in Solomon Islands after RAMSI', *Asia and the Pacific Policy Studies*, 1 (2), 395–408.

Barnett, Michael N. (1997), 'Bringing in the New World Order: Liberalism, Legitimacy, and the United Nations', *World Politics*, 49 (4), 526–51.

Barron, Patrick and Clark, Samuel (2006), *Decentralizing Inequality? Center-Periphery Relations, Local Governance, and Conflict in Aceh*, (Jakarta: World Bank).

Batley, James (2005), 'The Role of RAMSI in Solomon Islands: Rebuilding the State, Supporting Peace', Paper delivered by James Batley, RAMSI Special Coordinator at the Peace, Justice and Reconciliation Conference (Brisbane: Australian Government, Department of Foreign Affairs and Trade).

Batley, Richard (2004), 'The Politics of Service Delivery Reform', *Development and Change*, 35 (1), 31–56.

Batley, Richard, McCourt, Willy and McLoughlin, Claire (2012), 'Editorial: The Politics and Governance of Public Services in Developing Countries', *Public Management Review*, 14 (2), 131–44.

Bellamy, Alex J., Williams, Paul and Griffin, Stuart (2004), *Understanding Peacekeeping* (Cambridge: Polity Press).

Belloni, Roberto (2012), 'Hybrid Peace Governance: Its Emergence and Significance', *Global Governance: A Review of Multilateralism and International Organizations*, 18 (1), 21–38.

Bennett, Judith (1987), *Wealth of the Solomons: A History of a Pacific Archipelago, 1800–1978* (Honolulu: Hawai'i University Press).

(2000), *Pacific Forest: A History of Resource Control and Contest in Solomon Islands, c. 1800–1997* (Cambridge and Leiden: White Horse Press and Brill Academic Publishers).

(2002), 'Roots of Conflict in Solomon Islands – Though Much Is Taken Much Abides: Legacies of Tradition and Colonialism', *State, Society and Governance in Melanesia Discussion Paper 2002/5* (Canberra: Research School of Pacific and Asian Studies, Australian National University).

Berger, Mark T. and Weber, Heloise (2014), *Rethinking the Third World: International Development and World Politics* (Basingstoke: Palgrave Macmillan).

Bergling, Per, Wennerstroem, Erik O. and Sannerholm, Richard Zajac (2010), 'Rule of Law in Public Administration: Problems and Ways Ahead in Post-Conflict Peace-Building', *Hague Journal on the Rule of Law*, 2 (2), 171–202.

Bickerton, Christopher J. (2007), 'State-Building: Exporting State Failure', in Christopher J. Bickerton, Philip Cunliffe and Alexander Gourevitch (eds.), *Politics Without Sovereignty: A Critique of Contemporary International Relations* (London: University College Press), 93–111.

Bickerton, Christopher J., Cunliffe, Philip and Gourevitch, Alexander (2007), 'Introduction: The Unholy Alliance Against Sovereignty', in Christopher J. Bickerton, Philip Cunliffe and Alexander Gourevitch (eds.), *Politics Without Sovereignty: A Critique of Contemporary International Politics* (London: University College London Press), 1–19.

Biddle, Stephen (2008), Stabilizing Iraq from the Bottom Up, Statement before the Committee on Foreign Relations United States Senate, Second Session, 110th Congress (Washington, DC).

Bivar, Caroline (2005), 'Emerging from the Shadows: The EU's Role in Conflict Resolution in Indonesia', *European Policy Paper* 44 (Brussels: European Policy Centre).

Bliesemann de Guevara, Berit (2010), 'Introduction: The Limits of Statebuilding and the Analysis of State-Formation', *Journal of Intervention and Statebuilding*, 4 (2), 111–28.

(2012), 'Introduction: Statebuilding and State-formation', in Berit Bliesemann de Guevara (ed.), *Statebuilding and State-Formation: The Political Sociology of Intervention* (Abingdon and New York: Routledge), 1–19.

Blomberg, Matt and Roeum, Van (2015), 'Grand Concessions: The Vietnamese People's Army Has Quietly Assumed Control of Nearly 40,000 Hectares of Land in Ratanakiri'. *Cambodia Daily*, 24 December, www.cambodia daily.com/grandconcessions/, accessed 10 November 2016.

Boege, Volker, Brown, M. Anne, Clements, Kevin P. and Nolan, Anna (2008), 'On Hybrid Political Orders and Emerging States: State Formation in the

Context of "Fragility"', in *Berghof Handbook Dialogue No. 8* (Berlin: Berghof Research Center for Constructive Conflict Management).

Boege, Volker, Brown, M. Anne and Clements, Kevin P. (2009), 'Hybrid Political Orders, Not Fragile States', *Peace Review*, 21 (1), 13–21.

Booth, David (2011), 'Aid, Institutions and Governance: What Have We Learned?', *Development Policy Review*, 29 (S1), S5–S26.

Boutros-Ghali, Boutros (1992), 'An Agenda for Peace: Preventive Diplomacy, Peacemaking and Peace-Keeping', A/47/277 – S/24111 (New York: United Nations).

Bratton, Michael and van de Walle, Nicolas (1994), 'Neopatrimonial Regimes and Political Transitions in Africa', *World Politics*, 46 (04), 453–89.

Bräutigam, Deborah, Fjeldstad, Odd-Helge and Moore, Mick (2008), *Taxation and State-Building in Developing Countries: Capacity and Consent*.

Brenner, Neil (2001), 'The Limits to Scale? Methodological Reflections on Scalar Structuration', *Progress in Human Geography*, 25 (4), 591–614.

Brenner, Neil and Elden, Stuart (2009), 'Henri Lefebvre on State, Space, Territory', *International Political Sociology*, 3 (4), 353–77.

Brenner, Neil, Jessop, Bob, Jones, Martin and MacLeod, Gordon (2003), 'Introduction: State Space in Question', in Neil Brenner, Bob Jessop, Martin Jones and Gordon MacLeod (eds.), *State/Space: A Reader* (Malden, MA: Blackwell Publishing), 1–26.

Brigg, Morgan (2009), '*Wantokism* and State Building in Solomon Islands: A Response to Fukuyama', *Pacific Economic Bulletin*, 24 (3), 148–61.

Brinkerhoff, Derick W. (2005), 'Organisational Legitimacy, Capacity and Capacity Development', *Discussion Paper No. 58A* (Maastricht: European Centre for Development Policy Management).

(2008), 'The State and International Development Management: Shifting Tides, Changing Boundaries, and Future Directions', *Public Administration Review*, 68 (6), 985–1001.

Brinkerhoff, Derick W. and Brinkerhoff, Jennifer M. (2002), 'Governance Reforms and Failed States: Challenges and Implications', *International Review of Administrative Sciences*, 68 (4), 511–31.

Brinkerhoff, Derick W. and Wetterberg, Anna (2013), 'Performance-Based Public Management Reforms: Experience and Emerging Lessons from Service Delivery Improvement in Indonesia', *International Review of Administrative Sciences*, 79 (3), 433–57.

Brinkerhoff, Derick W., Wetterberg, Anna and Dunn, Stephen (2012), 'Service Delivery and Legitimacy in Fragile and Conflict-Affected States: Evidence from Water Services in Iraq', *Public Management Review*, 14 (2), 273–93.

Brown, Graham (2005), 'Horizontal Inequalities, Ethnic Separatism, and Violent Conflict: The Case of Aceh, Indonesia', *Human Development Report Office Occasional Paper* (Jakarta: UNDP).

Brown, Taylor, Rudland, Emily and Bazeley, Peter (2012), *Working Collaboratively for Economic Reform in Solomon Islands: A Case Study of the Core Economic Working Group* (Canberra: Office of Development Effectiveness, Australian Agency for International Development).

BRR (2009), *10 Management Lessons for Host Governments Coordinating Post-Disaster Reconstruction* (Jakarta: Badan Rehabilitasi dan Rekonstruksi NAD-Nias).

Buehler, Michael (2011), 'Indonesia's Law on Public Services: Changing State–Society Relations or Continuing Politics as Usual?', *Bulletin of Indonesian Economic Studies*, 47 (1), 65–86.

Burnside, Craig and Dollar, David (1997), 'Aid, Policies, and Growth', *Policy Research Paper* 1777 (Washington DC: World Bank).

Bush, George H. W. (2005), 'New World Order', Speech to Congress, www.al-bab.com/arab/docs/pal/pal10.htm, accessed 9 June 2016.

Cahyono, Heru (2016), 'Evaluasi atas pelaksanaan otonomi khusus Aceh: Gagal menyejahterakan rakyat dan sarat konflik internal [Evaluation of the Implementation of Special Autonomy in Aceh: Failed People's Welfare and Internal Conflicts]', *Jurnal Penelitian Politik*, 9 (2), 1–22.

Cammack, Paul (2004), 'What the World Bank Means by Poverty Reduction, and Why It Matters', *New Political Economy*, 9 (2), 189–211.

Campbell, Susanna, Chandler, David and Sabaratnam, Meera (eds.) (2011), *A Liberal Peace? The Problems and Practices of Peacebuilding* (London and New York: Zed Books).

Carothers, Thomas (1998), 'The Rule of Law Revival', *Foreign Affairs*, 77 (2), 95–106.

Carothers, Thomas and De Gramont, Diane (2013), *Development Aid Confronts Politics: The Almost Revolution* (Washington DC: Carnegie Endowment for International Peace).

Carroll, Toby (2010), *Delusions of Development: The World Bank and the Post-Washington Consensus in Southeast Asia* (Basingstoke: Palgrave Macmillan).

CBSI (2014), 'Annual Report 2013', (Honiara: Central Bank of Solomon Islands).

CCHR (2013), *Cambodia: Land in Conflict. An Overview of the Land Situation* (Phnom Penh: Cambodian Center for Human Rights), http://cchrcambodia.org/admin/media/report/report/english/CCHR%20Report%20%20Cambodia%20Land%20in%20Conflict%20An%20Overview%20of%20the%20Land%20Situation%20ENG.pdf, accessed 10 November 2016.

Cerny, Philip G. (1997), 'Paradoxes of the Competition State: The Dynamics of Political Globalization', *Government and Opposition*, 32 (2), 251–74.

Chabal, Patrick and Daloz, Jean-Pascal (1999), *Africa Works: The Political Instrumentalization of Disorder* (Bloomington: Indiana University Press).

Chayes, Abram and Chayes, Antonia Handler (1995), *The New Sovereignty: Compliance with International Regulatory Agreements* (Cambridge and London: Harvard University Press).

Chhotray, Vasudha and Hulme, David (2009), 'Contrasting Visions for Aid and Governance in the 21st Century: The White House Millennium Challenge Account and DFID's Drivers of Change', *World Development*, 37 (1), 36–49.

Chopra, Jarat and Hohe, Tanja (2004), 'Participatory Intervention', *Global Governance*, 10 (3), 289–305.

Clark, Colin and Levy, Ken (2012), 'Improving Accountability in the Solomon Islands: A Review of Auditor-General Enabling Legislation', *Asia Pacific Law Review*, 20 (1), 45–62.

Cock, Andrew (2016), *Governing Cambodia's Forests: The International Politics of Policy Reform* (Copenhagen: NIAS Press).

Colás, Alejandro (2008), 'Open Doors and Closed Frontiers: The Limits of American Empire', *European Journal of International Relations*, 14 (4), 619–43.

Cooper, Neil (2007), 'Review Article: On the Crisis of the Liberal Peace', *Conflict, Security and Development*, 7 (4), 605–16.

Coppel, Nicholas (2012), 'Transition of the Regional Assistance Mission to Solomon Islands', State, Society and Governance in Melanesia Programme, Discussion Paper 2012/10, (Acton, ACT: Australian National University).

Corbett, Jack (2013), '"Everybody Knows Everybody": Practising Politics in the Pacific Islands', *Democratization*, 1–22.

Corbett, Jack and Wood, Terence (2013), 'Profiling Politicians in Solomon Islands: Professionalisation of a Political Elite?', *Australian Journal of Political Science*, 48 (3), 320–34.

Cornell, Agnes (2014), 'Why Bureaucratic Stability Matters for the Implementation of Democratic Governance Programs', *Governance*, 27 (2), 191–214.

Corrin, Jennifer (2007), 'Breaking the Mould: Constitutional Review in Solomon Islands', *Revue Juridique Polynésienne*, 13, 143–68.

Coventry, Peter (2009), 'The Hidden Mechanics of Solomon Islands Budget Processes – Understanding Context to Inform Reform', State Society and Governance in Melanesia, Discussion Paper 2009/3, (Acton, ACT: Australian National University).

Cox, John (2015), 'The Politics of Distribution in Solomon Islands: North Vella Lavella Constituency', State, Society and Governance in Melanesia Working Brief 1/2015, (Canberra: Australian National University).

Cox, John and Morrison, Joanne (2004), 'Solomon Islands Provincial Governance Information Paper', (Canberra: Australian Agency for International Development).

Craig, David and Pak Kimchoeun (2011), 'Party Financing of Local Investment Projects: Elite and Mass Patronage', in Caroline Hughes and Kheang Un (eds.), *Cambodia's Economic Transformation* (Copenhagen: NIAS Press), 219–45.

Craig, David and Porter, Doug (2006), *Development Beyond Neoliberalism? Governance, Poverty Reduction and Political Economy* (London and New York: Routledge).

Craig, David and Porter, Doug (2014), 'Post-Conflict Pacts and Inclusive Political Settlements: Institutional Perspectives from Solomon Islands', Effective States and Inclusive Development, ESID Working Paper No. 39, (Manchester: University of Manchester).

CRU (2014), 'Fourth Joint Plenary Endorses 2014 Draft', Solomon Islands Government, Constitutional Reform Unit, *Quarterly Newsletter*, 1 (17), 1.

Dahl, Robert A. (1971), *Polyarchy: Participation and Opposition* (New Haven: Yale University Press).

Dahl-Østergaard, Tom, et al. (2005), '*Lessons Learned on the Use of Power and Drivers of Change Analyses in Development Cooperation: Review Commissioned by the OECD DAC Network on Governance (GOVNET)*', (Paris: Organisation for Economic Cooperation and Development, Development Assistance Committee).

Daly, Patrick, Feener, Michael, Jauhola, Marjaana and Thorburn, Craig. (2016), 'Blue Prints for Change in Post-Tsunami Aceh, Indonesia', in Patrick Daly and Michael R. Feener (eds.), *Rebuilding Asia Following Natural Disasters: Approaches to Reconstruction in the Asia-Pacific Region* (Cambridge: Cambridge University Press).

Dawea, Elliot (2013), 'Solomons Constituency Development Fund Bill Passed', *Solomon Star*, 29 March, available at http://pidp.eastwestcenter.org/pireport/2013/March/03-29-03.htm, accessed 10 November 2016.

Department of Army (2006), 'Counterinsurgency, US Army Field Manual 3–24 and Marine Corps Warfighting Publication 3–33.5', in *Department of the Army* (ed.), (Washington, DC).

Devesi, Jude Solomon (2013), 'Getting Leaders to Lead: How Do We Get Solomon Islands Politicians to Think and Behave in the National

Interest?', *RAMSI 10th Anniversary Seminar* (Honiara, Forum Fisheries Agency Complex).

DFID (2004), 'Drivers of Change', *Public Information Note* (London: UK Department for International Development).

(2005), 'Why We Need to Work More Effectively in Fragile States' (London: UK Department for International Development).

Diamond, Larry (1999), *Developing Democracy: Towards Consolidation* (Baltimore: Johns Hopkins University Press).

Dinnen, Sinclair and Allen, Matthew G. (2013), 'Paradoxes of Postcolonial Police-Building: Solomon Islands', *Policing and Society*, 23 (2), 222–42.

Dodge, Toby (2005), 'Iraqi Transitions: From Regime Change to State Collapse', *Third World Quarterly*, 26 (4–5), 705–21.

(2007), 'The Causes of US Failure in Iraq', *Survival*, 49 (1), 85–106.

(2009), 'Coming Face to Face with Bloody Reality: Liberal Common Sense and the Ideological Failure of the Bush Doctrine in Iraq', *International Politics*, 46 (2), 253–75.

Downer, Alexander (2007), 'Open Letter to Solomon Islands', 13 July, www.pireport.org/articles/2007/07/19/alexander-downer-open-letter-solomon-islands, accessed 25 March 2017.

Doyle, Michael W. (1986), 'Liberalism and World Politics', *American Political Science Review*, 80 (04), 1151–69.

Duffield, Mark (2001), *Global Governance and the New Wars: The Merging of Development and Security* (London: Zed Books).

(2007), *Development, Security and Unending War: Governing the World of Peoples* (Cambridge: Polity Press).

Ear Sophal (2011), 'Growth in the Rice and Garment Sectors', in Caroline Hughes and Kheang Un (eds.), *Cambodia's Economic Transformation* (Copenhagen: NIAS Press), 70–94.

(2013), *Aid Dependence in Cambodia: How Foreign Assistance Undermines Democracy* (New York: Columbia University Press).

Easterly, William (2013), *The Tyranny of Experts: Economists, Dictators, and the Forgotten Rights of the Poor* (New York: Basic Books).

Economist Intelligence Unit (1989–90), *Country Profile: Indochina – Vietnam, Laos, Cambodia* (London: The Economist).

Edi, Jepri and Setianingtias, Ayu (2007), *Donor Proliferation and Donor Coordination in Indonesia: The Case of Governance Reform* (Brighton: Institute of Development Studies).

Egnell, Robert and Haldén, Peter (2013), 'Introduction: The Need for New Agendas in Statebuilding', in Robert Egnell and Peter Haldén (eds.), *New Agendas in Statebuilding: Hybridity, Contingency and History* (Abingdon and New York: Routledge), 1–10.

Ehrenberg, John (1999), *Civil Society: The Critical History of an Idea* (New York: New York University Press).

EIA and Telepak (2005), *The Last Frontier: Illegal Logging in Papua and China's Massive Timber Theft* (London and Bogor, Indonesia: Environmental Investigation Agency).

Emmerson, Donald K. (1983), 'Understanding the New Order: Bureaucratic Pluralism in Indonesia', *Asian Survey*, 23 (11), 1220–41.

Eng Netra and Craig, David (2009), *Accountability and Human Resource Management in Decentralising Cambodia*, Working Paper no. 40 (Phnom Penh: Cambodia Development Resource Institute).

Eng Netra, Vong Mun and Hort Navy (2015), *Social Accountability in Service Delivery in Cambodia*, Working Paper no. 102 (Phnom Penh: Cambodia Development Resource Institute).

Essex, Jamey (2013), *Development, Security, and Aid: Geopolitics and Geoeconomics at the U.S. Agency for International Development* (Athens: Georgia University Press).

EU (2003), 'A Secure Europe in a Better World: European Security Strategy', (Paris: European Union Institute for Security Studies).

European Court of Auditors (2008), 'European Commission Rehabilitation Aid Following the Tsunami and Hurricane Mitch', *Special Report No 6* (Luxembourg: European Court of Auditors).

Evans, Peter B., Rueschemeyer, Dietrich and Skocpol, Theda (eds.) (1985), *Bringing the State Back In* (Cambridge: Cambridge University Press).

Everest-Phillips, Max (2010), 'State-Building Taxation for Developing Countries: Principles for Reform', *Development Policy Review*, 28 (1), 75–96.

Everett, Silas (2015), 'The Rise of Smart Phones in Cambodia Challenges Social Norms', *In Asia: Weekly Insight and Analysis*, Asia Foundation, 16 December, http://asiafoundation.org/2015/12/16/the-rise-of-smart-phones-in-cambodia-challenges-social-norms/, accessed 10 November 2016.

Fadillah, Almira (2016), 'Korupsi di Aceh: Ironi Pembangunan Aceh [Corruption in Aceh: The Irony of Aceh Development]'. *The Global Review*. www.theglobal-review.com/content_detail.php?lang=id&id=19020&type=5#.V8kEGPl95D8, accessed 9 May 2016.

Falleti, Tulia G. (2010), *Decentralization and Subnational Politics in Latin America* (New York: Cambridge University Press).

Faust, Jörg (2010), 'Policy Experiments, Democratic Ownership and Development Assistance', *Development Policy Review*, 28 (5), 515–34.

FCM and VNG International (2010), 'Strengthening Local Governance and Decentralization: Lessons and Experiences from Local Government Associations in Asia' (Ottawa and Nassaulaan, the Netherlands:

Federation of Canadian Municipalities and the International Cooperation Agency of the Association of Netherlands Municipalities).

Feener, Michael, Daly, Patrick and Reed, Anthony (eds.) (2011), *Mapping the Acehnese Past* (Leiden: Brill).

Fono, Fred (2007), 'A Perspective on Constituency Development in Solomon Islands', *Pacific Economic Bulletin*, 22 (2), 127–30.

Fraenkel, Jon (2004), *The Manipulation of Custom: From Uprising to Intervention in the Solomon Islands* (Wellington, NZ: Victoria University Press).

(2011), 'The Atroph ied State: A Supply-Side Perspective on Politician "Slush Funds" in Western Melanesia', in Ron Duncan (ed.), *The Political Economy of Economic Reform in the Pacific* (Manila: Asian Development Bank), 303–26.

Fraenkel, Jon, Madraiwiwi, Joni and Okole, Henry (2014), 'The RAMSI Decade: A Review of the Regional Assistance Mission to Solomon Islands, 2003–2013', (Suva: Pacific Islands Forum).

Frazer, Ian (1997), 'The Struggle for Control of Solomon Island Forests', *The Contemporary Pacific*, 9 (1), 39–72.

Freire, Maria Raquel and Lopes, Paula Duarte (2013), 'Peacebuilding in Timor-Leste: Finding a Way Between External Intervention and Local Dynamics', *International Peacekeeping*, 20 (2), 204–18.

Frieson, Kate (1996), 'The Politics of Getting the Vote in Cambodia', in Steve Heder and Judy Ledgerwood (eds.), *Propaganda, Politics and Violence in Cambodia: Democratic Transition under United Nations Peacekeeping* (London: M. E. Sharpe), 183–207.

Frings, Viviane (1994), 'Cambodia after Decollectivization (1989–1992)', *Journal of Contemporary Asia* 24 (1): 49–66.

Fritz, Verena and Menocal, Alina Rocha (2007), 'Developmental States in the New Millennium: Concepts and Challenges for a New Aid Agenda', *Development Policy Review*, 25 (5), 531–52.

Fry, Greg and Kabutaulaka, Tarcisius Tara (2008), 'Political Legitimacy and State-Building Intervention in the Pacific', in Greg Fry and Tarcisius Tara Kabutaulaka (eds.), *Intervention and State-Building in the Pacific: The Political Legitimacy of 'Cooperative Intervention'* (Manchester: Manchester University Press), 1–36.

Fukuyama, Francis (1992), *The End of History and the Last Man* (London: Penguin).

(2004), *State-Building: Governance and World Order in the 21st Century* (Ithaca, NY: Cornell University Press).

(2008), 'State Building in Solomon Islands', *Pacific Economic Bulletin*, 23 (3), 18–34.

(2013), 'What Is Governance?', *Governance*, 26 (3), 347–68.

Gaillard, Jean-Christophe, Clavé, Elsa and Kelman, Ilan (2008), 'Wave of Peace? Tsunami Disaster Diplomacy in Aceh, Indonesia', *Geoforum*, 39 (1), 511–26.

Garrett, Jemima (2015), 'Solomon Islands Chief Justice Calls for Action on Corruption as Millions of Government Funding "Unaccounted for"', www.abc.net.au/news/2015-01-22/solomon-islands-chief-justice-calls-for-action-on-corruption/6036168, accessed 20 November 2015.

Gaus, Nurdiana, Sultan, Sultan and Basri, Muhammad (2016), 'State Bureaucracy in Indonesia and Its Reforms: An Overview', *International Journal of Public Administration*, 1–12.

Gelb, A., Knight, J. B. and Sabot, R. H. (1991), 'Public Sector Employment, Rent Seeking and Economic Growth', *The Economic Journal*, 101 (408), 1186–99.

GeRAK Aceh (2016), 'GeRAK: Pemerintah Aceh Adalah Pemerintah Yang Gemar Gonta-Ganti Kabinet [Gerakan Anti Korupsi Aceh (GeRAK): Aceh Government Loves Reshuffling the Cabinet]', 4 April.

Gershman, John (2002), 'Is Southeast Asia the Second Front?' *Foreign Affairs* July/August 2002, www.foreignaffairs.com/articles/asia/2002-07-01/southeast-asia-second-front, accessed 10 November 2016.

Ghani, Ashraf and Lockhart, Clare (2008), *Fixing Failed States: A Framework for Rebuilding a Fractured World* (Oxford: Oxford University Press).

Gibson, Edward L. (2013), *Boundary Control: Subnational Authoritarianism in Federal Democracies* (Cambridge: Cambridge University Press).

Giddens, Anthony (1985), *The Nation-State and Violence* (Berkley: University of California Press).

Gill, Stephen (1995), 'Globalisation, Market Civilisation, and Disciplinary Neoliberalism', *Millennium – Journal of International Studies*, 24 (3), 399–423.

Girishankar, Navin, DeGroot, David Desai, Raj Stout, Susan and Westcott, Clay (2011), *Cambodia: World Bank Country-Level Engagement on Governance and Anti-Corruption*, IEG Working Paper no. 2011/6, (Washington DC: World Bank Independent Evaluation Group), http://documents.worldbank.org/curated/en/127591468232490752/pdf/666760NWP00PUB0B0GACCambodiaWPFinal.pdf accessed 10 November 2016.

Gisselquist, Rachel M. (2015), 'Varieties of Fragility: Implications for Aid', *Third World Quarterly*, 36 (7), 1269–80.

Gisselquist, Rachel M. and Resnick, Danielle (2014), 'Aiding Government Effectiveness in Developing Countries', *Public Administration and Development*, 34 (3), 141–48.

Global Witness (1998), 'Co-Prime Ministers Sign Illegal US$60 Million Timber Deal', press release, 20 March, www.globalwitness.org/en-gb/archive/

co-prime-ministers-sign-illegal-us60-million-timber-deal/, accessed 10 November 2016.

(2002), 'Senior Global Witness Personnel Attacked in Phnom Penh, Cambodia', press release, 3 May, www.globalwitness.org/en-gb/archive/senior-global-witness-personnel-attacked-phnom-penh-cambodia/, accessed 10 November 2016

(2007), 'Cambodia's Family Trees', Report, 31 May 2007, www.globalwitness.org/en-gb/reports/cambodias-family-trees/, accessed 10 November 2016.

(2009), 'Country for Sale: How Cambodia's Elite has Captured the Country's Extractive Industries', Report, 5 February 2009, www.globalwitness.org/en/reports/country-sale/, accessed 30 March 2017.

Goldfinch, Shaun, DeRouen, Karl and Pospieszna, Paulina (2013), 'Flying Blind? Evidence For Good Governance Public Management Reform Agendas, Implementation And Outcomes In Low Income Countries', *Public Administration and Development*, 33 (1), 50–61.

Gottesman, Evan (2003), *Cambodia after the Khmer Rouge: Inside the Politics of Nation-Building* (New Haven, CT: Yale University Press).

Gough, Jamie (2004), 'Changing Scale as Changing Class Relations: Variety and Contradiction in the Politics of Scale', *Political Geography*, 23 (2), 185–211.

Gramsci, Antonio (1971), *Selections from the Prison Notebooks* (London: Lawrence and Wishart).

Grenfell, Damian (2008), 'Governance, Violence and Crises in Timor-Leste: Estadu Seidauk Mai', in David Mearns (ed.), *Democratic Governance in Timor-Leste: Reconciling the Local and the National* (Darwin, Australia: Charles Darwin University Press), 85–97.

Grindle, Merilee S. (2004), 'Good Enough Governance: Poverty Reduction and Reform in Developing Countries', *Governance*, 17 (4), 525–48.

(2009), *Going Local: Decentralization, Democratization, and the Promise of Good Governance* (Princeton: Princeton University Press).

Grindle, Merilee S. and Hilderbrand, Mary E. (1995), 'Building Sustainable Capacity in the Public Sector: What Can Be Done?', *Public Administration and Development*, 15 (5), 441–63.

Hadiz, Vedi R. (2010), *Localising Power in Post-Authoriatrian Indonesia: A Southeast Asia Perspective* (Stanford, CA: Stanford University Press).

(2016), *Islamic Populism in Indonesia and the Middle East* (Cambridge: Cambridge University Press).

Hadiz, Vedi R. and Robison, Richard (2005), 'Neo-Liberal Reforms and Illiberal Consolidations: The Indonesian Paradox', *Journal of Development Studies*, 41 (2), 220–41.

Hai, Immanuel Sok (2014), 'Facebook Statistics Cambodia 2014', www.geeksincambodia.com/facebook-statistics-in-cambodia-2014, accessed 10 November 2016.

Hameiri, Shahar (2007), 'The Trouble with RAMSI: Reexamining the Roots of Conflict in Solomon Islands', *The Contemporary Pacific*, 19 (2), 409–41.

(2009), 'Capacity and Its Fallacies: International State Building as State Transformation', *Millennium: Journal of International Studies*, 38 (1), 55–81.

(2010), *Regulating Statehood: State Building and the Transformation of the Global Order* (Basingstoke: Palgrave Macmillan).

(2014a), 'The Crisis of Liberal Peacebuilding and the Future of Statebuilding', *International Politics*, 51 (3), 316–33.

(2014b), 'Avian Influenza, "Viral Sovereignty", and the Politics of Health Security in Indonesia', *Pacific Review*, 27 (3), 333–56.

Hameiri, Shahar and Jones, Lee (2013), 'The Politics and Governance of Non-Traditional Security', *International Studies Quarterly*, 57 (3), 462–73.

(2014), 'Murdoch International: the 'Murdoch School' in International Relations', Working Paper No. 178 (Perth: Asia Research Centre, Murdoch University).

(2015), *Governing Borderless Threats: Non-Traditional Security and the Politics of State Transformation* (Cambridge: Cambridge University Press).

(2016), 'Rising Powers and State Transformation: The Case of China', *European Journal of International Relations*, 22 (1), 72–98.

Hap Phalthy (2010), *The Implementation of Cambodia's Laws on Land Tenure*, LLD Dissertation, Nagoya University, www.theredddesk.org/sites/default/files/the_implementation_of_cambodias_laws_on_land_tenure_0.pdf, accessed 10 November 2016.

Haque, Tobias A. (2012), 'The Influence of Culture on Economic Development in Solomon Islands: A Political-Economy Perspective', Discussion Paper 2012/1 (Acton: Australian National University, State, Society and Governance in Melanesia Programme).

(2013), 'Economic Transition in Solomon Islands', Discussion Paper 2013/10 (Acton: Australian National University, State, Society and Governance in Melanesia Programme).

Harrison, Graham (2004), *The World Bank and Africa: The Construction of Governance States* (New York and London: Routledge).

Harun, Harun, An, Yi, and Kahar, Abdul (2013), 'Implementation and Challenges of Introducing NPM and Accrual Accounting in Indonesian Local Government', *Public Money & Management*, 33 (5), 383–88.

Harvey, David (2001), 'Globalization and the "Spatial Fix"', *Geographische Revue*, 3 (2), 23–20.

(2006), *The Limits to Capital* (London: Verso).

Hay, Colin (2002), *Political Analysis: An Introduction* (Basingstoke: Palgrave Macmillan).

(2006), '(What's Marxist about) Marxist State theory?', in Colin Hay, Michael Lister and David Marsh (eds.), *The State: Theories and Issues* (Basingstoke: Palgrave Macmillan), 59–78.

Hayward-Jones, Jenny (2014), *Australia's Costly Investment in Solomon Islands: The Lessons of RAMSI* (Sydney: Lowy Institute for International Policy).

Heathershaw, John (2008), 'Seeing like the International Community: How Peacebuilding Failed (and Survived) in Tajikistan', *Journal of Intervention and Statebuilding*, 2 (3), 329–51.

Hefner, Robert W. (2000), *Civil Islam: Muslims and Democratization in Indonesia* (Princeton and Oxford: Princeton University Press).

Heredia, Blanca and Schneider, Ben Ross (2003), 'The Political Economy of Administrative Reform in Developing Countries', in Ben Ross Schneider and Blanca Heredia (eds.), *Reinventing Leviathan: The Politics of Administrative Reform in Developing Countries* (Miami: North-South Center Press), 1–29.

Heriansyah, Mitro (2015), 'GeRAK Aceh Uraikan Dugaan Korupsi Mantan Wagub Senilai 60,6 Milyar [GeRAK Aceh Says Corruption by Former Aceh Vice Governor Worth 60.6 Billion]', 15 April. http://acehpost.co.id/gerak-aceh-uraikan-dugaan-korupsi-mantan-wagub-senilai-606-milyar/.

Hewison, Kevin, Robison, Richard and Rodan, Garry (1993), 'Changing Forms of State Power in Southeast Asia', in Kevin Hewison, Richard Robison and Garry Rodan (eds.), *Southeast Asia in the 1990s: Authoritarianism, Democracy and Capitalism* (St Leonards, Australia: Allen and Unwin), 2–8.

Hibou, Béatrice (2004), 'From Privatising the Economy to Privatising the State: An Analysis of the Continual Formation of the State', in Béatrice Hibou (ed.), *Privatising the State* (London: Hurst and Co.), 1–46.

Hickey, Sam (2009), 'The Return of Politics in Development Studies (II): Capturing the Political?', *Progress in Development Studies*, 9 (2), 141–52.

(2012), 'Turning Governance Thinking Upside-down? Insights from "The Politics of What Works"', *Third World Quarterly*, 33 (7), 1231–47.

Hillman, Ben (2011), 'The Policy-Making Dimension of Post-Conflict Governance: The Experience of Aceh, Indonesia', *Conflict, Security & Development*, 11 (5), 533–53.

(2012), 'Power-Sharing and Political Party Engineering in Conflict-Prone Societies: The Indonesian Experiment in Aceh', *Conflict, Security & Development*, 12 (2), 149–69.

(2013), 'Public Administration Reform in Post-Conflict Societies: Lessons from Aceh, Indonesia', *Public Administration and Development*, 33 (1), 1–14.

Hobsbawm, Eric J. (1994), *The Age of Extremes: A History of the World, 1914–1991* (New York: Pantheon Books).

Hohe, Tanja (2002), 'The Clash of Paradigms: International Administration and Local Political Legitimacy in East Timor', *Contemporary Southeast Asia*, 24 (3), 569–89.

Hooghe, Liesbet and Marks, Gary (2003), 'Unraveling the Central State, But How? Types of Multi-Level Governance', *American Political Science Review*, 97 (2), 233–43.

Hor Hab (2009), 'Fibre-Optic Cable Links Region's Data Networks', *Phnom Penh Post*, 16 July, www.phnompenhpost.com/business/fibre-optic-cable-links-regions-data-networks, accessed 10 November 2016.

Hout, Wil (2004), 'Political Regimes and Development Assistance: The Political Economy of Aid Selectivity', *Critical Asian Studies*, 36 (4), 591–613.

Hout, Wil and Robison, Richard (2008), *Governance and the Depoliticisation of Development* (London: Taylor & Francis).

HRW (2004), 'Aceh at War: Torture, Ill-Treatment, and Unfair Trials' (Washington, DC: Human Rights Watch).

(2010), 'Unkept Promise: Failure to End Military Business Activity in Indonesia', (New York: Human Rights Watch).

(2013), 'Cambodia: Land Titling Campaign Open to Abuse', June 12, www.hrw.org/news/2013/06/12/cambodia-land-titling-campaign-open-abuse, accessed 21 August 2016.

(2015), 'Thirty Years of Hun Sen: Violence, Repression and Corruption in Cambodia', (Washington DC: Human Rights Watch), www.hrw.org/sites/default/files/reports/cambodia0115_ForUpload.pdf, accessed 10 November 2016.

Hughes, Caroline (2003), *The Political Economy of Cambodia's Transition 1991–2001*, (London: Routledge).

(2006), 'The Politics of Gifts: Tradition and Regimentation in Cambodia', *Journal of Southeast Asian Studies* 37 (3): 469–89.

(2008), 'Cambodia in 2007: Development and Dispossession', *Asian Survey* 48 (1): 69–74.

(2013), 'Friction, Good Governance and the Poor: Cases from Cambodia', *International Peacekeeping*, 20 (2), 144–58.

Hughes, Caroline and Conway, Tim (2003), 'Understanding Pro-Poor Political Change: The Policy Process in Cambodia', 2nd Draft. DFID

Drivers of Change report. (London: ODI), www.gsdrc.org/docs/open/doc11.pdf, accessed 10 November 2016.

Hughes, Caroline and Eng Netra (2015), 'Facebook and the Elections in Cambodia', paper delivered at the workshop on The Political Economy of Poor People's Politics in South East Asia, University of Birmingham, 30 September 2015.

Hughes, Caroline and Hutchinson, Jane (2012), 'Development Effectiveness and the Politics of Commitment', *Third World Quarterly*, 33 (1), 17–36.

Hughes, Caroline and Sedara, Kim (2004), *The Evolution of Democratic Process and Conflict Resolution in Cambodia*, Working Paper no. 30. (Phnom Penh: Cambodia Development Resource Institute).

Hughes, Caroline, Eng Netra, Thon Vimealea, Ou Sivhuoch and Ly Tem (2011), 'Leaders and Big Business in Three Communes', in Caroline Hughes and Kheang Un (eds.), *Cambodia's Economic Transformation* (Copenhagen: NIAS Press), 245–65.

Hughes, Caroline, Öjendal, Joakim, and Schierenbeck, Isabell (2015), 'The Struggle versus the Song – The Local Turn in Peacebuilding: An Introduction', *Third World Quarterly*, 36 (5), 817–24.

Hughes, John (2003), *The End of Sukarno: A Coup That Misfired, a Purge That Ran Wild* (New York: Archipelago Press).

Hughes, Tony (2013), 'Against Public Objections, Solomons MPs Give Themselves Bigger Slush Funds', *DEVPOLICY* Blog, 10 April, www.devpolicy.org/against-public-objections-solomons-mps-give-themselves-bigger-slush-funds-20130410-2, accessed 10 November 2016).

(2014), 'No Constitutional Reform, So Upgrade Provincial Government', *Solomon Star*, 22 August, www.solomonstarnews.com/viewpoint/letters-to-the-editor/3618-no-constitutional-reform-so-upgrade-provincial-government, accessed 10 November 2016.

Hughes, Tony, Crawford, Paul, Sutch, Helen and Tacconi, Luca (2010), 'SI Forest Management Project II (FMP2): Independent Completion Report (ICR)', (Canberra: Australian Agency for International Development).

Hunter, Helen-Louise (2007), *Sukarno and the Indonesian Coup: The Untold Story* (Westport, CT: Praeger Security International).

Huntington, Samuel P. (1968), *Political Order in Changing Societies* (New Haven, CT: Yale University Press).

Hutchison, Jane, Hout, Wil, Hughes, Caroline and Robison, Richard (2014), *Political Economy and the Aid Industry in Asia* (Palgrave Macmillan).

ICG (2007a), 'Aceh: Post-Conflict Complications' (Jakarta and Brussels: International Crisis Group).

(2007b), 'Indonesia: How GAM Won in Aceh' (Jakarta and Brussels: International Crisis Group).

(2008), 'Iraq after the Surge I: The New Sunni Landscape', *Middle East Report No74* (Brussels: International Crisis Group).

(2009), 'Indonesia: Deep Distrust in Aceh as Elections Approach' (Jakarta and Brussels: International Crisis Group).

(2013), 'Indonesia: Tensions Over Aceh's Flag' (Jakarta and Brussels: International Crisis Group).

Ichimura, Shinichi and Bahl, Roy (eds.) (2009), *Decentralization Policies in Asian Development* (Hackensack, NJ and London: World Scientific Publishing).

IPAC (2014), 'Aceh's Surprising Election Results' (Jakarta: Institute for Policy Analysis of Conflict).

(2015), 'Political Power Struggles in Aceh' (Jakarta: Institute for Policy Analysis of Conflict).

(2013), 'IRD launches its Tax Compliance Focus for 2013 to 2015', Solomon Islands Inland Revenue Division, www.ird.gov.sb/Resource.aspx?ID=113, accessed 10 November 2016.

Islahuddin (2010), 'Some Preliminary Notes on the Aceh Special Autonomy Fund and the Shared Oil and Gas Earning Fund' (Banda Aceh: Syiah Kuala University).

Jafaruddin (2013), 'Otonomi Daerah, Solusi atau Problem? [Local Autonomy, Problem or Solution?]'. *Serambi Indonesia*, 23 July, http://aceh.tribunnews.com/2013/07/23/otonomi-daerah-solusi-atau-problem.

Jayasuriya, Kanishka (2006), *Statecraft, Welfare and the Politics of Inclusion* (Houndmills: Palgrave Macmillan).

Jeldres, Julio (2003), 'China-Cambodia: More than Just Friends?' *Asia Times*, 16 September, www.atimes.com/atimes/Southeast_Asia/EI16Ae03.html, accessed 10 November 2016.

Jessop, Bob (1990), *State Theory: Putting the Capitalist State in Its Place* (Cambridge: Polity Press).

(2002), *The Future of the Capitalist State* (Cambridge: Polity Press).

(2008), *State Power* (Cambridge: Polity Press).

(2009), 'Avoiding Traps, Rescaling States, Governing Europe', in Roger Keil and Rianne Mahon (eds.), *Leviathan Undone? Towards a Political Economy of Scale* (Vancouver: University of British Columbia Press), 87–104.

Johnson, Kristin and Hutchison, Marc L. (2012), 'Hybridity, Political Order and Legitimacy: Examples from Nigeria', *Journal of Peacebuilding & Development*, 7 (2), 37–52.

Jung, Dietrich (2008), 'State Formation and State-Building: Is There a Lesson to Learn from Sociology?', in Lars Engberg-Pedersen, et al. (eds.), *DIIS*

Report 2008: Fragile Situations Background Papers (Copenhagen: Danish Institute for International Studies), 33–42.

Kabutaulaka, Tarcisius Tara (2001), 'Beyond Ethnicity: The Political Economy of the Guadalcanal Crisis in Solomon Islands', *State Society and Governance in Melanesia Project Working Paper 1/2001* (Canberra: Research School of Pacific and Asian Studies, Australian National University).

(2006), 'Global Capital and Local Ownership in Solomon Islands' Forestry Industry', in Stewart Firth (ed.), *Globalisation and Governance in the Pacific Islands* (Canberra: Asia Pacific Press), 239–57.

Kando, Tony (2014), '36 Former MPs Retain Seat', *Solomon Times Online*, 24 November, www.solomontimes.com/news/36-former-mps-retain-seat/8327, accessed 10 November 2016).

Kantor Berita Radio Antero (2013), 'Gubernur: APBA 2014 Tercepat Dalam 8 Tahun Terakhir [Governor: Budget 2014 Fastest in Eight Years]', 31 December, http://portal.radioantero.com/index.php?option=com_content&view=article&id=2119:gubernur-apba-2014-tercepat-dalam-8-tahun-terakhir&catid=35:demo-content.

Kaufman, Daniel (2003), 'Rethinking Governance: Empirical Lessons Challenge Orthodoxy' (Washington, DC: World Bank).

Keesing, Roger M. (1989), 'Creating the Past: Custom and Identity in the Contemporary Pacific', *The Contemporary Pacific*, 1 (1), 19–42.

Kell, Tim (2010 [1995]), *The Roots of Acehnese Rebellion, 1989–1992* (Jakarta and Kuala Lumpur: Equinox Publishing).

Khan, Mushtaq (2010), 'Political Settlements and the Governance of Growth-Enhancing Institutions', working paper (London: SOAS), http://eprints.soas.ac.uk/9968/, accessed 11 November 2016.

Kilcullen, David (2009), *The Accidental Guerrilla: Fighting Small Wars in the Midst of a Big One* (Oxford: Oxford University Press).

Kingsbury, Damien (2007), 'The Free Aceh Movement: Islam and Democratisation', *Journal of Contemporary Asia*, 37 (2), 166–89.

klikkabar.com (2015), 'Mualem Minta SKPA Berapor Merah Percepat Realisasi Anggaran [Mualem Asks SPKA in Red to Accelerate Budget Realisation]', 25 September, http://klikkabar.com/2015/09/25/mualem-minta-skpa-berapor-merah-percepat-realisasi-anggaran/.

Klitzsch, Nicole (2014), 'Disaster Politics or Disaster of Politics? Post-Tsunami Conflict Transformation in Sri Lanka and Aceh, Indonesia', *Cooperation and Conflict*, 49 (4), 554–73.

Knapman, Bruce and Saldanha, Cedric D. (1999), 'Reforms in the Pacific: An Assessment of the Asian Development Bank's Assistance to Reform Programs in the Pacific', (Manila: Asian Development Bank).

Kontras(2004), 'When Gun Point Joins the Trade; Military Business Involvement in Bojonegoro, Boven Digoel and Poso', (Jakarta: Komisi untuk Orang Hilang dan Korban Tindak Kekerasan (Kontras)).

Krasner, Stephen D. and Risse, Thomas (2014), 'External Actors, State-Building, and Service Provision in Areas of Limited Statehood: Introduction', *Governance*, 27 (4), 545–67.

Kumar, Chetan and De la Haye, Jos (2012), 'Hybrid Peacemaking: Building National "Infrastructures for Peace"', *Global Governance: A Review of Multilateralism and International Organizations*, 18 (1), 13–20.

Kwon, Huck-ju and Kim, Eunju (2014), 'Poverty Reduction and Good Governance: Examining the Rationale of the Millennium Development Goals', *Development and Change*, 45 (2), 353–75.

Kyed, Helene Maria and Albrecht, Peter (2015), 'Introduction: Policing and the Politics of Order-Making on the Urban Margins', in Peter Albrecht and Helene Maria Kyed (eds.), *Policing and the Politics of Order-Making* (Abingdon and New York: Routledge), 1–23.

Laking, Rob (2010), 'State performance and capacity in the Pacific' (Manila: Asian Development Bank).

Lancaster, Carol (2007), *Foreign Aid: Diplomacy, Development, Domestic Politics* (Chicago: Chicago University Press).

Lawson, Stephanie (1996), *Tradition versus Democracy in the South Pacific: Fiji, Tonga, and Western Samoa* (Cambridge: Cambridge University Press).

Le Billon, Philippe (2000), 'The Political Ecology of Transition in Cambodia: War, Peace and Forest Exploitation, 1989–1999', *Development and Change* 31 (4): 785–805.

Leftwich, Adrian (2000), *States of Development: On the Primacy of Politics in Development* (Cambridge: Polity Press).

(2012), 'Coalitions in the Politics of Development: Findings, Insights and Guidance from the DLP Coalitions Workshop, 15–16 February, Sydney', Research and Policy Workshop Report (Melbourne: Developmental Leadership Program).

Lemay-Hébert, Nicolas (2009), 'Statebuilding Without Nation-Building? Legitimacy, State Failure and the Limits of the Institutionalist Approach', *Journal of Intervention and Statebuilding*, 3 (1), 21–45.

Leonardsson, Hanna and Rudd, Gustav (2015), 'The "Local Turn" in Peacebuilding: A Literature Review of Effective and Emancipatory Local Peacebuilding', *Third World Quarterly*, 36 (5), 825–39.

Leuprecht, Peter (2001), 'Situation of Human Rights in Cambodia', Report of the Special Representative (New York UN Economic and Social Council).

Levy, Brian (2004), 'Governance and Economic Development in Africa: Meeting the Challenge of Capacity-Building', in Brian Levy and Sahr

Kpundeh (eds.), *Building State Capacity in Africa: New Approaches, Emerging Lessons* (Washington, DC: World Bank Institute), 1–42.

Li, Tania Murray (2007), *The Will to Improve: Governmentality, Development, and the Practice of Politics* (Durham, NC: Duke University Press).

LICADHO (2005), 'Harmful Effects of Economic Land Concessions on Poor Cambodians', Briefing Paper, November, www.licadho-cambodia.org/reports/files/74LICADHOPaperLandIssues05.pdf, accessed 10 November 2016.

(2009), 'Landgrabbing and Poverty in Cambodia: The Myth of Development', Report, May, www.licadho-cambodia.org/reports/files/134LICADHOREportMythofDevelopment2009Eng.pdf, accessed 16 November 2016.

(2013), 'Human Rights in 2012: The Year in Review', February, www.licadho-cambodia.org/reports/files/176LICADHOReportHumanRightsReview2012English.pdf, accessed 16 November 2010.

Lillie, Nathan A. (2010), 'Bringing the Offshore Ashore: Transnational Production, Industrial Relations and the Reconfiguration of Sovereignty', *International Studies Quarterly*, 54 (3), 683–704.

LintasGayo.co (2016), 'Bersama Kegiatan Strategis APBA 2016 [Joint Strategic Activity Budget 2016]', 27 April. http://lintasgayo.co/2016/04/27/kontrak-bersama-kegiatan-strategis-apba-2016-gubernur-jangan-hanya-duduk-di-belakang-meja.

Mac Ginty, Roger (2006), *No War, No Peace* (Basingstoke: Palgrave Macmillan).

(2010), 'Hybrid Peace: The Interaction Between Top-Down and Bottom-Up Peace', *Security Dialogue*, 41 (4), 391–412.

(2011), *International Peacebuilding and Local Resistance: Hybrid Forms of Peace* (Basingstoke: Palgrave Macmillan).

Mac Ginty, Roger and Richmond, Oliver P. (2013), 'The Local Turn in Peace Building: A Critical Agenda for Peace', *Third World Quarterly*, 34 (5), 763–83.

(2016), 'The Fallacy of Constructing Hybrid Political Orders: A Reappraisal of the Hybrid Turn in Peacebuilding', *International Peacekeeping*, 23 (2), 219–39.

Mae, Paul (2010), 'Constitutional Reforms in Solomon Islands: An Analysis of Public Participation in the Reform Process', *Turmoil and Turbulence in Small Developing States: Going beyond Survival* (St Augustine: University of the West Indies, Sir Arthur Lewis Institute of Social and Economic Studies).

Majone, Giandomenico (1994), 'The Rise of the Regulatory State in Europe', *West European Politics*, 17 (3), 77–101.

Mann, Michael (1993), *The Sources of Social Power: The Rise of Classes and Nation-States, 1760–1914* (Cambridge: Cambridge University Press).

Marquette, Heather and Beswick, Danielle (2011), 'State Building, Security and Development: State Building as a New Development Paradigm?', *Third World Quarterly*, 32 (10), 1703–14.

Mayall, James (1996), 'Introduction', in James Mayall (ed.), *The New Interventionism, 1991–1994: United Nations Experience in Cambodia, Former Yugoslavia and Somalia* (Cambridge: Cambridge University Press), 1–24.

Mazarr, Michael J. (2014), 'The Rise and Fall of the Failed-State Paradigm: Requiem for a Decade of Distraction', *Foreign Affairs*, 93, 113–121.

McDougall, Debra (2014), 'Sub-National Governance in Post-RAMSI Solomon Islands', State Society and Governnace in Melanesia Working Paper 3/2014 (Canberra: Australian National University).

McLeod, Ross H. (2011), 'Institutionalized Public Sector Corruption: A Legacy of the Suharto Franchise', in Edward Aspinall and Gerry van Klinken (eds.), *The State and Illegality in Indonesia* (Leiden: KITLV Press), 45–63.

McLoughlin, Claire (2015), 'When Does Service Delivery Improve the Legitimacy of a Fragile or Conflict-Affected State?', *Governance*, 28 (3), 341–56.

MDF Secretariat (2005), 'Rebuilding Together: Multi-Donor Fund for Aceh and Nias | Progress Report No. 1 – December 2005' (Jakarta: Multi-Donor Trust Fund for Aceh and Nias).

(2009), 'Five Years after the Tsunami: Continuing the Commitment to Reconstruction' (Jakarta: Multi-Donor Trust Fund for Aceh and Nias).

MDP (2007), 'Solomon Islands Agriculture and Rural Development Strategy', (Honiara: Solomon Islands Government, Ministry of Development Planning and Aid Coordination).

Mietzner, Marcus (2009), *Military Politics, Islam, and the State in Indonesia: From Turbulent Transition to Democratic Consolidation* (Singapore: Institute of Southeast Asian Studies).

Millar, Gearoid (2014), 'Disaggregating Hybridity: Why Hybrid Institutions Do Not Produce Predictable Experiences of Peace', *Journal of Peace Research*, 51 (4), 501–14.

Millar, Gearoid, van der Lijn, Jaïr and Verkoren, Willemijn (2013), 'Peacebuilding Plans and Local Reconfigurations: Frictions Between Imported Processes and Indigenous Practices', *International Peacekeeping*, 20 (2), 137–43.

Miller, Byron (2009), 'Is Scale a Chaotic Concept? Notes on Processes of Scale Production', in Roger Keil and Rianne Mahon (eds.), *Leviathan*

Undone? Towards a Political Economy of Scale (Vancouver: University of British Columbia Press), 51–66.

Minas, Stephen (2010), 'Fiancing the Forests', *Inside Story*, 20 October. http://insidestory.org.au/financing-the-forests.

Minder, Raphael (2005), 'Aceh Role Force Boosts EU's Foreign Policy Credentials', *Financial Times*, 1 August.

Minogue, Martin (2001), 'The Internationalization of New Public Management', in Willy McCourt and Martin Minogue (eds.), *The Internationalization of Public Management* (Cheltenham: Edward Elgar), 1–19.

MOFT (2014), 'Annual Report 2013', (Honiara: Solomon Islands Government, Ministry of Finance and Treasury).

Moore, Clive (2004), *Happy Isles in Crisis: The Historical Causes for a Failing State in Solomon Islands, 1998–2004* (Canberra: Asia Pacific Press).

Moore, Mick (2004), 'Revenue, State Formation, and the Qualilty of Governance in Developing Countries', *International Political Science Review*, 25 (3), 297–319.

Morgan, Lindsay, Brinkerhoff, Derick and Najib, Mohammad (2012), 'Community engagement and performance-based incentives: the view from Indonesia', *PBI Case Studies* (Washington, DC: USAID).

Morgan, Michael and McLeod, Abby (2006), 'Have We Failed Our Neighbour?', *Australian Journal of International Affairs*, 60 (3), 412–28.

Morton, Adam (2015), 'Solomon Islands: Where Power Brings Cash, but Not Answers', www.smh.com.au/world/solomon-islands-where-power-brings-cash-but-not-answers-20150820-gj3zq5.html, accessed 20 November 2015.

Murray, Kieran, Oliver, Robin and Wyatt, Sally (2014), 'Evaluation of Taxation Reform in the Pacific: Report Prepared for the Ministry of Foreign Affairs and Trade, New Zealand', (Wellington, NZ: Sapere Research Group).

Namosuaia, Daniel (2014), 'More Containers of Tubi Seized', *Solomon Star*, 23 September, www.solomonstarnews.com/news/national/4141-more-containers-of-tubi-seized, accessed 10 November 2016.

Nanau, Gordon Leua (2011), 'The *Wantok* System as a Socio-Economic and Political Network in Melanesia', *OMNES: Journal of Multicultural Society*, 2 (1), 31–55.

Neef, Andreas (2016), 'Cambodia's Devasting Economic Land Concessions', *East Asia Forum*, 29 June, www.eastasiaforum.org/2016/06/29/cambodias-devastating-economic-land-concessions, accessed 10 November 2016.

Newman, Edward (2009), '"Liberal" Peacebuilding Debates', in Edward Newman, Roland Paris and Oliver P. Richmond (eds.), *New Perspectives on Liberal Peacebuilding* (Tokyo and New York: United Nations University Press), 26–53.

Nicol, Bill (2013), *Tsunami Chronicles: Adventures in Disaster Management* (CreateSpace Independent Publishing Platform).

OECD (2006), 'Whole of Government Approaches to Fragile States' (Paris: Organisation for Economic Co-operation and Development).

(2010), 'The State's Legitimacy in Fragile States: Unpacking Complexity' (Paris: Organisation for Economic Co-operation and Development).

OECD DAC (n.d.), 'OECD.StatExtracts', http://stats.oecd.org/ (Paris: Development Assistance Committee, Organisation for Economic Co-operation and Development).

OECD High-Level Forum on Aid Effectiveness (2005), 'Paris Declaration on Aid Effectiveness: Ownership, Harmonisation, Alignment, Results and Mutual Accountability' (Paris: Organisation for Economic Co-operation and Development).

Oldham, Geoffrey and Delahunt, Brett (2004), *Cambodian Decorations of Honour*, (Auckland: Milymen Books).

Ottaway, Marina (2003), 'Rebuilding State Institutions in Collapsed States', in Jennifer Milliken (ed.), *State Failure, Collapse and Reconstruction* (Malden, MA: Blackwell Publishing), 245–66.

Otto, Syamsuddin Ishak (2007), 'Anatomy of Aceh Democracy', *Tempo Magazine* 16–22 January.

Öjendal, Joakim and Kim Sedara (2006), 'Korob, Kaud, Klach: In Search of Agency in Rural Southeast Asia,' *Journal of Southeast Asian Studies*, 37 (3), 507–526.

Özay, Mehmet (2012), 'The Historical Basis of Aceh Socio-Economics Development (1511–1904) ', *Journal of History Culture and Art Research*, 1 (2), 55–70.

Pacific Islands Forum Ministerial Standing Committee (2009), 'Partnership Framework Between Solomon Islands Government and Regional Assistance Mission to Solomon Islands' (Honiara: Pacific Islands Forum).

Paffenholz, Thania (2015), 'Unpacking the Local Turn in Peacebuilding: A Critical Assessment towards an Agenda for Future Research', *Third World Quarterly*, 36 (5), 857–74.

Pak Kimchoeun (2011), 'A Dominant Party in a Weak State: How the Ruling Party in Cambodia Manages to Become Dominant and Stay in Power', PhD thesis, Australian National University.

Paris, Roland (2004), *At War's End: Building Peace after Civil Conflict* (Cambridge: Cambridge University Press).

(2010), 'Saving Liberal Peacebuilding', *Review of International Studies*, 36 (2), 337–65.

Paris, Roland and Sisk, Timothy D. (2009), 'Introduction: Understanding the Contradictions of Postwar Statebuilding', in Roland Paris and Timothy D. Sisk (eds.), *The Dilemmas of Statebuilding: Confronting the Contradictions of Postwar Peace Operations* (London and New York: Routledge), 1–20.

Parks, Thomas and Cole, William (2010), 'Political Settlements: Implications for International Development Policy and Practice', *Occasional Paper* No. 2 (San Francisco: Asia Foundation).

Peck, Jamie (2002), 'Political Economies of Scale: Fast Policy, Interscalar Relations, and Neoliberal Workfare', *Economic Geography*, 78 (3), 331–60.

Peck, Jamie and Tickell, Adam (2002), 'Neoliberalizing Space', *Antipode*, 36 (3), 380–404.

Pender, John (2001), 'From "Structural Adjustment" to "Comprehensive Development Framework": Conditionality Transformed?', *Third World Quarterly*, 22 (3), 397–411.

Peterson, Jenny H. (2012), 'A Conceptual Unpacking of Hybridity: Accounting for Notions of Power, Politics and Progress in Analyses of Aid-Driven Interfaces', *Journal of Peacebuilding & Development*, 7 (2), 9–22.

Phnom Penh Post (1997), 'Why the IMF Pulled the Plug', *Phnom Penh Post*, 24 October, www.phnompenhpost.com/national/why-imf-pulled-plug, accessed 10 November 2016.

(2000), 'All That Glitters Seems to Be . . . Sokimex', *Phnom Penh Post*, 28 April, www.phnompenhpost.com/national/all-glitters-seems-be-sokimex, accessed 10 November 2016.

Pieterse, Jan Nederveen (2001), 'Hybridity, So What?: The Anti-Hybridity Backlash and the Riddles of Recognition', *Theory, Culture & Society*, 18 (2–3), 219–45.

Pollitt, Chrisopher and Bouckaert, Geert (2011), *Public Management Reform: A Comparative Analaysis: New Public Management, Governance and the Neo-Weberian State, Third Edition* (New York: Oxford University Press).

Poulantzas, Nicos (1978), *State, Power, Socialism* (London and New York: Verso).

Pritchett, Lant and Woolcock, Michael (2004), 'Solutions When *the* Solution is the Problem: Arraying the Disarray in Development', *World Development*, 32 (2), 191–212.

Pryke, Jonathan (2013), 'Rising Aid Dependency in the Pacific', *DEVPOLICY Blog*, 17 September, http://devpolicy.org/rising-aid-dependency-in-the-pacific-20130917, accessed 10 November 2016.

Pugh, Michael (2005), 'The Political Economy of Peacebuilding: A Critical Theory Perspective', *International journal of Peace Studies*, 10 (2), 23–42.

Pusat Pengembangan Keuangan Daerah (2016), '*Kajian Pelaksanaan Dana Otonomi Khusus Kabupaten/Kota [Study on the Implementation of Special Autonomy Fund Regency / City]*' (Banda Aceh: Bappeda).

Pye, Daniel and Pech Sotheary (2015), 'NGO: Data Shows "Wholesale Sell-off"', *Phnom Penh Post*, 31 March, www.phnompenhpost.com/national/ngo-data-shows-wholesale-sell, accessed 10 November 2016.

Rachman, Risman A. (2012), *TOMMY Si Agen Tak Tuk [Tommy, the 'Tak Tuk' agent]* (Banda Aceh: P2 K-ABBA, Aceh Provincial Government).

Randazzo, Elisa (2016), 'The Paradoxes of the 'Everyday': Scrutinising the Local Turn in Peace Building', *Third World Quarterly*, 37 (8), 1351–70.

Reid, Anthony (ed.), (2006), *Verandah of Violence: The Background to the Aceh Problem* (Singapore: Singapore University Press).

Reilly, Benjamin (2006), *Democracy and Diversity: Political Engineering in the Asia-Pacific* (Oxford: Oxford University Press).

Reno, William (1998), *Warlord Politics and African States* (Boulder, CO: Lynne Rienner Publishers).

Richmond, Oliver P. (2005), *The Transformation of Peace* (Basingstoke: Palgrave Macmillan).

(2009a), 'Becoming Liberal, Unbecoming Liberalism: Liberal-Local Hybridity via the Everyday as a Response to the Paradoxes of Liberal Peacebuilding', *Journal of Intervention and Statebuilding*, 3 (3), 324–44.

(2009b), 'Beyond Liberal Peace? Responses to "backsliding"', in Edward Newman, Roland Paris, and Oliver P. Richmond (eds.), *New Perspectives on Liberal Peacebuilding* (Tokyo and New York: United Nations University Press), 54–77.

(2011), 'De-romanticising the Local, De-mystifying the International: Hybridity in Timor Leste and the Solomon Islands', *Pacific Review*, 24 (1), 115–36.

(2014), *Failed Statebuilding: Intervention, the State, and the Dynamics of Peace Formation* (New Haven and London: Yale University Press).

Richmond, Oliver P. and Mitchell, Audra (2012), 'Introduction – Towards a Post-Liberal Peace: Exploring Hybridity via Everyday Forms of Resistance, Agency and Autonomy', in Oliver P. Richmond and Audra Mitchell (eds.), *Hybrid Forms of Peace: From Everyday Agency to Post-Liberalism* (Basingstoke: Palgrave Macmillan), 1–38.

Rieffel, Alexis and Pramodhawardani, Jaleswari (2007), *Out of Business and on Budget: The Challenge of Military Financing in Indonesia* (New York: Brookings Institution Press).

Rist, Manfred (2010), 'The Economic Development of Aceh since 1945', in Arndt Graf, Susanne Schroter and Edwin Wieringa (eds.), *Aceh: History, Politics and Culture* (Singapore: Institute of Southeast Asian Studies), 99–119.

Robison, Richard (1986), *Indonesia: The Rise of Capital* (Sydney: Allen and Unwin).

Robison, Richard and Hadiz, Vedi R. (2004), *Reorganising Power in Indonesia: The Politics of Power in an Age of Markets* (London and New York: RoutledgeCurzon).

Rodan, Garry (ed.), (1996), *Political Oppositions in Industrialising Asia* (London and New York: Routledge).

Rodan, Garry and Hughes, Caroline (2012), 'Ideological Coalitions and the International Promotion of Social Accountability: The Philippines and Cambodia Compared 1', *International Studies Quarterly*, 56 (2), 367–80.

Rodrik, Dani, Subramanian, Arvind and Trebbi, Rancesco (2002), 'Institutions Rule: The Primacy of Institutions over Geography and Integration in Economic Development', *CID Working Paper* 97, (Cambridge: Center for International Development, Harvard University).

Ross, Michael L. (2005), 'Resources and rebellion in Aceh', in Paul Collier and Nicholas Sambanis (eds.), *Understanding Civil War* (Washington, DC: World Bank).

Rosser, Andrew (2008), 'Neo-Liberalism and the Politics of Australian Aid Policy-Making', *Australian Journal of International Affairs*, 62 (3), 372–85.

Routley, Laura (2012), 'Developmental States: A Review of the Literature', *ESID Working Paper* No. 03 (Manchester: Effective States and Inclusive Development Research Centre, University of Manchester).

Royal Government of Cambodia, Ministry of Commerce (2012), *Rubber Sector Profile*, July, www.moc.gov.kh/Tradeswap/userfiles/Media/file/Projects/TDSP/Top Ten Products/2012-07-26 Rubber Sector profile.pdf, accessed 10 November 2016.

RTI International (2007), '2007 Annual Report Local Governance Support Program' (Washington, DC: USAID).

(2009), 'Final Report Local Governance Support Program' (Washington, DC: USAID).

Ruggie, John Gerard (1982), 'International Regimes, Transactions, and Change: Embedded Liberalism in the Postwar Economic Order', *International Organization*, 36 (2), 379–415.

Sabarini, Prodita (2010), 'Kuntoro Mangkusubroto: Integrity, Simplicity and Asceticism', *Jakarta Post*, 15 February.

Santoso, Aboeprijadi (2006), 'GAM and Former Rebels in Elections Victory', *Jakarta Post*, 16 December.

SAPRIN (2004), *Structural Adjustment: The Structural Adjustment Participatory Review International Network report. The Policy Roots of Economic Crisis, Poverty and Inequality* (London and New York: Zed Books).

Scales, Ian (2003), *The Social Forest: Landowners, Development Conflict and the State in Solomon Islands* (Canberra: Australian National University).

Scarpello, Fabio (2009), *Aid, Politics, and the Multidonor Trust Fund for Aceh and Nias*, (Jakarta: World Bank).

Schultz, Jonathan (2012), *Overseeing and Overlooking: Australian Engagement with the Pacific islands 1988–2007* (Melbourne: University of Melbourne).

Schulze, Kirsten E. (2004), *The Free Aceh Movement (GAM): Anatomy of a Separatist Organization* (Washington, DC: East-West Center).

(2007), 'Mission Not So Impossible: The Aceh Monitoring Mission and Lessons Learned for the EU', *International Policy Analysis* (Berlin: Friedrich-Ebert-Foundation).

Scott, Zoe (2011), *Evaluation of Public Sector Governance Reforms 2001–2011* (Oxford: Oxford Policy Management).

Seabrooke, Leonard (2002), 'Bringing Legitimacy Back in to Neo-Weberian State Theory and International Relations', *Department of International Relations Working Paper 2002/6* (Canberra: Australian National University).

Serambi Indonesia (2012a), 'Provinsi tidak Boleh Kaku Soal Dana Otsus [Province Cannot Impose Inflexible Special Autonomy Fund Earmarking]', 9 November. http://aceh.tribunnews.com/2012/11/09/provinsi-tidak-boleh-kaku-soal-dana-otsus.

(2012b), 'Anggota Dewan Protes Otsus Kabupaten Dikurangi [Board Members Protests Cuts to Districts Allocation of Special Autonomy Fund]', 21 December. http://aceh.tribunnews.com/2012/12/21/anggota-dewan-protes-otsus-kabupaten-dikurangi.

(2012c), 'Kabupaten Pertanyakan Perubahan Rasio Dana Otsus [Districts Question the Change in Special Autonomy Fund Allocation Ratio]', 11 October. http://aceh.tribunnews.com/2012/10/11/kabupaten-pertanyakan-perubahan-rasio-dana-otsus.

(2012d), 'Pemerintah Aceh Akan Revisi Qanun Otsus [Aceh Government to revise Special Autonomy Fund Bylaw]', 4 August. http://aceh.tribunnews.com/2012/08/04/pemerintah-aceh-akan-revisi-qanun-otsus.

(2013), 'Dana Otsus Ditransfer ke Daerah [Special Autonomy Fund Transferred to Disctricts]', 19 March. http://aceh.tribunnews.com/2013/03/19/dana-otsus-ditransfer-ke-daerah.

(2015a), 'Reformasi Birokrasi Tetap Jadi Prioritas [Bureaucratic Reform Remains a Priority]', 14 December. http://aceh.tribunnews.com/2015/12/14/reformasi-birokrasi-tetap-jadi-prioritas.

(2015b), 'Gubernur: Birokrasi tidak Berkualitas Bisa Rusak Program [Unqualified Bureaucracy Can Damage Programs]', 12 June. http://aceh.tribunnews.com/2015/06/12/gubernur-birokrasi-tidak-berkualitas-bisa-rusak-program.

(2015c), 'Saatnya KPK Action di Aceh [Time for KPK Action in Aceh]', 26 October. http://aceh.tribunnews.com/2014/10/26/saatnya-kpk-action-di-aceh.

(2016), 'Gubernur: Tenaga Honor yang Malas Distop Saja [Governor: Committed to Stop Lazy Workers]', 22 March. http://aceh.tribunnews.com/2016/03/22/gubernur-tenaga-honor-yang-malas-distop-saja.

Shah, Anwar (ed.), (2006), *Local Governance in Developing Countries* (Washington, DC: World Bank).

SIG (2014), 'Solomon Islands Budget 2014: Budget Strategy and Outlook Budget Paper: Volume 1' (Honiara: Solomon Islands Government, Ministry of Finance and Treasury).

Sindre, Gyda Marås (2016), 'In Whose Interests? Former Rebel Parties and Ex-combatant Interest Group Mobilisation in Aceh and East Timor', *Civil Wars*, 18 (2), 192–213.

Slater, Dan (2010), *Ordering Power: Contentious Politics and Authoritarian Leviathans in Southeast Asia* (New York: Cambridge University Press).

Smith, Neil (1992), 'Contours of a Spatialized Politics: Homeless Vehicles and the Production of Geographical Scale', *Social Text*, (33), 55–81.

(2003), 'Remaking Scale: Competition and Cooperation in Pre-National and Post-National Europe', in Neil Brenner, Bob Jessop, Martin Jones and Gordon MacLeod (eds.), *State/Space: A Reader* (Malden, MA: Blackwell Publishing), 227–38.

(2010), *Uneven Development: Nature, Capital, and the Production of Space*, 3rd ed. (London: Verso).

Sokunpanha You (2015), 'Review of Aid Dependence in Cambodia', http://asiapacific.anu.edu.au/newmandala/2013/11/14/review-of-aid-dependence-in-cambodia-tlc-nmrev-lxiii/, accessed 1 December 2015.

Solomon Islands National Parliament (2013), 'Report on the Constituency Development Funds Bill 2013: Bills and Legislation Committee', Paper No. 2 of 2013 (Honiara: National Parliament of Solomon Islands).

Solomon Star (2014), 'Government Sued: Ousted AG Challenges Sacking in High Court', 27 November.

Stedman, Stephen J. (1992/1993), 'The New Interventionists', *Foreign Affairs*, 72 (1), 1–16.

(1997), 'Spoiler Problems in Peace Processes', *International Security*, 22 (2), 5–49.

Steeves, Jeffrey (2011), '"Unbounded Politics" and the Democratic Model in Solomon Islands: The 2010 National Elections', *Commonwealth and Comparative Politics*, 49 (3), 342–58.

Stiglitz, Joseph E. (1998), 'Towards a New Paradigm for Development: Strategies, Policies and Processes', *The 1998 Prebisch Lecture* (Geneva: United Nations Conference on Trade and Development).

(2002), *Globalization and Its Discontents* (New York: W.W. Norton).

Streeck, Wolfgang (2014), *Buying Time: The Delayed Crisis of Democratic Capitalism* (London: Verso).

Stuart-Fox, Martin and Ung Bunheang (1998), *The Murderous Revolution* (Chiang Mai: Orchid Press).

Stubbs, Richard (2009), 'Whatever Happened to the East Asian Developmental State? The Unfolding Debate', *Pacific Review*, 22 (1), 1–22.

Suhrke, Astri (2007), 'Reconstruction as Modernisation: The "Post-Conflict" Project in Afghanistan', *Third World Quarterly*, 28 (7), 1291–308.

Sukma, Rizal (2005), *Security Operations in Aceh: Goals, Consequences, and Lessons* (Washington, DC: East-West Center).

Sulistiyanto, Priyambudi (2001), 'Whither Aceh?', *Third World Quarterly*, 22 (3), 437–52.

Swyngedouw, Erik A. (1997), 'Neither Global nor Local: "Glocalization" and the Politics of Scale', in Kevin R. Cox (ed.), *Spaces of Globalization: Reasserting the Power of the Local* (New York: Guildford), 137–66.

Tadjbakhsh, Shahrbanou (ed.), (2011), *Rethinking the Liberal Peace: External Models and Local Alternatives* (Abingdon and New York: Routledge).

Talierio, Robert (2009), 'Unlocking Capacity and Revisiting Political Will: Cambodia's Public Financial Management Reforms', *International Public Management Review*, 10 (1): 90–118.

Tamsitt, Mark (2014), 'Solomon Islands Needs a Parliament That Will Deliver Results', 25 November, *The Interpreter*, Lowy Institute for International Policy, www.lowyinstitute.org/the-interpreter/solomon-islands-needs-parliament-will-deliver-results, accessed 10 November 2016.

Taqwaddin, Akbar (2010), 'Pengelolaan Dana Otsus [The Managment of the Special Autonomy Fund]'. https://pekikdaerah.wordpress.com/artikel-makalah/pengelolaan-dana-otsus/.

Teschke, Benno (2003), *The Myth of 1648: Class, Geopolitics, and the Making of Modern International Relations* (London: Verso).

The Jakarta Globe (2013), 'Sweeping Civil Service Reform Gathers Pace in Indonesia', 18 October, http://jakartaglobe.beritasatu.com/news/sweeping-civil-service-reform-gathers-pace-in-indonesia/.

The Solomon Islands Core Economic Working Group (2011), 'Report of the Economic and Financial Reform Program: Second Annual Joint Review' (Canberra: Australian Government, Department of Foreign Affairs and Trade).

Thon Vimealea, Ou Sivhuoch, Eng Netra and Ly Tem (2009), 'Leadership in Local Politics of Cambodia: A Study of Leaders in Three Communes of Three Provinces', Working Paper no. 42. (Phnom Penh: Cambodia Development Resource Institute).

Thorburn, Craig and Bryan, Rochelle (2014), 'The Acehnese Gampong Ten Years On: A Post-Post Tsunami Assessment' (Melbourne: Monash University).

Tilly, Charles (1990), *Coercion, Capital and European States,* AD *900–1990* (Oxford: Wiley-Blackwell).

Toye, John (1987), *Dilemmas of Development: Reflections on the Counter-Revolution in Development Theory and Policy* (Oxford: Basil Blackwell).

Transparency Solomon Islands (2013), 'RCDF Audit Must be Released', Transparency Solomon Islands Facebook page, 29 November, www.facebook.com/TransparencySI/posts/248703081953696, accessed 10 November 2016.

Tryatmoko, Mardyanto Wahyu (2016), 'Problematika peran ganda gubernur di daerah otonomi khusus [The problematic double role of the governor in the special autonomy areas]', *Jurnal Penelitian Politik*, 9 (2), 75–89.

Turner, Mark, Imbaruddin, Amir and Sutiyono, Wahyu (2009), 'Human Resource Management: The Forgotten Dimension of Decentralisation in Indonesia', *Bulletin of Indonesian Economic Studies*, 45 (2), 231–49.

UNDP (2004), 'Practice Note on Public Administration Reform' (New York: United Nations Development Programme).

(2008), 'Aceh Government Transformation Programme Project Appraisal Document' (Jakarta: United Nations Development Programme).

(2010), 'Aceh Government Transformation Programme Annual Report: January–December 2010' (Jakarta: United Nations Development Programme).

(2012a), 'Aceh Government Transformation Programme Final Evaluation' (Jakarta: United Nations Development Programme).

(2012b), 'The Legacy of AGTP' (Jakarta: United Nations Development Programme).

UNDP Monitoring Staff (2010), 'Otsus Migas Field Monitoring Report' (Banda Aceh: United Nations Development Programme).

United Nations (2004), 'A More Secure World: Our Shared Responsibility. Report of the Secretary-General's High-Level Panel on Threats, Challenges and Change' (New York: United Nations).

(2013a), 'A New Global Partnership: Eradicate Poverty and Transform Economies through Sustainable Development: The Report of the High-Level Panel of Eminent Persons on the Post-2015 Development Agenda' (New York: United Nations).

(2013b), 'Responsibility to protect: State responsibility and prevention: Report of the Secretary-General', in *UN General Assembly and Security Council* (ed.), A/67/929–S/2013/399 (New York: United Nations).

Unsworth, Sue (2009), 'What's Politics Got To Do With It?: Why Donors Find It So Hard To Come To Terms With Politics, And Why This Matters', *Journal of International Development*, 21 (6), 883–94.

URS Australia (2013), 'Pacific Horticultural and Agricultural Market Access Program (PHAMA) Technical Report 42: Development of Forestry Certification for Exports of Value-Added Timber Products from Solomon Islands: Report prepared for AusAID' (Adelaide: URS Australia).

USAID (2005), *Fragile States Strategy* (Washington, DC: US Agency for International Development).

Vaux, Tony and Visman, Emma (2005), 'Service Delivery in Countries Emerging from Conflict' (London: UK Government, Department for International Development).

Vickery, Michael (1984), *Cambodia 1975–1982*, (Boston: South End Press).

Visoka, Gëzim (2012), 'Three Levels of Hybridisation Practices in Post-Conflict Kosovo', *Journal of Peacebuilding & Development*, 7 (2), 23–36.

vom Hau, Matthias (2012), 'State Capacity and Inclusive Development: New Challenges and Directions', ESID Working paper No. 2 (Manchester: Effective States and Inclusive Development Research Centre, University of Manchester).

von Einsiedel, Sebastian (2005), 'Policy Responses to State Failure', in Simon Chesterman, Michael Ignatieff and Ramesh Thakur (eds.), *Making States Work: State Failure and the Crisis of Governance* (Tokyo: United Nations University Press), 13–35.

Vrieze, Paul and Naren, Kuch (2012), 'Carving Up Cambodia', *Cambodia Daily*, 10–11 March, www.cambodiadaily.com/cdfiles/wp-content/uploads/2012/10/Carving-Up-Cambodia.pdf, accessed 25 March 2017.

Wainwright, Elsina (2003), 'Our Failing Neighbour: Australia and the Future of Solomon Islands', *Strategy and International Program ASPI Policy Report* (Canberra: Australian Strategic Policy Institute).

Walker, R. B. J. (1993), *Inside/Outside: International Relations as Political Theory* (Cambridge: Cambridge University Press).

Wallis, Joanne (2012), 'A Liberal-Local Hybrid Peace Project in Action? The Increasing Engagement Between the Local and Liberal in Timor-Leste', *Review of International Studies*, 38 (4), 735–61.

Wallis, Joanne and Wesley, Michael (2016), 'Unipolar Anxieties: Australia's Melanesia Policy after the Age of Intervention', *Asia & the Pacific Policy Studies*, 3 (1), 26–37.

Warner, Nick (2003), 'Message to the People of Solomon Islands: Speech by Nick Warner, Special Coordinator, Regional Assistance Mission to Solomon Islands', http://dfat.gov.au/news/speeches/Pages/message-to-the-people-of-solomon-islands.aspx, accessed 10 November 2016.

Weber, Heloise (2014), 'When Goals Collide: Politics of the MDGs and the Post-2015 Sustainable Development Goals Agenda', *SAIS Review of International Affairs*, 34 (2), 129–39.

Weiss, Linda (1999), *The Myth of the Powerless State* (Ithaca, NY: Cornell University Press).

Whalan, Jeni (2011), 'Aid for Education in Post-Conflict Solomon Islands', *Prospects*, 41 (2), 237–47.

White House (2002), 'National Security Strategy of the United States' (2005).

Whitfield, Lindsay and Therkildsen, Ole (2011), 'What Drives States to Support the Development of Productive Sectors? Strategies Ruling Elites Pursue for Political Survival and Their Policy Implications', *DIIS Working Paper* No 2011:15 (Copenhagen: Danish Institute for International Studies).

Williams, David (2003), 'Managing Sovereignty: The World Bank and Development in Sub-Saharan Africa', *Mondes en Developpement*, 3 (123), 5–21.

(2013), 'Development, Intervention, and International Order', *Review of International Studies*, 39 (05), 1213–31.

Wimmer, Andreas and Glick Schiller, Nina (2002), 'Methodological Nationalism and Beyond: Nation-State Building, Migration and the Social Sciences', *Global Networks*, 2 (4), 301–34.

World Bank (2004), 'Cambodia at the Crossroads: Strengthening Accountability to Reduce Poverty', Report no. 30636-KH (Washington, DC: World Bank), http://documents.worldbank.org/curated/en/504481468015856100/pdf/306360ENGLISH0KH0white0cover01public1.pdf, accessed 10 November 2016.

(2005), 'Civil Service – A Win–Win Reform' (Jakarta: World Bank).

(2006), 'Aceh Public Expenditure Analysis Spending for Reconstruction and Poverty Reduction' (Jakarta: World Bank).

(2008), 'Public Sector Reform: What Works and Why? An IEG Evaluation of World Bank Support' (Washington DC: World Bank Group).

(2010), 'Solomon Islands Development Challenges: Analysis and Supporting Materials' (Honiara: World Bank).

(2011a), *World Development Report 2011: Conflict, Security and Development* (Washington DC: World Bank Group).

(2011b), 'Public Expenditure Review for the Solomon Islands Government, Revised June 2011' (Honiara: World Bank).

(2012), 'SPADA Implementation and Completion Report' (Jakarta: World Bank).

(2013), 'Where have all the poor gone? Cambodia Poverty Assessment 2013' (Washington, DC: World Bank), http://documents.worldbank.org/curated/en/824341468017405577/Where-have-all-the-poor-gone-Cambodia-poverty-assessment-2013, accessed 10 November 2016.

(2014), 'Well-Being from Work in the Pacific Island Countries' (Washington, DC: World Bank).

(2015a), *World Development Report 2015: Mind, Society and Behavior* (Washington, DC: World Bank Group).

(2015b), 'Cambodia: Country Summary Brief' (Washington, DC: World Bank Group), updated 22 June, http://siteresources.worldbank.org/EXTCDD/Resources/430160-1435154813801/Cambodia_Country_Brief.pdf, accessed 10 November 2016.

Zartman, I. William (1995), 'Introduction: Posing the Problem of State Collapse', in I. William Zartman (ed.), *Collapsed States: The Disintegration and Restoration of Legitimate Authority* (Boulder, CO: Lynne Rienner), 1–14.

Zaum, Dominik (2012), 'Review Essay: Beyond the "Liberal Peace"', *Global Governance*, 18 (1), 121–32.

Ziegenhain, Patrick (2010), 'The Aceh Conflict during the New Order and the Following Democratization Process', in Arndt Graf, Susanne Schroter and Edwin Wieringa (eds.), *Aceh: History, Politics and Culture* (Singapore: Institute of Southeast Asian Studies), 120–34.

Zyad, Teungku (2014), 'The Aceh Exception', *New Mandala*, 29 April. www.newmandala.org/the-aceh-exception.

Index

For EU product safety concerns, contact us at Calle de José Abascal, 56–1°, 28003 Madrid, Spain or eugpsr@cambridge.org.

www.ingramcontent.com/pod-product-compliance
Lightning Source LLC
LaVergne TN
LVHW100300210926
848480LV00003B/980

* 9 7 8 1 1 0 8 4 0 3 4 1 2 *